T0339576

*Cyber Security Management*

*Peter Albert John Trim*
*With love and much gratitude*

# Cyber Security Management

## A Governance, Risk and Compliance Framework

**PETER TRIM**
*University of London, UK*

**YANG-IM LEE**
*University of Westminster, UK*

Routledge
Taylor & Francis Group

LONDON AND NEW YORK

First published 2014 by Gower Publishing

2 Park Square, Milton Park, Abingdon, Oxfordshire OX14 4RN
52 Vanderbilt Avenue, New York, NY 10017

*Routledge is an imprint of the Taylor & Francis Group, an informa business*

First issued in paperback 2020

**British Library Cataloguing in Publication Data**
A catalogue record for this book is available from the British Library.

**The Library of Congress has cataloged the printed edition as follows:**
Trim, Peter R. J.
 Cyber security management : a governance, risk and compliance framework / by Peter R.J. Trim and Yang-Im Lee.
  pages cm
 Includes bibliographical references and index.
 ISBN 978-1-4724-3209-4 (hardback) -- ISBN 978-1-4724-3210-0 (ebook) -- ISBN 978-1-4724-3211-7 (epub)  1.  Business enterprises--Computer networks--Security measures. 2. Computer security. 3.  Computer crimes--Prevention. 4.  Corporations--Security measures. I. Lee, Yang-Im. II. Title.
 HF5548.37.T74 2014
 658.4'78--dc23

                                                                    2014008666


ISBN 13: 978-1-4724-3209-4 (hbk)
ISBN 13: 978-0-367-60616-9 (pbk)

# Contents

# List of Figures and Diagrams

## Figures

# Diagrams

# List of Tables

# List of Appendices

# *About the Authors*

**Dr Peter Trim** is currently a Senior Lecturer in Management at Birkbeck, University of London and Director of the Centre for Advanced Management and Interdisciplinary Studies (CAMIS). He has studied at a number of institutions including Cranfield Institute of Technology (MSc and PhD), City University (MBA) and the University of Cambridge (MEd). Peter is Managing Director of GAMMA (Global Alliance of Marketing and Management Associations) Europe and is a Fellow of the Higher Education Academy and the Royal Society of Arts, and a Member of the Information Assurance Advisory Council (IAAC) Academic Liaison Panel. He has published over 50 academic articles in a range of journals including *Industrial Marketing Management*, the *European Journal of Marketing, Security Journal, International Journal of Intelligence and Counter Intelligence, Disaster Prevention and Management, Cross-Cultural Management: An International Journal, Journal of Business Continuity & Emergency Planning, Simulation & Gaming: An International Journal of Theory, Practice and Research*, and the *Journal of Global Scholars of Marketing Science: Bridging Asia and the World*. Peter has produced a number of single authored, co-authored and edited books. He has co-authored, with David Upton, a book entitled *Cyber Security Culture: Counteracting Cyber Threats through Organizational Learning and Training* (Farnham: Gower Publishing), which was published in 2013; and co-edited a book with Jack Caravelli entitled *Strategizing Resilience and Reducing Vulnerability* (New York: Nova Science Publishers Inc.), which was published in 2009.

Peter contributed the Cyber Attacks section of the University College London report *Scientific Advice and Evidence in Emergencies*, which was edited by Professor McGuire and submitted to the House of Commons Science and Technology Committee as written evidence in 2010. He has been Principal Investigator on two research projects: one was funded by the UK's Technology Strategy Board and the other was funded by the Technology Strategy Board and SEEDA (South East England Development Agency). In addition to this, he has been involved in a number of initiatives such as the Canada-UK Partnership for Knowledge Forum, and the Law Enforcement and National Security Global Forum. He is now involved in the Anglo-Korean government approved university–business project entitled *Increasing Cyber Security Provision in the UK and Korea: Identifying Market Opportunities for SME's*, which is co-funded by the UK's Department of Business Innovation & Skills and involves managing the UK component of the UK-Korea Cyber Security Research Network.

**Dr Yang-Im Lee** is a Senior Lecturer in Marketing at Westminster Business School, University of Westminster and is a specialist in strategic marketing and culture. Yang-Im has studied and worked in Korea, Japan and the UK. She undertook studies at the School of Oriental and African Studies in London (where she has also given a number of guest lectures); and was awarded a scholarship by Stirling University to undertake a PhD at that institution. Yang-Im has worked for both Brunel University and Royal Holloway, University of London and has published over 30 articles in a range of academic journals including the *European Journal of Marketing, Industrial Marketing Management,* and the *Journal of Global Scholars of Marketing Science: Bridging Asia and the World.* She has also co-authored a book and co-edited a book.

Yang-Im is a Fellow of the Higher Education Academy and the Royal Society of Arts and was involved in the iGRC Consortium three-year research project funded by the Technology Strategy Board and SEEDA. She also provided research input into the Technology Strategy Board Fast Track project undertaken by Peter Trim and David Upton entitled 'Develop proven software system to improve emergency response exercises, and extend it to develop robustness in critical information infrastructure'. Yang-Im is a member of the UK-Korea Cyber Security Research Network and a Visiting Fellow at Birkbeck, University of London. Yang-Im has provided support for the Information Assurance Advisory Council and has been their Academic Liaison Panel Co-ordinator for a number of years.

# *Preface*

*Cyber Security Management: A Governance, Risk and Compliance Framework* has been written for a wide audience including academics, researchers, practising managers and government representatives. Derived from research, it places security management in a holistic context and outlines how the strategic marketing approach can be used to underpin cyber security in partnership arrangements. The approach used is unique because it integrates material that is of a highly specialized nature but which can be interpreted by those with a non-specialist background in the area. Indeed, those with a limited knowledge of cyber security will be able to develop a comprehensive understanding of the subject and will be guided into devising and implementing relevant policy, systems and procedures that make the organization better able to withstand the increasingly sophisticated forms of cyber attack that are being launched upon organizations in both the public and private sectors.

A range of topics have been given attention including: the types of threat managers in organizations are confronted with; managing threats; building trust based relationships; business continuity planning; risk communication; resilience policy; risk assessment and enterprise risk management; corporate governance and compliance; security awareness and organizational learning; unmet customer needs and strategic marketing; competitor analysis; resilience policy and strategy mapping; and project liaison management.

The book is unique and includes a sequence-of-events model; an organizational governance framework; a business continuity management planning framework; a multi-cultural communication model; a cyber security management model and strategic management framework; an integrated governance mechanism; an integrated resilience management model; an integrated management model and system; a communication risk management strategy; and recommendations for counteracting a range of cyber threats.

One of the benefits of the book is that it simplifies complex material and provides explanation and interpretation of how managers can manage cyber threats in a proactive manner. Advice is provided through reasoned argument, and the diagrams, figures and tables can be considered highly relevant as they will allow a multi-disciplinary perspective to be utilized to counteract cyber threats both now and in the future.

## Acknowledgements

The work is derived from the iGRC programme, and was funded by the UK government's Technology Strategy Board and the South East England Development Agency (SEEDA) under the grant TP14/IIP/6/I/BJ029H. Sponsor and financial support acknowledgment goes to the iGRC Consortium and especially to the leading organization, Information Governance Limited (now known as Infogov). The title of the research project was 'Integrated model for the management of the complexity, risk and resilience of secure information infrastructure'.

We are extremely grateful to staff at the Information Assurance Advisory Council (IAAC) for allowing us to attend the Consumerisation of IT research workshops and a number of other workshops and to collect, analyse and interpret data that was used at various stages of the research project.

Peter R.J. Trim and Yang-Im Lee
22 April 2014

# Foreword

MIKE POPHAM

*MBA, FRSA, Project Manager, iGRC Consortium 2009–2012*

The research referred to in this book forms the social science cyber security component of the iGRC Consortium project entitled 'Integrated model for the management of the complexity, risk and resilience of secure information infrastructure'. The project was made possible by the overt and essential support of the UK government's Centre for the Protection of National Infrastructure (CPNI), and funding was provided by the UK's Technology Strategy Board and the South East England Development Agency (SEEDA). The iGRC Consortium project was led by Infogov (www.infogov.co.uk), and included HP Enterprise Services (previously EDS), Assuria and Nexor, and the Universities of Cranfield, Loughborough and London (Birkbeck). Using an already advanced governance, risk and compliance technology in Proteus® Enterprise, iGRC was conceived to bridge the gap between the governance of information security controls and risk treatments and the systems, devices, agents and sensors deployed in systems, networks and endpoints to highlight breaches and incidents for rapid remedial actions.

The iGRC project was an exemplar to cooperation between industry and academia producing an innovation to assist business counteract the actions of those engaging in cyber crime. The extension into real time risk management of the already developed Proteus® Enterprise governance risk and compliance suite represents a substantial step towards eradicating managerial, operational and technical vulnerabilities that make organizations susceptible to cyber attack. The work of Trim and Lee is informative, as it outlines, through linking theory and practice, what factors, issues and challenges senior management need to take into account when formulating and implementing a cyber security management policy and strategy. By structuring the material in the way that they have, Trim and Lee outline clearly the research they undertook, explain how they undertook it and what emerged from it. It is clear when reading *Cyber Security Management: A Governance, Risk and Compliance Framework*, that security is a core activity and management need to view it as such. Of particular interest is how the authors integrate the various strands of knowledge to produce insights into how managers and those involved in security generally, can develop a multi-faceted, enterprise wide real time, information security related risk management approach to counteracting the acts of those engaging in cyber crime.

On reflection, it can be argued that the iGRC Consortium is a superb example of teamwork and dedication in fulfilling cutting edge innovation conceived and designed to help solve a major international security problem that has been troubling government officials for a number of years. Indeed, managers in both the private sector and the public sector need to understand that those engaging in acts of cyber crime will become more focused and continually find ways to disrupt and to gain from their illicit actions.

The main advantage of *Cyber Security Management: A Governance, Risk and Compliance Framework* is that it draws on a range of published material and includes insights from people that are aware of current and future cyber security issues, and offers a holistic view as to how managers can go about increasing the level of cyber security provision in their organization so that the organization does not fall victim to what are becoming more and more sophisticated attacks.

As well as providing a number of useful insights and frameworks, Trim and Lee provide guidance as to how senior management, irrespective of the level of cyber security in place, can devise and coordinate cyber security policy so that they work effectively with staff in partner organizations to ensure that the supply chain is protected against attack. The strategic approach advocated by the authors will provide direction as regards what needs to be done in order that the organization's security objectives can be realized.

# 1

# *Introduction and Background to the Research*

## 1.0 Introduction

The authors of this book undertook a social science cyber security analysis and interpretation, which formed an integral part of and contribution to the iGRC (integrated governance, risk and compliance) Consortium research project that was composed of Information Governance Limited (Infogov), Assuria, HP Enterprise Services, Nexor, Cranfield University, Loughborough University and Birkbeck, University of London. The consortium also benefited from a link with a number of small associate security companies. The social science cyber security researchers contributed to the project in a number of ways and provided insights into how senior managers and government representatives can identify and deal with various cyber and non-cyber threats that organizations are confronted with.

It is, we feel, useful to point out that the iGRC Consortium was established to develop 'an open standard to enable the integration of governance, risk and compliance technology with complementary network sensor technologies to produce an integrated model for the management of the complexity, risk and resilience of secure information infrastructure' (http://www.igrc.co.uk/). The software tool at the centre of the research and development process was Proteus and information about Proteus is available in Appendix 1.

This chapter starts by placing cyber threats and the research in context (Section 1.1) and continues with promoting a holistic view of security (Section 1.2). Next, reference is made to the research plan (Section 1.3) and the methodological approach and data collection process (Section 1.4). A conclusion is provided (Section 1.5).

## 1.1 Placing Cyber Threats and the Research in Context

The following examples, provided by Elrod (2010: 2), show how vulnerable small and medium sized companies are to cyber attack and highlight the consequences associated with such attacks.

> *Companies that put off essential security standards can suffer drastic consequences, as can be seen in a case of a California escrow firm. Last March, computer bandits broke into the online banking network of Village View Escrow Inc., a company based out of Redondo Beach, stealing a total amount of $465,000.*

*The culprits then proceeded to make 26 wire transfers to 20 various individuals around the globe who have no relation to the company. Unlike consumers, when businesses lose money online there really isn't a sure way of retrieving it.*

*Since the incident, the owner of Village View Escrow has had to take out a $395,000 loan at 12% interest to get back on track, and it will surely be some time before that ever happens.*

*Another similar incident occurred last April at DKG Enterprises, an Oklahoma City party supplies firm. David Green, a manager for DKG, usually only accessed the company's bank account from a Mac computer in the office.*

*Last April, however, while he was sick and working from his home he found he needed to authorize a company transfer. He decided to use his wife's PC because he could not get to the office that day. Of course, this was the same computer his children play on, and it had at that time contracted a password-stealing Trojan horse. A few days later, computer hackers had stolen $100,000 from the company account using their stolen password. As of yet, DKG has been able to recover only $22,000 of their losses.*

Andrew Powell, a senior manager at the UK's CPNI (Centre for the Protection of National Infrastructure), is clear about the risks associated with e-communication, and has made public the fact that preventing criminals from carrying out attacks via existing networks is a priority (ENISA, 2008: 4). Furthermore, Powell also highlights the potential problem associated with terrorist attacks on communication networks (ENISA, 2008: 4). This focuses attention on two areas: interdependence and interchange. Speaking at the Cyber Security Challenge UK event, which was officially launched by The Rt Hon. Baroness Neville-Jones, Minister for Security on 26 July 2010 at University College London, the Rt Hon. John Reid (Lord Reid of Cardowan), indicated that whereas 'interchange' provided opportunity, 'interdependence' gave rise to vulnerability (Reid, 2010). Bearing in mind the fact that interdependencies exist between nations, organizations and infrastructures, it is important to note that CPNI is active in international CERT communities (ENISA, 2008: 4) and that a nation's cyber security strategy needs to be placed in the context of an international cyber security strategy because a certain percentage of attacks on a country are planned and implemented by people based in other countries. However, those involved in cyber security are aware that as well as individuals and companies being vulnerable to attack, a range of organizations and industries are at risk. The organizational, management and resource concerns relating to cyber security in the context of the US nuclear programmes was cited in the report entitled *National Nuclear Security Administration: Additional Actions Needed to Improve Management of the Nation's Nuclear Programs* (United States Government Accountability Office, 2007: 23). It is also evident from the report that nuclear counter-intelligence is necessary, as some incidents have already occurred (United States Government Accountability Office, 2007: 40).

Reflecting on the above, it can be stated that by facilitating cooperation and information sharing between governments and organizations, and other relevant bodies, it is possible for government representatives to put in place a cyber security management system and framework that counteracts illegal cyber activities. This is a key point to note because senior managers need to pay increased attention to both the type and degree of cyber threat and possible attack(s), and the ramifications associated with these attacks.

One area of concern which has already been highlighted is the dearth of skilled people able to deal with cyber attacks and cyber related problems. For example, Judy Baker, Director of the Cyber Security Challenge UK, has indicated that companies are finding it difficult to recruit specialist and skilled labour in this area (Baker, 2010) and at the same venue, Alan Paller, Director of the Sans Institute, indicated that the US needed many thousands of individuals with the necessary skill base to counteract the work of those involved in cyber crime, including experts in: system forensics; network forensics; deep pocket installations; Windows; UNIX; PDA defence configurations; log analysis; script development; exploitation and penetration testing; service coding; reverse engineering; and counter-intelligence (Paller, 2010).

The Rt Hon. Baroness Neville-Jones (2010a), when she was Minister for Security stated: 'Cyberspace is woven into the fabric of our society; it is integral to our economy, our communities and our security. Defending all of our interests in cyberspace is a relatively small cadre of talented and highly skilled public sector and private sector cyber security professionals. This pool of professionals must grow and the Cyber Security Challenge UK offers an innovative and exciting way of attracting talented individuals to take up rewarding careers in this field.' Indeed, as regards cyber security leadership, it is clear that government will provide the lead and that society will be involved in cyber security initiatives because cyber is central to the economy and the fact that it encompasses daily life. It also needs to be remembered that a nation can move from an existing state of development to that of embracing interconnectivity within a short time span (Neville-Jones, 2010b).

Another point that needs to be borne in mind is that it is not always possible to determine who is behind a cyber attack or how the attack originates. For example, the attack on Estonia in April 2007 was thought to have been launched by nationals from a specific country but to date nobody has accepted responsibility for the attack (Brenner, 2009). Botnets have also been used to launch attacks on the Netherlands, Sweden and the US, and other countries. What does need clarifying is whether such an attack is intended to disrupt or to cause serious damage or both. Bearing this in mind, policy makers need to think in terms of whether an attack is linked with cyber warfare, cyber crime, or cyber terrorism; and whereas traditional warfare can be considered 'overt and destructive', cyber warfare can be viewed as 'subtle and erosive' (Brenner, 2009: 9–10). This distinction is important due to the complexity of the problem, the consequences and ramifications associated with the unknowns involved, and the mobilization of what would be international resources because the issue of interdependency is key.

Brenner (2009: 13), referring to the work of Alice Lipowicz, reported the Federal Bureau of Investigation had estimated cyber crime to have cost the US citizen US$400 billion in 2004. However, it is not possible to provide an accurate picture of the problem because cyber crime carried out both against individuals and indeed against corporations is not fully reported and any figures supplied are likely to underestimate the problem. It is also not possible to outline how many criminal gangs and individuals are involved in cyber crime, but the activities of the main criminal syndicates are well known and have been studied. What is of concern is the size of the problem (cyber crime may well amount to between US$45 billion and US$75 billion per year in the UK, but the lion's share of this emanates from the UK's financial square mile and may be directed at banks and financial institutions). This would bring to notice the international dimension of the problem, as London is an international trading centre, and the way in which the law enforcement and other authorities can deal with the problem depends to a certain extent on how organizations share information or are prevented from doing so by their legal advisors. What worries experts is the fact that malware (malicious code) is escalating and it seems that those perpetrating such activity are not likely to be caught and held to account. The worrying aspect of this is that it does not just concern large corporations, but criminal acts are also being focused on small companies and key industrial sectors (e.g. pharmaceuticals) (Lyne, 2010). Referring back to the threat posed to small companies, Kevin Elrod (2010: 1–3) has stated that:

> For many small business owners, the recent economic downturn has brought a sea of economic challenges. A new threat, however, has emerged which may be the nail in the coffin, and it has come in the form of cybercrime.

> Hackers and computer criminals have lately been turning away from the impenetrable security systems of large corporations in order to reap the fruits of the vulnerable small business sector.

> To the careless, or even prepared, entrepreneur this may spell bankruptcy, and the effects could trickle down causing further harm to local economies.

> Action must be taken in order to insure financial security for small business owners, especially in our current economic climate.

Evidence of this comes from the Canadian Chamber of Commerce, which has indicated that '85% of all business fraud occurs in small to medium-sized businesses' (Elrod, 2010: 2). According to the World Economic Forum, online theft stood at over US$1 trillion in 2009 (Elrod, 2010: 2) and what this highlights is that managers do not take security adequately into account; they do not invest adequately in anti-virus software; they have not undertaken a partial or complete risk analysis; they are using networks which they have limited understanding of; they are unaware of activist groups that may consider that they should be attacked because the industry they are in is harmful in some way; they are in an industry which is susceptible to attacks by criminal syndicates; they are harbouring disgruntled employees who may decide to engage in the sabotage of company records and data or sell it to competitors or place it on the Internet to damage the image of the company.

Owing to the fact that a cyber attack can be launched from any part of the world at any time, it is clear that governments and international institutions need to work more closely together, first to raise public awareness and second, to put in place more effective counter-attack measures. This means that a change in organizational culture is needed in order to ensure that staff become much more aware of such threats and also, people in positions of responsibility communicate issues or highlight problems before they become full blown problems.

## 1.2 Promoting a Holistic View of Security

When seeking a solution to these issues and problems, managers throughout the private and public sectors will be challenged to find solutions that work in all cases. Indeed, cyber attacks differ in degree, type and context, and establishing blanket solutions may only be part of the solution. What such attacks do is force managers to review and revisit the issue of security. Security needs to be viewed from a holistic perspective, if, that is, confronting such issues is to be embedded within the psyche of the organizational value system. Both internal considerations and external considerations need to be taken into account, and this suggests a strategic approach to the problem. For example, reference has been made to 'an appropriate chain of trust' to be established and more specifically (NIST, 2009: 13–14): 'A chain of trust requires that the organization establish and retain a level of confidence that each participating service provider in the potentially complex consumer-provider relationship provides adequate protection for the services rendered to the organization.'

When considering what form a risk management strategy should take, it is important to (i) categorize information systems, and then to (ii) select the security controls, (iii) implement the security controls, (iv) assess the security controls, (v) authorize the information systems, and (vi) monitor the security controls, and then (vii) categorize information systems, all of which is encapsulated within a risk management framework (NIST, 2009: 13–14). This raises a variety of questions regarding who in an organization is responsible for internal security? And who is responsible for external security? Is it one and the same person or a group of skilled individuals. Also, how are internally resulting security issues related to external law enforcement and industry specific security organizations? And how are attacks communicated between organizations? Cyber security needs to be thought of internationally and crisis management is usually confined or limited to being regional or national. How should the data in the computer logs be made international? For example, evidence of government orchestrated attacks, successful defences, disasters and errors all need to be made known.

Glasser and Kelso (2010: 9–10) have indicated that at present the Revolutionary Armed Forces of Columbia (FARC), the Basque Fatherland and Liberty (ETA), Aum Shinrikyo (Japan), al Qaeda and Hezbollah are the main terrorist groups responsible for terrorist attacks; however, high levels of poverty in Muslim countries are a cause for concern as young adults in particular seem to be drawn into becoming active terrorist members because of this. Of less concern are the activities of the Irish Republican Army and Shining Path (Peru) (Glasser and Kelso, 2010: 9). By focusing on the threat posed by poverty, policy makers need to think in terms of implementing a microcredit (small loans) programme, which has been proposed in order that the US government can reduce the possibility of people joining Islamic extremist terrorist networks and thus reduce the chance that they will become active terrorist members (Glasser and Kelso, 2010: 9–15). Countries identified as possible areas of extremist behaviour or as being non-cooperative with the US government are Algeria, Iran, Syria, Libya and Yemen, Palestine, Tunisia, Lebanon, Afghanistan, Pakistan, Bangladesh, Cuba and Sudan (Glasser and Kelso, 2010: 9–15).

Jack Caravelli (2009: 4 and 6–7) has indicated that nuclear and radiological threats to the US take a number of forms and has indicated that both North Korea and Iran 'may harbor their own plans for using their current or future nuclear capabilities for political or military advantage, but the expertise and materials developed in those national programs could be transferred to and used by sub-national groups such as al Qaeda'.

The infrastructural bombings in Afghanistan and Iraq need to be put in context. Going back in history it can be remembered that the Irish Republican Army unleashed actual and attempted attacks on the UK's critical infrastructure (the electricity distribution infrastructure in Northern Ireland in 1971 and a similar but foiled attempt on London's critical infrastructure in 1996 (Craig, 2010: 309–326)). Indeed, from May to November 1971 there were 13 successful attacks on Northern Ireland's main electricity distribution system (Craig, 2010: 317–322) and it goes without saying that the outcome could have been more severe and debilitating than the set of attacks actually were.

## 1.3 Research Plan

Having placed the research in a wider security context, reference will now be made to the research plan and the social science cyber security research component of the project. The social science researchers undertook four work packages: (1) WP1a, (2) WP1b, (3) WP2 and (4) WP3. Each of these is outlined below.

1. WP1a Cyber Security SLEPT (Social, Legal, Economic, Political, Technological) analysis and a vulnerability Sequence-of-Events Model.
   The objectives of WP1a were to identify the emerging trends in criminal and terrorist behaviour; identify potential system(s) failure; identify legal vulnerability; establish the effect on society in economic terms should a major cyber attack/series of attacks occur; establish the main vulnerability and threat drivers confronting senior management; and produce a vulnerability Sequence-of-Events Model. The deliverables were defined in terms of an academic-led Cyber Security SLEPT (Social, Legal, Economic, Political, Technological) analysis; a vulnerability Sequence-of-Events Model; and topics and questions to be integrated into the research strategy.

2. WP1b Cyber Security SWOT Analysis.
   The objectives of WP1b were to produce an organizational strategic governance framework; a business continuity management contingency planning framework; a communication risk management strategy; and a generic cyber security management model and strategic management framework. The deliverables included an academic-led cyber security SWOT (Strengths, Weaknesses, Opportunities and Threats) analysis from a hands on operational perspective; a communications risk management strategy; and a generic cyber security management model and strategic management framework.

3. WP2 Cyber Security Decision Analysis.
   The objectives of WP2 were to map resilience policy and strategy; produce a risk assessment policy; an integrated governance mechanism; integrated security; identify threats; produce an integrated resilience management model; and produce an integrated management model and system. The deliverable was defined in terms of an academic-led Cyber Security Decision Analysis.

4. WP3 Strategic Marketing Management Framework.
   The objectives of WP3 were to identify unmet customer needs; produce a competitor and marketing analysis; outline how a project liaison team is managed; outline what a governance and compliance decision making process is; produce insights into how to communicate a risk management strategy; outline the content for a masters degree in security management; outline a publishing plan; and make recommendations

for counteracting cyber threats. The deliverables included a strategic marketing management framework; and a publishing plan.

# 1.4 Methodological Approach and Data Collection Process

There were seven main data collection periods during the three-year period that the social science cyber security research was undertaken. A number of fit-for-purpose qualitative research methods were used to collect the data, and the analysis and interpretation produced were incorporated into the deliverables. The main data collection periods and research methods used are outlined below.

### FIRST DATA COLLECTION PERIOD.

The first data collection period was composed of the following main events: (i) a small group interview with two industry experts lasting two hours and twenty minutes (25 March 2011); (ii) two informal, in-depth one-to-one interviews with an industry expert that lasted five hours, (iii) participation in the 'People-Centric Information Assurance Workshop: Helping People Fend for Themselves Online' organized by the Information Assurance Advisory Council (IAAC) at the BCS, The Chartered Institute for IT in London (14 July 2010); (iv) attendance at an all day iGRC workshop in Reading; (v) attendance at the 'Technology Strategy Board and Digital Systems KTN Digital Content Knowledge Workshop' at the Westminster Conference Centre in London (27 May 2010); (vi) attendance at the 'Technology Strategy Board and Digital Systems KTN Privacy in the Digital Society: A fine balance 2000 Conference' at the BIS Conference Centre in London (8 June 2010), (vii) attendance at the 'Technology Strategy Board and Digital Communications KTN Collaboration Across Digital Industries Workshop' held in London at the Radisson Hampshire Hotel (5 July 2010), (viii) two iGRC webliners organized by Information Governance Limited (Infogov) (28 April 2011 and 5 May 2011).

### SECOND DATA COLLECTION PERIOD.

The second data collection period saw the researchers collect data via (i) a small group interview that included a telephone conference and (ii) involvement in an IAAC Consumerisation Research Workshop held at the BCS, The Chartered Institute for IT in London (17 November 2011).

### THIRD DATA COLLECTION PERIOD.

A questionnaire composed of six questions entitled 'Preventing Cyber Attacks' was distributed to 25 of the delegates attending the CAMIS Integrated Governance, Risk and Compliance Conference and Knowledge Sharing Event, incorporating the iGRC Consortium demonstration and network sensor devices at Birkbeck, University of London (15 December 2011). Twelve completed questionnaires were returned representing a response rate of 48 per cent.

## FOURTH DATA COLLECTION PERIOD.

The researchers attended and participated in three Information Assurance Advisory Council (IAAC) workshops: (i) IAAC Consumerisation and Information Sharing Workshop 'What Happens When it Goes Wrong?' held in London at the BCS, The Chartered Institute for IT (17 January 2012); (ii) IAAC Academic Liaison Panel, which was held in London at the BCS, The Chartered Institute for IT (25 January 2012); (iii) the IAAC-Cabinet Office key issues seminar entitled 'Opportunities and Tasks in Implementing the UK Cyber Security Strategy' at the BCS, The Chartered Institute for IT (31 January 2012). It is important to note that an ethical and responsible approach was taken to data and information collection throughout the life of the research project and on occasion, owing to the sensitivity of what was involved, data and information was only made use of if it was in the public domain and/or permission had been given to make use of it.

## FIFTH DATA COLLECTION PERIOD.

The researchers attended two Information Assurance Advisory Council (IAAC) Consumerisation and Information Sharing Workshops: (i) 'Governance and Consumerisation: Who Should do What?' held in London at the BCS, The Chartered Institute for IT (15 February 2012), and (ii) 'Understanding, Explaining and Counteracting Inappropriate User Behaviour', which was held in London at the BCS, The Chartered Institute for IT (13 March 2012).

## SIXTH DATA COLLECTION PERIOD.

The researchers (i) undertook an international telephone interview with an industry expert, which lasted 32 minutes (28 May 2012); (ii) participated in a teleconference and web demonstration with an industry expert (22 June 2012); and (iii) attended the Information Assurance Advisory Council research workshop entitled 'Communication Warnings, Providing Advice and Reporting Incidents', held in London at the BCS, The Chartered Institute for IT (9 October 2012).

## SEVENTH DATA COLLECTION PERIOD.

The researchers attended the Cyber Security Conference and Workshop at Birkbeck, University of London (16 November 2012). Two research groups were established, one composed of five people and the other composed of seven people. Each group provided answers to four questions and shared their analysis and interpretation with the other group.

As well as the above, a number of seminars, workshops and conferences proved beneficial with respect to providing background information and updating the researchers vis-à-vis the subject and related subject areas. These have been listed in Appendix 2.

# 1.5 Conclusion

It is clear that organizations and individuals need to safeguard themselves against cyber attack because cyber attacks are growing in sophistication and intensity, and are focused and carefully planned to inflict the maximum discomfort on their victims. An holistic approach  to security will allow cyber security professionals  to unravel the complexities involved and link with other bodies of knowledge in order that we can derive relevant insights into attack modes and prepare our defences so that we are able to deal with an attack more effectively than is the case at present. By adopting a broad based social science cyber security approach it is possible that other areas of interest (socio-cultural, geo-political, human behaviour and factors, and market opportunities) will be better understood and the security systems that are developed and put in place will be better able to safeguard data and information and make individuals less vulnerable to attack. It is also envisaged that more robust information systems will enable organizations to withstand constant attack, make them more resilient and allow them to continue in business.

# References

Baker, J. 2010. Talk at the Cyber Security Challenge UK, University College London (26 July).

Brenner, S.W. 2009. *Cyberthreats: The Emerging Fault Lines of the Nation State*. Oxford: Oxford University Press.

Caravelli, J. 2009. *Nuclear Insecurity: Understanding the Threat from Rogue Nations and Terrorists*. Westport, CT: Praeger.

Craig, T. 2010. Sabotage! The origins, development and impact of the IRA's infrastructural bombing campaigns 1939–1997. *Intelligence and National Security*, 25 (3), 309–326.

Elrod, K. 2010. Small business – The new target for cybercriminals, pp. 1–3. https://infosecisland.com/blogview/5760-Small-Business-The-New-Target-for-cybercriminals.html [accessed 27 July 2010].

ENISA. 2008. *Report on 4th ENISA CERT Workshop*. Athens: European Network and Information Security Agency (June).

Glasser, M. and Kelso, C. 2010. Terrorism and US-sponsored microcredit program: Macroglobal returns. *Journal of Emergency Management*, 8 (3), 9–15.

Lyne, J. 2010. Talk at the Cyber Security Challenge UK, University College London (26 July).

Neville-Jones, P., Rt Hon. 2010a. Minister of Security. Cyber Security Challenge.Org.Uk (26 July).

Neville-Jones, P., Rt Hon. 2010b. Minister of Security, talk at the Cyber Security Challenge UK, University College London (26 July).

NIST. 2009. *Recommended Security Controls for Federal Information Systems and Organizations – NIST Information Security Special Publication 800-53 Revision 3*. Gaithersburg, MD: National Institute of Standards and Technology, US Department of Commerce (August).

Paller, A. 2010. Talk at the Cyber Security Challenge UK, University College London (26 July).

Reid, J., Rt Hon. 2010. Opening speech. Cyber Security Challenge UK, University College London (26 July).

United States Government Accountability Office. 2007. *National Nuclear Security Administration: Additional Actions Needed to Improve Management of the Nation's Nuclear Programs, GAO-07-36*. Washington, DC: GAO (January).

# Websites

http://www.igrc.co.uk/ [accessed 5 May 2010]

http://rm-inv.enisa.europa.eu/tools/t_proteus.html [accessed 18 September 2013]

# Appendix 1
# Information About Proteus

Tool name: Proteus
Vendor name: Infogov (Information Governance Limited)
Country of origin: United Kingdom

Level of reference of the tool
Details about the coverage or the 'originators' of the solution

Coverage: Worldwide (State oriented)
Supported by organization, club... (e.g. as sponsor): British Standards Institution (BSI) – Information Security Forum (ISF) – Holistic Information Security Practitioner Institute (HISP institute)

Brief description of the product
Give a brief description of the product containing general information, overview of functions

- Proteus Enterprise is a comprehensive web server based compliance, information security and risk management, and corporate governance tool developed by Information Governance Ltd. The entire range of Proteus products, and its preceding versions, have been branded and distributed by the British Standards Institution since 1995, although most enterprise level sales are direct via Information Governance Ltd and its global distribution network managed by Veridion Inc., Canada. Proteus allows organizations to implement the controls of any standard or regulation, e.g. BS ISO/IEC 17799 and BS ISO/IEC 27001, BS 25999, SOX, CobiT, PCI DSS etc.

Supported functionality
Specify the functionality this tool provides.

R.A. Method phases supported

- Risk identification: Both Qualitative and Quantitative Risk Assessment techniques supported. Both being fully integrated with Asset Management, Threats, Countermeasures, Risk Treatment Plans and Incident Management.
- Risk analysis: Relative and Absolute risk scales can be used to adapt to corporate 'risk appetite'.
- Risk evaluation: 5 types: Physical, Information, Service, Application and Group (combination) Assets are supported. Threats can be automatically inherited via asset relationships, location and asset profile.

Other phases

- Asset inventory & evaluation: Supported by location but cross-referenced across an entire, multi-national or distributed, organisation. External, open interface, to import data and to integrate with third party applications such as network scanning and penetration testing applications.

R.M. Method phases supported

- Risk assessment: 5 stage generic process, easily mapped to BS ISO 27001, IRAM or other methodologies.
- Risk treatment: 'Action Plans' are fully integrated with Compliance, Risk Assessment, Business Impact Analysis, Business Continuity and Incident Management.
- Risk acceptance: Full audit trail of ALL system changes. Every process is automatically captured as a time stamped PDF, and full sign-off & acceptance is supported via email and workflow management.
- Risk communication: Every aspect of the system can be reported or viewed by 'secure' PDFs, fully customisable Business Objects reporting, and via the optional Proteus RiskView™ management information graphical 'dashboard'.

Other phases

- N/A

Other functionality

- Document Management
- Business Continuity
- Remote auditing: Distribute questionnaires
- Incident Management
- Automated Alert Management (SMS and email) : Incidents can be captured via custom intranet Portal pages and automated alerts (by SMS or email) sent to relevant individuals according to the affected (or potentially affected) assets and business processes.

Information processed

- Global Views: Compliance Status, Financial Exposure, Threats, Incidents etc.
- Compliance: Documentation (policies, procedures, evidence, testing) and Corrective Actions.
- Assets: Related Controls and Tasks.
- Incident Management: Analysed by incident type and/or losses, with identified control failures and related assets
- Business Impact: Processes by Risk or with Assets affected by Incidents
- Business Continuity: Critical process exposures
- Risk Analysis: Threat Exposure
- Action Plans: Task Summary

- Incidents: Event types and losses
- Document Control: Review Status

Lifecycle
Date of the first edition, date and number of actual version

Date of first release: March 1995 – CoP-iT, original Compliance 'gap analysis' tool, launched concurrently with BS7799:1995.
Date and identification of the last version: June 2007 – Proteus Alert Management™ (P.A.M.) Fully integrated automated alert management linked to custom client intranet web 'portal' pages for Incident capture.

Useful links
Link for further information

Official web site: http://www.infogov.co.uk
User group web site: N/A
Relevant web site: http://www.veridion.net – http://www.bsi-global.co.uk – http://www.hispi.org

Languages
List the available languages that the tool supports

Languages available: English – French – Spanish – Japanese – Chinese

Pricing and licensing models
Specify the price for the product (as provided by the company on December 2005)

- Proteus Solo: £599 per year
- Proteus Professional: £6000 per year or £600 per month
- Proteus Enterprise: p.o.a.

Sectors with free availability or discounted price: N/A

Trial before purchase
Details regarding the evaluation period of the tool

CD or download available: 1.Webex Demo or Evaluation by request – 2.Pilot Project p.o.a.
Identification required: N/A
Trial period: N/A

Tool architecture
Specify the technologies used in this tool

- Database: MS SQL
- Web server: IIS or Apache
- Application Server: PHP

- Client: I.E., Firefox etc.

Scope
Target public
Defines the most appropriate type of communities for this tool

- Government, agencies
- Large scale companies
- SME

Specific sector: Finance, TelCo, Pharmaceutical, Retail, Government

Spread
Information concerning the spread of this tool

General information: Worldwide in many different organizations
Used inside EU countries: N/A
Used outside EU countries: N/A

Level of detail
Specify the target kind of people for this tool based on its functionality

Management: yes
Operational: yes
Technical: N/A

Compliance to IT Standards
List the national or international standard this tool is compliant with

- BS ISO 17799 & 27001: Licensed by BSI
- BS 25999: Licensed by BSI
- SoGP: Licensed by ISF
- PCI DSS
- SOX
- Many others

Tool helps towards a certification
Specify whether the tool helps the company toward a certification according to a standard

- BS ISO 27001

Training
Information about possible training courses for this tool

Course: Proteus Enterprise
Duration: 2 Days
Skills: InfoSec

Expenses: Public courses free of charge

Course: Holistic Information Security Practitioner
Duration: 5 Days
Skills: HISP
Expenses: £1,500

Users viewpoint

Skills needed
Specify the skills needed to use and maintain the solution

- To install: Web & Database Servers, Business Objects on own server, or can be hosted on Infogov secure servers
- To use: Standard web browser
- To maintain: Standard web browser

Tool Support
Specify the kind of support the company provides for this product

Support: Telephone, email (local language support by international distributors)

Organization processes integration
Describe user roles this tool supports

Supported Roles

- N/A

Integration in organization activities

- N/A

Interoperability with other tools
Specify available interfaces or other ways of integration with other tools

- Integration Method
- Active directory
- Single Sign-on
- External Network Audit: API
- External ERP: API
- External Bespoke: Database Replication / Synchronisation

Sector adapted knowledge databases supported
Name and describe the sector adapted databases that this tool provides

- Full Authoring Facilities included

Flexibility of tool's database
Can the database be customized and adapted to client requirements?

- Fully Customisable: Supports multi-languages, menu and forms customisation.

*Source*:    http://rm-inv.enisa.europa.eu/tools/t_proteus.html    [accessed    on    18 September 2013]. Reproduced with permission.

# Appendix 2
# Additional Seminars, Workshops and Conferences Attended

The Digital Communications Knowledge Transfer Network Future Internet Initiative – *What does it mean for the UK?* BIS Conference Centre, London (26 February 2010).

The Information Assurance Advisory Council (IAAC) Annual Symposium, *Information Assurance – Valuing and Protecting Information*, BT Centre, London (8 September 2010).

Royal United Services Institution, *The Future of Critical National Infrastructure - The View to 2015 Conference*, RUSI, London (13–14 October 2010).

The *Cyber Security Summit 2010*, Queen Elizabeth II Conference Centre, London (11 November 2010).

Royal United Services Institution, *The Emergency Response 2010: Emergency Services: A 2020 Vision Conference*, RUSI, London (2 December 2010).

Royal United Services Institution, *The Virtual Emergencies: Simulation Technology for Emergency Planning and Response Conference*, RUSI, London (8 April 2011).

The *Information Assurance Advisory Council - GCHQ Workshop*, BCS, The Chartered Institute for IT, London (30 June 2011).

The *National Security Conference*, Queen Elizabeth II Conference Centre, London (5 July 2011).

The Information Assurance Advisory Council (IAAC) First Consumerisation Research Workshop: *Information Assurance (IA) and Consumerisation – Impact on IA of the Sea Change in the Use of Information*, BCS, The Chartered Institute for IT, London (13 October 2011).

The Information Assurance Advisory Council (IAAC) Second Consumerisation Research Workshop: *Common and Shared Services in the Context of Cloud Computing*, BCS, The Chartered Institute for IT, London (17 November 2011).

The Information Assurance Advisory Council (IAAC) Third Consumerisation Research Workshop: *Risk and Advanced Persistent Threat Agent*, BCS, The Chartered Institute for IT, London (6 December 2011).

The *SMi Cyber Defence 2012 Conference*, Copthorne Tara Hotel, London (18–19 June 2012).

Information Assurance Advisory Council. *IAAC Consumerism of IT: Same Old IA Issues … or Not?* BCS, The Chartered Institute for IT, London (19 June 2012).

The Information Assurance Advisory Council (IAAC) Annual Symposium: *Securing the Cloud – Securing Me*, Royal College of Physicians, London (12 September 2012).

Information Assurance Advisory Council. *IAAC Consumerisation of IT Workshop: Business Continuity and the Main Information Risk Issues*. BCS, The Chartered Institute for IT, London (15 January 2013).

# 2 *Sequence-of-Events Model*

## 2.0 Introduction

This chapter draws on work undertaken by Trim and Lee (2010). When producing the Sequence-of-Events Model, attention was given to how various managers in an organization can put in place a framework for reducing organizational vulnerability. The Sequence-of-Events Model was designed specifically so that managers could devise and implement policy that enables the organization to counteract cyber threats and at the same time allows senior managers and top management in particular to devise a resilience oriented strategy that incorporates a sustainable counter-intelligence policy and strategy, and which places the management of risk in a business–industry framework. By drawing on earlier work undertaken by Trim and Lee (2010) relating to a cyber security SLEPT analysis and a cyber security SWOT analysis, and taking into account the emerging security paradigm as outlined by Baroness Pauline Neville-Jones (2009), managers can develop and implement a cyber security strategy that is company and industry specific. In order to do this effectively, it is necessary for senior managers to think in terms of developing a security culture, which is underpinned by an intelligence oriented organizational value system and which ensures that a strategic intelligence focus is evident. By adopting and embracing a workable organizational learning approach it is possible for senior managers to devise a security management model and to integrate the organization's cyber security strategy with those of partner organizations and to work closely with government representatives when necessary.

This chapter starts with cyber security analysis (Section 2.1) and continues with corporate security and corporate intelligence (Section 2.2). Attention is then given to cyber security threats (Section 2.3); issues, developments and considerations needing answers (Section 2.4); and enterprise risk management (Section 2.5). Next, issues for commerce and industry, and government (Section 2.6) precedes building trust based relationships (Section 2.7). The protective umbrella (Section 2.8) is followed by justifying the approach (Section 2.9) and the Sequence-of-Events Model (Section 2.10). A conclusion (Section 2.11) is provided.

## 2.1 Cyber Security Analysis

By adopting an integrated management approach it is possible for managers to use the outputs of a cyber security SLEPT (Social, Legal, Economic, Political, Technological) analysis and the outputs of a cyber security SWOT (Strengths, Weaknesses, Opportunities and Threats) analysis (Trim and Lee, 2010: 1–3).

## 2.1.1 CYBER SECURITY SLEPT ANALYSIS

A cyber security SLEPT analysis can be considered an integral component of a corporate intelligence activity and incorporates environmental scanning that is aimed at (Trim and Lee, 2010: 1–2):

1. identifying the emerging trends in criminal and terrorist behaviour;
2. identifying potential systems failure;
3. identifying legal vulnerability;
4. establishing the effect on society in economic terms should a major cyber attack/series of attacks occur;
5. establishing the main vulnerability and threat drivers confronting senior management; and
6. resulting in a vulnerability Sequence-of-Events Model.

By harnessing the knowledge of staff based in external organizations (companies, private consultancies, government agencies, international institutions, universities, trade associations, embassies and chambers of commerce and industry for example), Corporate Intelligence Officers and their support staff can synthesise the results of a cyber security SLEPT analysis into a Sequence-of-Events Model. The Sequence-of-Events Model can be used by senior managers (IT, finance, marketing, corporate law, security and corporate intelligence for example) to highlight current and future cyber security threats and to provide guidance for prioritizing each risk identified. Following an analysis and interpretation of expected outcomes, recommendations can be made to counter the threats identified. Managers lower down the organization's hierarchy can be engaged in identifying areas of vulnerability, and senior managers based in various departments and functions can work with organizational strategists to devise and implement countermeasures that help the organization to become resilient.

In order to understand what can be deemed influencing factors, managers need to take into account social factors, and this means analysing and interpreting customer buying habits/needs (achieved through segmentation) and devising and implementing knowledge support mechanisms (linking digital marketing campaigns with online payment systems). Managers will through time understand and interpret the behaviour of customers (marketing domain) and establish how they make the buying decisions that they do. Of importance is how knowledge support mechanisms (social websites for example) support and facilitate the flow of data and information, and in particular, how knowledge is transferred among and between people and used in order to support the decision-making process.

As regards what may be referred to as legal factors, managers need to be aware of the influence (direct and indirect) that industry standards have on how the organization functions and how current and future regulations place constraints on organizations. Protecting and sharing intellectual property rights will receive attention through time, and as regards economic factors, managers need to pay careful attention to how organizational costs can be kept to a minimum. This is an important consideration because additional costs can be incurred through initiating/maintaining corporate governance mechanisms and processes; devising a risk management strategy; communicating response measures; and devising and implementing a resilience policy.

Increased interaction between government agencies aimed at combatting the spread of cyber crime warrants increased attention to country specific laws and the myriad relationships that an organization will establish both in the domestic market and the overseas market. It also brings into play the role of political factors. Managers need to be aware of how governments influence e-commerce policy and this highlights the need to understand the role that technological factors play (the integration of people, processes and technological applications, which includes recovery, for example).

## 2.1.2 CYBER SECURITY SWOT ANALYSIS

A cyber security SWOT (Strengths, Weaknesses, Opportunities and Threats) (Trim and Lee, 2010: 2–3) forms an integral part of corporate intelligence activity and underpins:

1. an organizational strategic governance framework;
2. a business continuity management contingency planning framework;
3. a communication risk management strategy; and
4. a generic cyber security management model and strategic management framework.

When assessing organizational strengths, managers will authorize an audit to be undertaken that requires that a corporate security function is established (if it does not exist already) and in addition a governance framework is put in place or implemented. Attention will also be given to how resilience and business continuity policies are formulated and implemented, and how a risk communication policy is communicated. As regards identifying and eradicating organizational weaknesses, it is important that corporate security gaps and deficiencies are identified and rectified, and there is a continual focus to eradicate faulty software because faulty software can be used to penetrate an organization's computer networks and systems.

Managers also need to keep an eye out for the opportunities that exist, and this means identifying best practice outlined in industry standards; evaluating various cyber law initiatives; identifying evolving market opportunities at home and abroad; and cooperating with government agencies and international organizations. With respect to threats, staff need to constantly monitor the external environment and identify the actions of organized crime syndicates; gauge the way in which state sponsored organizations carry out acts of industrial espionage and sabotage; identify the actions associated with terrorist networks and money laundering activities; understand how and why activists and small criminals engage in disruptive behaviour; and provide support and assistance to government agencies at home and abroad that implement initiatives aimed at eradicating cyber crime.

# 2.2 Corporate Security and Corporate Intelligence

By linking a cyber security SLEPT analysis with a cyber security SWOT analysis, it is possible to produce a Generic Cyber Security Management Model (GCSMM), which is placed in a Cyber Security Management Framework (CSMF) (Trim and Lee, 2010: 5). The easiest way in which to do this is for senior managers to review the literature relating to relevant bodies of knowledge and to draw on existing models and frameworks that have a security and intelligence focus/dimension. By amending and utilizing an existing model or framework, it is easier to develop an appropriate model or framework in the sense that it can be made company and industry specific. In order that managers throughout the organization participate fully in the model or framework building process, it is necessary for a holistic view of security to be adopted and for a management logic to be incorporated that ensures that the corporate security framework or model that materializes is robust. Trim (2005: 496) has stated that:

> *Senior management cannot sit back and wait for security systems to evolve naturally, the necessary commitment and stimulation needs to be put in place so that a security culture is created that incorporates an intelligence dimension. The organization's intelligence function needs to have a specific organizational-environment focus. Hence it needs to be organizational specific, industry specific, technology specific and country specific. This being the case, corporate intelligence and security will automatically be linked to governmental transnational intelligence. Transnational intelligence deals with the many but integrated threats that emerge to debilitate a system. Once a system is debilitated, it is both defenceless and vulnerable.*

By accepting that security is a core activity, it should be possible to put in place a corporate security function that assumes responsibility for security policy and strategy (internally oriented policy and externally oriented policy) (Trim, 2005: 502). What has to be remembered is that for security to be viewed as an essential component of management, it is necessary for senior managers to promote the organizational learning concept that ensures that the organization's cultural value system embraces the sharing of information, the aim of which is to make people aware of immediate and future cyber threats, and condition people to act responsively and to work together to eradicate organizational vulnerabilities. For example, staff in the finance department will from time to time have personal knowledge of the various forms of financial fraud that are in being and will no doubt liaise with information technology professionals who are aware of hacking and cracking tools and techniques, and will need to liaise with colleagues in the corporate legal department to determine what deterrents can be put in place to counteract such activity. Organizational staff will from time to time need to talk with external legal representatives and may need to work with law enforcement officers.

What is evident from the above is that managers will, in order to put an effective corporate security framework in place, need to embrace the concept of organizational learning so that the level of security awareness is raised. Should this be the case, one can assume that the business model that is developed, and which may embrace outsourcing and/or offshoring, will be sustainable.

## 2.3 Cyber Security Threats

A wide range of diverse cyber threats confronting senior managers and government representatives have been identified and are listed below.

1. Counterfeiting and brand piracy. In particular, the pharmaceutical industry is heavily targeted and this is worrying because certain drugs are banned or restricted in some countries or highly priced, and spurious companies are now offering fake

drugs which appear to be the real product and are being purchased both face to face and over the Internet.

2. Insider crime. A disillusioned employee or espionage agent will find a way to gain access to records and sensitive data. Data can be altered or copied or stolen or placed on the worldwide web. It is clear that fraud is increasing and that the insider (an employee or contractor with access to codes and passwords) may occupy a position of responsibility and be able to cover their tracks. They will engage in transferring data and money and/or use programs to skim accounts or sell data and information to a competitor or an overseas government agency.

3. Fraud orchestrated by organized crime syndicates is becoming a way of life and the stealing and resale of people's identities is big business and is likely to continue.

4. Cyber attacks from hackers and crackers and government front companies is continuing, aided by the Internet, and in some cases cannot be immediately detected. Hence the need for information sharing on an intra- and inter-industry basis. Note: some companies that are hacked do not report the incident to the authorities but hack the offending company in return.

5. It is evident that there is a lack of skilled cyber security professionals and therefore a gap vis-à-vis people writing secure computer programs; managers with the ability and awareness to understand the technical gaps and the human deficiencies; administrators who are not motivated to look into problems or ensure that recovery action and/or follow-up action is taken when necessary; and there is a shortage of people who can write secure code and those that can produce secure websites.

6. It is easy for malware (malicious code) to get into the system and the chance of the perpetrator being caught is very remote so hackers and crackers do not consider that they are at risk of being caught and prosecuted. This is likely to be of concern for many years.

7. The increasing number of fake software products is causing concern and more education is needed to inform the public about this and raise awareness.

8. Companies do not have adequate cyber security policies and security plans in place, and do not implement recovery plans rapidly enough.

9. Initiatives such as cloud computing appear fine, however, how is cloud computing managed? When answering this question a number of sub-issues emerge such as placing data in the system, accessing data, who and when and where are the backup and recovery systems located. Also, the issue of who else has access to the data and information surfaces. It could be, for example, that somebody in the UK enters data which is stored in another European country and there is a backup system in the US. How is this managed? How is it controlled?

10. Poor or ineffective patching can result in additional problems and a sense of apathy, as managers believe they have solved the problem when in fact additional problems (viruses) have been created or have penetrated the system.

11. The increasing targeting of social networking activities and resulting identify theft and fraud is worrying the authorities.

12. Product testing and evaluation, and validation against national and international standards, especially intrusion detection devices and web applications and network devices. Issues remain and need to be addressed.

13. The mitigation of risk, and the link with contingency planning and disaster recovery planning, needs to be embedded firmly in the organization's cyber security policy.

The need exists to create a security culture that accepts that the human factor(s) and the technology factor(s) are linked.

14. In order to ensure that a robust cyber security policy is in place that links with the security policy of partner organizations in the supply chain and marketing channel organizations, and feeds data and information to law enforcement agencies, an organizational monitoring system needs to be in place that is visible and operational within the organization's structure.

15. Ensure that the necessary staff development and training  programmes are available for  skill enhancement, and ensure that the organization's culture is robust (e.g. a collectivist organizational cyber security culture is in being).

16. The transparency of operations is key with respect to internal and external auditors understanding how cyber security assessment and security controls are applied in an  industry specific context.

17. The importance of Supervisory Control and Data Acquisition (SCADA) systems and the risk associated with vendors developing faulty products that are integrated into control systems, or of individuals/organizations that aim to exploit a vulnerability having gained prior knowledge of a fault waiting to be patched needs to be borne in mind.

18. Technological developments which could result in an untested product or technology being made available before it is proven and its knock on effects. For example, the increasing trend towards the use of remote connections and the vulnerabilities associated with these is a cause for concern and a priority for attention.

19. Encouraging and supporting communication between organizations, institutions, private sector companies and government departments is necessary, if, that is, assurance is to be achieved and people trust that the systems in place are robust and can withstand various types of cyber attack.

20. Develop an organizational security culture that embeds information security/ assurance policy within the risk management strategy and which embraces the concept of continual improvement and perfection seeking as opposed to quick fixes. This needs to be organizational specific.

21. As regards terrorist networks, it is important to think in terms of which organizations are actively involved in terrorist attacks, what their motives are, and who funds these activities. Also, which countries support terrorist groups and why; and how terrorist organizations are likely to move resources and people, and set up operational or active commands in various (possibly neutral) countries. Another key issue is the relationship between governments, which governments are actively promoting international cyber security cooperation and what support they need.

22. Countries with a persistently poor economic performance may become centres for organized crime syndicates or terrorist groups in the sense that well educated professional people (e.g. those with computer and IT skills especially) are able to sell their knowledge to those that pay well above market rates, or in the case where no or limited work is available, are prepared to sell their knowledge in return for a substantial one-off payment (countries to be watched include Russia and other poorly performing European countries).

23. Industrial espionage companies deal openly in stolen data and information, as is happening in China.

24. Continued threat of attacks against infrastructure (critical national infrastructure, or CNI, and critical information infrastructure, CII) and tourist attractions (e.g.

Egypt, Uganda and Indonesia) and leisure facilities, in order to disrupt and to maximize publicity and thereby facilitate recruitment of gullible individuals into the terrorist operation.

25. Continued expansion of organized crime (money laundering, fraud, kidnapping and extortion), and corruption of government representatives and officials (e.g. Eastern Europe and various parts of the world where law enforcement is weak or a political dictator or military group is in power).

26. Computer abuse by employees is expected to increase because the penalties are insufficient and organizations do not wish to make matters public (e.g. banks and pharmaceutical companies operate their own security and industry monitoring systems).

27. The degree of risk and severity associated with cyber attacks could increase because of a rogue government's backing of an attack on another nation's CNI and CII, and/or disruption of a nation's infrastructure. Possible penetration of a nuclear missile system and the triggering of an attack on another country thus causing a war and then escalating the war is now being considered as happening at some point in time in the future.

28. Identity fraud linked to benefit fraud. Decreases have resulted due to tougher government action; however, criminals are likely to develop new approaches to identify fraud as it can be lucrative and the general public remain unaware of the dangers.

29. Spyware is expected to increase as industrial espionage is perceived by some governments to be legitimate and government agencies consider that stealing technological secrets is one way to reduce the technology gap between nations.

30. The threat posed by terrorist networks and organized crime syndicates that penetrate and work for legitimate specialist defence contractors and then sabotage or debilitate or activate a nuclear missile system with devastating consequences is worrying governments around the world as it is linked with a government's need to engage in cost cutting and to be more efficient. The resulting business model is untested and may increase risk and result in several emerging vulnerabilities (e.g. converging threats and unpredicted and unknown events).

31. The threat posed by terrorist networks and criminal syndicates that work for legitimate specialist defence contractors and then knowingly through wireless control systems block a missile attack on a country where they are based and which means that the defence systems of the country that was attacked are rendered useless. The military in that country would not be able to respond to defend the country against further attacks, and cannot launch reciprocal attacks, and the political consequences would be enormous (e.g. some nations may change sides).

32. An increased need to develop timely nuclear counter-intelligence policy and responses and to place these within a strategic intelligence context and to link the management process with operational management and develop a highly skilled proactive management team reinforced by the concept of organizational learning.

33. The growth in the idea of cyber sex; for example, academics and adult entertainment providers have recognized that there is a growing trend among people to engage in cyber sex as a substitute for building real and long-lasting relations with other people (Yesterday Television Channel, 2010). This is worrying because of the possible link with child abuse and the possibility of an escalation in Internet pornography and how people can be recorded and blackmailed into delivering secrets and engaging in antisocial practice in order to disrupt business activity.

34. The growing trend in hoaxing relating to computer viruses is likely to cause chaos and confusion, and management time is wasted solving non-existent problems.
35. Growing vigilante movement to expose Internet bullies to their employers and the problems associated with this. For example, people may be suspended from work when they should not be and if coordinated with a cyber attack, it could be devastating for a business, especially if it is a small business.
36. Spurious emails from supposed relatives or those supposedly representing family members that cause relatives/friends/employers to send money for false reasons to bank accounts from where the money goes missing.
37. Money laundering and drug trafficking are international in scope and are increasingly likely to move from location to location and trap politicians, businessmen and bankers. Acts of corruption are likely to become more frequent and to intensify.
38. An organized crime syndicate may undertake both legitimate and illegal activities in one country or a group of countries, and forge associations with terrorist networks.

## 2.4 Issues, Developments and Considerations Needing Answers

Cloud computing is perceived by some as a necessary and obvious way forward. However, certain points need to be considered. For example, three different models have been identified (Global Knowledge, 2010: 1–2):

1. Infrastructure-as-a-Service (IaaS), which is where the company owns the software and purchases 'virtual power to execute as needed'. An example is Amazon Web Services.
2. Platform-as-a-Service (PaaS), where the provider is responsible for the platform for the service and in particular the system development life cycle, application program interfaces, website portals, and gateway software. GoogleApps is an example.
3. Software-as-a-Service (SaaS), where a complete service is offered via a front end or web portal. Salesforce.com provide this type of service.

A number of issues and concerns have been raised about cloud computing which bring to the fore the subject of security controls. It is important to note that (NIST, 2010: 1):

*Security controls are the management, operational, and technical safeguards or countermeasures prescribed for an information system to protect the confidentiality, integrity (including non-repudiation and authenticity), and availability of the system and its information. Once employed within an information system, security controls are assessed to provide the information necessary to determine their overall effectiveness; that is, the extent to which the controls are implemented correctly, operating as intended, and producing the desired outcome with respect to meeting the security requirements for the system. Understanding the overall effectiveness of the security controls implemented in the information system and its environment of operation is essential in determining the risk to the organization's operations and assets, to individuals, to other organizations, and to the Nation resulting from the use of the system.*

Understanding the risk associated with operational activities is key and requires senior managers to place risk assessment and prioritization within a logical context and to place risk mitigation within a security management framework and process. As regards cloud computing services, several questions can be posed regarding whether an organization should engage partially or fully in cloud computing activities and services. The National Institute of Standards and Technology (NIST, 2010: 4) indicates that cryptographic modules and information technology products can be tested, evaluated and validated and these include: 'operating systems, database systems, firewalls, intrusion detection devices, Web browsers, Web applications, smart cards, biometrics devices, personal identity verification devices, network devices, and hardware platforms using national and international standards'.

In the US, the Process Control Security Requirements Forum (PCSRF) was established by the National Institute of Standards and Technology (Stouffer, 2005: 2): 'to increase the security of industrial process control systems through the definition and application of a common set of information security requirements for these systems. This will reduce the likelihood of successful cyber-attack on the nation's critical infrastructures'. Owing to the fact that cyber security needs to be placed within an international as opposed to a national context, it is not surprising to learn that (Stouffer, 2005: 2): 'Members of the PCSRF represent the critical infrastructures and related process industries, including oil and gas, water, electric power, chemicals, pharmaceuticals, metals and mining, and pulp and paper. There are currently over 650 members, from 32 countries in the PCSRF representing government, academic, and private sectors.'

Stouffer (2005: 4–6) has provided some valuable insights into SCADA:

*Supervisory Control and Data Acquisition (SCADA) systems integrate data acquisition systems with data transmission systems and Human-Machine Interface (HMI) software in order to provide a centralized monitor and control system for numerous process inputs and outputs. SCADA systems are designed to collect information, transfer it back to a central computer, and display the information to the operator(s) graphically or textually, thereby allowing the operator to monitor and/or control an entire system from a central location in real time. Based on the sophistication and set-up of the individual system, control of any individual system, operation or task can be automatic, or it can be initiated by operator commands.*

*SCADA systems are often used for electronic tagging of control and data points. Tags can include control inhibit, alarm and scan inhibit, as well as caution and informational messages as allowed in a utility's operational procedures. SCADA systems are used to control dispersed assets where centralized data acquisition is as important as control and are used in the distribution operations of water supply systems, oil/gas pipelines, electrical systems and rail systems. ....A large, complex, and geographically dispersed infrastructure system can be operated by a small number of people in a Control Centre.......Most current SCADA field devices are highly insecure because encryption, authentication, and other security measures were not designed into the devices. An adversary could potentially exploit these insecurities by inserting false commands and responses, modifying legitimate communication, or altering field device behaviour.*

Common vulnerabilities in SCADA field devices include (but are not limited to):

- *TCP/IP addressability*
- *Weak or non-existent authentication*
- *Remote configuration capabilities and modem access*

- *O-pen FTP, Telnet, SNMP and HTML ports that allow for remote configuration*
- *Configuration modes that are protected by passwords sent in clear text*
- *Unencrypted communications with SCADA MTU*
- *Lack of configuration backups*
- *E-mbedded web servers*
- *Default OS security configurations*
- *Uncollected or unexamined system logs.*

Power outage, followed by terrorism, bird flu and extreme weather conditions are considered the main threats to businesses and are now placed within the context of risk management processes (EIU, 2006). A combined event, a natural disaster which coincides with a major terrorist attack and reinforced by hacker/criminal activity, is part of the scenario planning of business continuity experts. It has to be said that senior managers in the US view the risk of terrorism and its consequences differently to European and Asian managers, but there is recognition that disaster recovery plans are important and need to be implemented (EIU, 2006).

The 'system of systems' view, explained by Stouffer (2005: 7) is relevant, as experts often refer to the US critical infrastructure in this way because 'of the interdependencies that exist between its various industrial sectors. Critical infrastructures are highly interconnected and mutually dependent in complex ways, both physically and through a host of information and communications technologies. What happens to one infrastructure can directly and indirectly affect other infrastructures through cascading and escalating failures'.

Stouffer (2005: 9–10) is right to recommend that management think in terms of management, operational and technical security controls (countermeasures) in order that they mitigate the risk associated with the vulnerabilities identified, and has this to say about the controls:

*Management controls are the security controls (countermeasures) for an industrial control system that focus on the management of risk and the management of the industrial control system. The main management controls focus around the following areas:*
- *Risk Assessment*
- *Developing and implementing a security program*
- *System and services acquisition*
- *Security assessments*

*Operational controls are the security controls (countermeasures) for an industrial control system that are primarily implemented and executed by personnel as opposed to the system. The main operational controls focus around the following areas:*
- *Personnel security*
- *Patch and configuration management*
- *Checklists*
- *Maintenance*
- *Network segmentation*
- *Incident response and disaster recovery*
- *Physical protection*
- *Media protection*

- *Awareness and training*

*Technical controls are the security controls (countermeasures) for an industrial control system that are primarily implemented and executed by the industrial control system through mechanisms contained in the hardware, software or firmware components of the system. The main technical controls focus around the following areas:*
- *User identification, authentication and authorization*
- *Data identification and authorization*
- *Device identification, authentication and authorization*
- *Logging and audit*
- *Secure communications*
- *Access control*
- *Intrusion detection and prevention*
- *Virus, worm and malicious code detection.*

## 2.5 Enterprise Risk Management (ERM)

Bearing the above in mind and the fact that terrorist attacks have been launched on private enterprises in a range of countries, it is important to reflect on what risk management involves. Risk can be interpreted from an organizational perspective, as many functions of the organization are vulnerable to attack and various managers within the organization are involved in monitoring and reporting incidents. It is for this reason that a collectivist risk management strategy can be developed and the enterprise risk management (ERM) concept can be considered useful with respect to providing guidance. Fox and Epstein (2010: 3) have placed risk within the organization's 'unique strategy, tolerance, culture and governance' and build on the work of The Risk and Insurance Management Society, Inc. Fox and Epstein (2010: 3) have outlined how ERM can be used to establish what an organization can tolerate in the way of risk, and how risk can be related to the businesses goals and objectives. Fox and Epstein (2010) advocate an approach whereby senior managers apply an environmental and intelligence scanning system to identify risks and match the threat of risks with internal organizational vulnerabilities, and develop and implement an enterprise risk management cyber strategy (ERMCS) that ensures that prioritized risks are documented, evaluated and contingency plans are drawn up relating to possible outcomes. Hence scenario planning and future research are useful, as they provide insights and add depth to our understanding of what vulnerabilities exist and what needs to be done to eradicate the organizational weaknesses. Those organizations that are involved in producing security tools and systems, and/or involved in working on cyber security projects, need to ensure that they are certified and meet compliance standards, because they too are at risk from sophisticated attacks.

The subject of risk covers a wide and sometimes multifaceted area of study and activity, and it is well known that 'the adoption of consistent processes within a comprehensive framework can help to ensure that risk is managed effectively, efficiently and coherently across an organization' (ISO/FDIS, 2009: v). It is clear that the management of risk encourages a proactive management approach; increases the likelihood that the organization will achieve its objectives; and improves the identification of opportunities and threats, financial reporting, governance, stakeholder confidence and trust, controls, operational effectiveness and efficiency, loss prevention and incident management, organizational learning and organizational resilience. It will make managers aware of the need to identify and to treat risk throughout the organization; managers will be forced to comply with relevant legal and regulatory requirements and also international norms; management will establish a reliable basis for decision making and planning; managers will be able to effectively allocate and use resources for risk treatment; enhance health and safety performance, and enhance environmental protection; and minimize losses (ISO/FDIS, 2009: v–vi). Taking this into account makes it clear that: 'Risk management is part of the responsibilities of management and an integral part of all organizational processes, including strategic planning and all project and change management processes' (ISO/FDIS, 2009: 7).

From the above, it is possible to deduce that organizational learning is embedded in and underpins the cultural value system of an organization and that transformation change requires that a collectivist approach is taken towards security management. This being the case, it can be argued that a holistic view of risk will be developed. For example, an organization confronting a cyber attack defined as coded threat A-17 (penetration of a marketing database containing customer details) may not know that a potential threat coded P-25A (a computer program designed to link and erase certain supplier/customer details and replace them with incorrect details) is possibly going to cause widespread damage to the organization's supply base. As a consequence of staff not monitoring the threat(s) in the way that they should, and not linking threats as they should, the risk and vulnerability increases and the sustainability of the organization is put into question. The interdependency aspect has been missed because the acquisition activity plan that was in being, and which focused on integrating more fully a limited number of suppliers with the organization in terms of a partnership arrangement, did not take into account the existing weaknesses of supplier organizations, and when the acquisition was completed, six months later, it was only after this point that the potential threat was realized and that action was taken. Taking action late can be costly in financial terms (system upgrading, management time and the hiring of experts for example) and could result in bad publicity depending on how the threat has materialized and what the outcome was.

Taking action late can be problematic in the sense that management become thinly spread (e.g. dealing with the emergency situation) and as a consequence the management of the business on a day to day basis is diluted. If a risk has not been identified and analysed, it cannot be evaluated and the necessary contingency plans cannot be drawn up, or those that are drawn up will be incomplete and ineffective. Monitoring is key and requires that a formal and systematic approach to environmental scanning (both internal to the organization and external to the organization) are in existence. A monitoring system will ensure that (ISO/FDIS, 2009: 20): the controls in place are effective and efficient, both in design and operation; further information is obtained and this improves the risk assessment process; analysing and learning from events, changes, trends, successes and failures allows lessons to be learned; changes in the internal and the external context are detected – risk criteria, the actual risk, and revision of risk treatments and priorities; and the identification of emerging risks is automatic.

## 2.6 Issues for Commerce, Industry and Government

There are two types of intellectual property (IP) crime: counterfeiting and piracy. According to York (IPO, 2009: 6): 'Counterfeiting involves the illegal copying of trade marks on products such as clothing and pharmaceuticals. Piracy involves the illegal copying of content such as music, film, sports events, literary works, broadcasts, computer games and software for commercial gain. Copyright infringement also includes illegal copying and downloading of digital content.' Referring to the Rogers Review, York (IPO, 2009: 9) suggests that criminal gain from intellectual property was estimated at £1.3 billion in 2006, with £900 million going direct to organized crime groups – however, some considered these figures to be underestimates. The following reinforces the scale of the problem (IPO, 2009: 9): according to the British Software Alliance and International Data Corporation, about 26 per cent of software installed in the UK in 2007 was from non-legal sources; in monetary terms, the UK clothing and footwear industry suffered enormously (the figure is put at £3.5 billion a year); as has been known for some time, and has been confirmed by the World Health Organization (WHO), about 1 per cent of medicines in the developed world are counterfeit compared with up to one-third in some developing countries (globally the figure is put at 10 per cent), and what is worrying to say the least is that the WHO estimates up to 50 per cent of medicines sourced from websites that do not make their physical address known are indeed counterfeit. Internet fraud is also on the increase. For example, in the US, internet fraud was up 33 per cent in 2008 compared with 2007, and the losses associated with this type of crime were in the region of US$265 million (IPO, 2009: 9). The Fifth Annual Global Study of Software Piracy (produced by the Business Software Alliance and the International Data Corporation in May 2008) revealed that the amount of illegal/unlicensed software on personal computers in the EU was enormous and cost the industry £6 billion (IPO, 2009: 64).

Prior to taking up office in government, the Conservative Party (2009a: 2, 5 and 8) produced a report, *A Resilient Nation: National Security The Conservative Approach*, which contained references to the threat from cyber attack and the need to prevent such occurrences. The report states (Conservative Party, 2009a: 8):

> *The nine essential sectors of daily life – energy, food, water, transport, telecommunications, government and public services, emergency services, health and finance – must be able to withstand and respond to extreme events such as terrorist attacks and natural hazards. These sectors have international supply chains underpinning the delivery of their services to customers which must also be flexible enough to adapt to changes in supply and demand. With the cooperation of private sector owners, systematic mapping and modelling is urgently needed to include knowledge of the interdependencies, capacity and redundancy of essential sectors to withstand and respond to extreme events and long-term trends.*

The Conservative Party's (2009b) *A Resilient Nation: National Security Green Paper* placed in context the threats and potential threats that the UK is facing, and outlined in some detail the new approach to security and made it clear that change was needed. As well as highlighting the fact that policy makers needed to think in terms of us entering a new era of nuclear insecurity, it was made known that the Cyber Security and Information Unit would, amongst other objectives, develop a cyber security exercise programme (Conservative Party, 2009b: 14 and 18). The issue of non-proliferation has been discussed and policy advisors from the UK and China are in agreement that in order to avoid nuclear anarchy, it is important to continually engage in 'consistent, widely-based non-proliferation efforts' (Chalmers, 2009: 4).

It has been recognized both in the UK and the US that more needs to be done in order to encourage and develop the pool of cyber security professions. For example, the report entitled *Cyber In-Security: Strengthening the Federal Cybersecurity Workforce* by Booz, Allen and Hamilton (2009: ii) has estimated that both the quality and the quantity of staff entering cyber security jobs, in both the private and public sectors, needs to be addressed because of the apparent shortfall (both numbers and quality). Looked at worldwide, one could conclude that many thousands of cyber security professionals and experts are needed in both the private and public sectors, and a worrying point to note is that some criminal organizations have recruited top quality cyber and legal brains and have developed organizational structures that mean that they can operate from almost any country in the world. More specifically, countries with very poor or inferior regulation, compliance and governance, and high levels of corruption and inadequate law enforcement, are putting managers in companies at risk as they are allowing illegal entities to operate 'legally'.

Possibly the rewards available for those entering the private sector will always overshadow those offered by the public sector; however, the public sector will increasingly need to draw on the services of private sector companies to fill knowledge gaps and this has already happened in the US. For example, it is more expedient to hire outside professionals when an immediate need for advice arises and also, a certain type of expertise may be needed for only a short period of time, hence it would be logical to bring in the services of an outside contractor (Booz, Allen and Hamilton, 2009: 3). Taking stock of the situation, it appears that government needs to sponsor research which will, as best as possible, identify the main threats posed by cyber attacks, and work out what private enterprise, universities and public sector organizations need to do in order to ensure that those dealing with cyber security issues have the right number and quality of staff available, and that the proactive approach adopted results in a collectivist approach to security.

Computer abuse by employees has been increasing over the years and is of concern to employers. For example, a survey undertaken by the Computer Security Institute found that 64 per cent of the organizations that responded to the survey had encountered losses due to computer abuse, amounting to US$378 million in total in 2001 and well over half of the computer abuse was carried out not by external hackers, but by company employees (Lee and Lee, 2002: 57). Although attempts have been made to increase protection via more appropriate enforcement and operation of security policies, paying increased attention to the development and operation of secure systems, and targeted deployment of security awareness programmes, it is clear that human factors and in particular how individuals build relationships with each other is very important (Lee and Lee, 2002: 57–58). Research has indicated that in order to better understand the motives of those engaging in computer abuse, it is necessary to look at the problem from the perspective of what causes computer abuse – for example, individuals who have formed strong social bonds with their peers may not engage in such activity because they feel some degree of responsibility to the group, whereas an individual who does not bond with his/her work colleagues, or mixes socially with those that may be considered to be anti-social in nature, may well be inclined to engage in computer abuse (Lee and Lee, 2002: 59).

The various issues that arise are outlined below and a number of additional issues and questions are listed in Appendix 3.

- How robust is the recruitment process vis-à-vis the vetting of potential employees?
- How secure are computer systems vis-à-vis highly skilled and inquiring minds?
- How does the organizational value system embrace the aspirations of employees?
- If an employee is to engage in computer abuse, will the effects be limited only to the company/partner organizations? And how will this affect trust enhancement between partners?
- At what stage does the organization involve the police and/or make matters public?

## 2.7 Building Trust Based Relationships

It seems that in order to lower the risk of a computer abuser carrying out an attack on a company, it is necessary for management to think in terms of making computer systems as secure as possible and maintaining this level of robustness through time. The organization's cultural value system needs to embrace all staff and ensure that no single individual is alienated. The monitoring of staff and their behaviour is and will continue to be important and also, it is necessary to make the penalties for unacceptable behaviour very clear. One way that this can be done is by talking about future employment of the individual within the industry, so if somebody does behave in an inappropriate manner, their actions are widely known. However, research findings suggest that in situations of high perceived risk, people will deploy a risk-reducing strategy based on behavioural choices which lower their vulnerability to what are regarded as potentially negative outcomes (Cho and Lee, 2006: 119). Stating and reinforcing the threats and penalties relating to computer crime may be worthwhile and this can be done through company seminars, workshops and public awareness campaigns.

Building and maintaining trust based relationships with external partners is key to maintaining long-term sustainable working relationships. However, as well as thinking in terms of internal trust (brought about and reinforced through leadership and teamwork), managers need to focus on developing and maintaining external trust, that is trust developed with suppliers, joint venture partners and customers (Huff and Kelley, 2005: 97). Drawing on their research findings, Suh and Kwon (2006: 198–199) state:

> It is safe to say that the success of supply chain rests on the degree of trust that the supply chain partners believe is in the partnership. Many supply chain tools presuppose that each partner behaves in a manner consistent with expectation based on trust. For example, collaborative planning, forecasting and replenishment (CPFR), a main driver for structural change in the supply chain optimization process requires information sharing, and such information sharing demands trust among and between supply chain partners. Any lack of trust creates an informational balance between partners, which in turn produces unintended inequitable distribution of optimization results (profits) among the partners.

Successful partnership involves coordination and governance, and can be thought of as a form of cooperation (Rese, 2006: 74). It is important to note that those organizations involved in a cooperative partnership need to carry out the agreed policies in the way specified and must be convinced of the benefits accruing and also, they need to be convinced of the need for cooperation at all levels within the partnership arrangement (Wucherer, 2006: 91–92). Senior managers need to think in terms of integrated solutions (e.g. cooperation between internal business units and departments), but in order for this to be achieved, it is essential that this view is extended to include end customers and partners of various kinds, including research institutes and government agencies (Windahl and Lakemond, 2006: 816–817).

## 2.8 The Protective Umbrella

Guarding against computer abuse may seem rather formidable when one takes into account the fact that e-commerce security in particular needs to take into account the interrelationship between applications development platforms, database management systems, systems software and network infrastructure (Someswar et al., 2002: 149). Someswar et al. (2002: 150) have indicated that when thinking about security access control, one needs to first think in terms of both physical access to a building and access to the computer system, which is underpinned by the concept of privacy (only those individuals listed as accessing information in a system should be allowed to do so); integrity ensures that only those individuals allowed to make changes to or amend records are permitted to do so; authentication is key as it ensures 'that the origin of an electronic message is correctly identified'; non-repudiation refers to the fact that the person that sends a message cannot deny sending it and also, the receiver is not able to deny receiving the message; the term availability refers to the fact that the systems are in place and are available when needed; and denial of service manifests in a corrupted hard disk or consumption of entire memory of the system as a result of the site being bombarded by large amounts of data. By taking into account the main components of an e-commerce system (e-commerce development platforms, database management systems, operating systems and infrastructure) (Someswar et al., 2002: 154) and how the various components and tools are linked, it is possible to outline the relationship between technologies and tools. The authors make clear the fact that the security needs of organizations differ and so too do the threats faced by different organizations, and it is necessary for senior management to decide what is useful and relevant, as duplication of effort needs to be avoided. Selecting what is appropriate is the main consideration, and implementing it effectively is another (Someswar et al., 2002: 157).

## 2.9 Justifying the Approach

Alpaslan et al. (2009: 41) are right to suggest that 'managerial tasks also include identifying potential/actual corporate stakeholders to a crisis and their concerns and interests, and involving these stakeholders in crisis preparation and response'. When addressing the topic of 'how to align security with the business', Briggs and Edwards (2006: 13) discovered that corporate security staff need to communicate widely and seek the views of non-security professionals in order that 'security is achieved through the everyday actions of employees right across the company'. One issue that needs to be addressed is that companies should invest in their local workforce because a high turnover of staff can result in security related problems (Briggs and Edwards, 2006: 44). Training and creating additional opportunities may cut down theft and absenteeism and acts of grievance (Briggs and Edwards, 2006: 44). Briggs and Edwards (2006: 49–52) have highlighted the fact that companies have included in their business model offshoring and they have also made reference to the fact that India, which has been a centre for offshoring activity, has been subject to a large number of terrorist attacks over the years and senior managers need to be aware of this, especially if they are working for organizations in sensitive industries.

Drawing on the UK Cybercrime Report 2008, Cornish et al. (2009: 3) indicate that 830,000 businesses in the UK in 2007–08 experienced an online/computer related security incident and in the order of 84,700 personal identity fraud cases took place online. Extremist groups are known to use the Internet and so too are organized crime gangs that engage in money laundering. Referring again to the UK Cybercrime Report 2008, Cornish et al. (2009: 7) have reported that in 2007 there were 255,800 online cases of financial fraud and that the losses associated with this activity were £535 million.

The fact that there are thousands of bot-infected computers in existence is of concern and Cornish et al. (2009: 8) make reference to the British North American Committee Cyber Attack Report which has indicated that 'the cost to business globally of malware and viruses was between US$169bn and US$204bn, and in 2005 the cost of spam transmissions alone was US$17bn in the US, US$2.5bn in the UK, and US$1.6bn in Canada'.

According to a survey undertaken by the Federal Bureau of Investigation (FBI) in 2005, the annual loss relating to computer crime to US organizations was put at US$67.2 billion (United States Government Accountability Office, 2007: 2). In 2006, US$49.3 billion of losses were reported and associated with identity theft and US$1 billion was associated with phishing (United States Government Accountability Office, 2007: 2). One issue that needs more attention is the fact that cybercrime laws vary from country to country (United States Government Accountability Office, 2007: 14) and in some countries it is not illegal to launch a cyber intrusion on another country.

Trim et al. (2009: 347), in their work relating to organizational resilience, make it known that a collectivist approach to security should reduce the prospect of a disaster occurring or if an incident does occur, result in more effective disaster recovery. The work of Turner (2006: 118) is useful, as the six stages of the sequence of events associated with a failure of foresight approach can be used to provide additional insights into how to manage a failure. The six stages have been defined as (Turner, 2006: 118): notionally normal starting point; incubation period; precipitating event; onset; rescue and salvage – first stage adjustment; and full cultural readjustment.

## 2.10 Sequence-of-Events Model

It is clear from the above that cyber security needs to be placed in a broad context, and that governments around the world are concerned about a range of issues that have cultural, economic, social, political and technological consequences. Table 2.1 outlines the main cyber characteristics and factors to be borne in mind by top managers, policy makers and their advisors, and security experts when considering the cyber threats outlined above and the holistic security approach advocated herewith. A diagrammatic representation is provided in Figure 2.1 and forms the actual Sequence-of-Events Model.

## Table 2.1   Cyber Sequence-of-Events Characteristics and Factors

| Current and Future Threats | (1) Current<br>Counterfeiting and brand piracy are harmful to brand leaders and can erode market share.<br>Insider crime is placing organizations at greater risk than crime committed by external individuals/organizations.<br>Fraud is increasingly linked with identity theft and is aided by technology.<br>Cyber attacks are carried out by individuals and organized crime syndicates.<br>A lack of skilled cyber security professionals has been noted.<br>Those producing malware (malicious code) are not at risk of being caught.<br>The amount of fake software coming onto the market is increasing.<br>The problems associated with ineffective patching are becoming more widely known.<br>Social networking activities are placing individuals and organizations at risk.<br>Product testing, evaluation and validation against standards are of concern.<br>Computer abuse by employees is a problem.<br>The actions of rogue governments have been reported.<br>Criminals are engaging in identity fraud.<br>Spyware exists.<br>Cyber sex is a possibility.<br>Child abuse is evident.<br>Hoaxing is evident.<br>A vigilante movement exposing Internet bullies is gaining momentum.<br>Money laundering and drug trafficking are evident.<br>Organized criminal syndicates operate both legitimate and illegal business activities.<br><br>(2) Future<br>Across industry cyber attacks are likely to be carried out more frequently by government established companies, terrorist networks and organized crime syndicates.<br>There is a pronounced lack of skilled cyber security professionals.<br>Those producing malware (malicious code) will intensify their activities.<br>The amount of fake software coming onto the market will increase dramatically.<br>Companies without adequate security will find it difficult to implement recovery plans.<br>Problems associated with the use of cloud computing will become known.<br>The problems associated with ineffective patching will intensify.<br>Social networking activities place individuals and organizations at increased levels of risk.<br>Issues remain relating to product testing, evaluation and validation against standards.<br>A security culture needs to embrace both human factors and technological factors.<br>A monitoring system with internal and external linkage needs to be visible and operational within the organization's structure.<br>Education, staff development and educational programmes need to be established.<br>Operational activities need to be understood by internal and external auditors.<br>More attention needs to be paid to SCADA and areas of vulnerability given priority.<br>The use of remote connections needs to be better understood.<br>Communication between organizations, institutions and governments needs to be improved. |
|---|---|

**Table 2.1**    *Concluded*

|  | Information security/assurance needs to be placed within a risk management strategy. Terrorist networks and their operations need to be better understood. The motives of countries with a poor economic performance and their nationals need more attention. Countries that tolerate markets in stolen data and information need to be watched. Attacks against infrastructure and tourist attractions are likely. The expansion of organized crime in countries with poor or inadequate law enforcement will intensify. Computer abuse by employees is likely to increase. The actions of rogue governments need to be monitored more fully. Criminals will develop new approaches to identity fraud. Spyware is expected to become increasingly sophisticated. Contractors are likely to be the target of terrorists and criminals seeking access to sensitive industries. The consequences facing governments not able to handle technology, terrorists groups and criminal syndicates will become known. Governments need to develop a nuclear counter-intelligence policy. The growth in cyber sex and its possible link with child abuse will become evident. Hoaxing will increase. A growing vigilante movement exposing Internet bullies will become more fully operational. New ways will be found to emotionally trap members of the public. Money laundering and drug trafficking will be increasingly mobile. Organized crime syndicates will be more involved in legitimate and illegal activities. |
|---|---|
| Immediate threats | Botnets attributed to:<br><br>    Cyber warfare<br>    Cyber crime<br>    Cyber terrorism. |
| Targets | Individuals. Organizations (large, small and medium sized). Government agencies. Banks and financial institutions. Pharmaceutical companies. Defence companies. |
| Opportunities | Information sharing facilitated by interchange in the supply chain/partnership arrangement. Organizational cyber security management system. An international cyber security strategy underpinned by counter-intelligence. Education and training. Scenario planning vis-à-vis security assessments. Improved crisis, disaster and business continuity planning. Enhanced communication translated into risk management strategy. |
| Mechanisms | Government funded awareness projects. A collectivist organizational security culture. Micro credit programmes. Organizational learning and governance, and trust based partnership arrangements. Strategic and organizational monitoring intelligence system. |
| Outcome | Generic Cyber Security Management Model (GCSMM) |

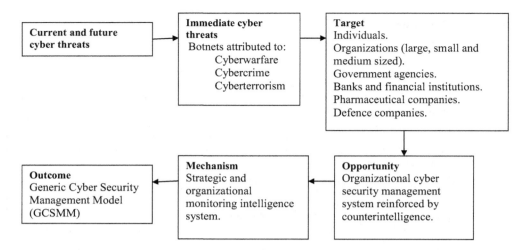

**Figure 2.1    Sequence-of-Events Model**

## 2.11 Conclusion

By undertaking a thorough cyber security SWOT and SLEPT analysis, it is possible to establish if the organization's corporate security and corporate intelligence functions are performing as expected. The analysis of events should also bring to the fore the knowledge and skill base of employees and pinpoint areas for improvement. In order that the analysis is thorough, it is important that such an analysis is undertaken at various stages throughout the year and that new cyber security threats are identified and the risk(s) ranked and priorities established.

Cloud computing is providing opportunities to transform the organization's business model into something dynamic; however, vigilance is required with respect to monitoring the environment for impacts and developments that result in organizational disruption. Having a sound appreciation of risk management should allow senior managers to better understand how an enterprise risk management (ERM) model or framework can be devised and implemented, and how risk analysis can be carried out. There is no doubt that organizational learning has a role to play and various managers throughout the organization should be engaged in forming trust based relationships that promote security awareness to the employees. A well designed and coordinated training programme can ensure that the expertise throughout the organization is utilized to maximum effect. A Sequence-of-Events Model, unique to the company and the industry in which it competes, can be developed and implemented to improve security awareness, and a Generic Cyber Security Management Model can be developed and put in place.

## References

Alpaslan, C.M., Green, S.E., and Mitroff, I.I. 2009. Corporate governance in the context of crises: Towards a stakeholder theory of crisis management. *Journal of Contingencies and Crisis Management,* 17 (1), 40–49.

Booz, Allen and Hamilton. 2009. *Cyber In-Security: Strengthening the Federal Cybersecurity Workforce.* Washington, DC: Booz, Allen and Hamilton.

Briggs, R., and Edwards, C. 2006. *The Business of Resilience: Corporate Security for the 21st Century.* London: Demos.

Chalmers, M. (editor). 2009. *Chinese and British Perspectives on the Road to the NPT 2010.* Workshop Report (November). London: Royal United Services Institute (RUSI).

Cho, J., and Lee, J. 2006. An integrated model of risk and risk-reducing strategies. *Journal of Business Research*, 59, 112–120.

Conservative Party (2009a). *A Resilient Nation: National Security the Conservative Approach.* London: The Conservative Party.

Conservative Party (2009b). *A Resilient Nation: National Security Green Paper.* Policy Green Paper No. 13. London: The Conservative Party.

Cornish, P., Hughes, R., and Livingstone, D. 2009. *Cyberspace and the National Security of the United Kingdom: Threats and Responses.* Chatham House Report. London: Royal Institute of International Affairs.

EIU. 2006. *Catastrophe Risk Management: Preparing for Potential Storms Ahead.* London: The Economist Intelligence Unit (EIU).

Fox, C.A., and Epstein, M.S. 2010. *Why is Enterprise Risk Management Important for Preparedness?* White Paper. New York: Risk Insurance Management Society, Inc.

Global Knowledge. 2010. Top 10 security concerns for cloud computing, pp. 1–2. https://infosecisland.com/blogview/5300-Top-10-Security-Concerns-for-Cloud-Computing.html [accessed on 27 July 2010].

Huff, L., and Kelley, L. 2005. Is collectivism a liability? The impact of culture on organizational trust and customer orientation: A seven-nation study. *Journal of Business Research*, 58, 96–102.

IPO. 2009. *Crime Group: 2008–2009 IP Crime Report.* Newport: Intellectual Property Office (IPO).

ISO/FDIS 2009. *International Standard: Risk Management – Principles and Guidelines.* Reference Number ISO/FDIS 31000: 2009 (E). Geneva: ISO.

Lee, J., and Lee, Y. 2002. A holistic model of computer abuse within organizations. *Information Management & Computer Security*, 10 (2), 57–63.

Neville-Jones, P. Rt Hon. 2009. *Security Issues: Interim Position Paper.* London: National and International Security Policy Group.

NIST. 2010. *Guide for Assessing the Security Controls in Federal Information Systems and Organizations: Building Effective Security Assessment Plans - Information Security Special Publication 800–53A Revision 1.* Gaithersburg, MD: National Institute of Standards and Technology, US Department of Commerce (June).

Rese, M. 2006. Successful and sustainable business partnerships: How to select the right partners. *Industrial Marketing Management*, 35, 72–82.

Someswar, K., Ramanujan, S., and Sridhar, N. 2002. A framework for analyzing e-commerce security. *Information Management & Computer Security*, 10 (4), 149–158.

Stouffer, K. 2005. NIST industrial control system security activities, pp. 1–12. *Proceedings of the ISA Expo*, Chicago, IL (25–27 October).

Suh, T., and Kwon, I-W., G. 2006. Matter over mind: When specific asset investment affects calculative trust in supply chain partnership. *Industrial Marketing Management*, 35, 191–201.

Trim, P.R.J. 2005 Managing computer security issues: preventing and limiting future threats and disasters. *Disaster Prevention and Management*, 14 (4), 493–505.

Trim., P.R.J., Jones, N., and K. Brear, 2009. Building organisational resilience through a designed-in security management approach. *Journal of Business Continuity & Emergency Planning*, 3 (4), 345–355.

Trim, P.R.J., and Lee, Y-I. 2010. A security framework for protecting business, government and society from cyber attacks, pages 1–6. *5th IEEE International Conference on System of Systems (SoSE): Sustainable Systems for the 21st Century*. Loughborough University (22–24 June).

Turner, B.A. 2006. The organization and interorganizational development of disasters, in *Key Readings in Crisis Management: Systems and Structures for Prevention and Recovery*, edited by D. Smith and D. Elliott, London: Routledge, 115–135.

United States Government Accountability Office 2007. *Cybercrime: Public and Private Entities Face Challenges in Addressing Cyber Threats*. GAO-07-705.: Washington, DC.: GAO.

Windahl, C., and Lakemond, N. 2006. Developing integrated solutions: The importance of relationships within the network. *Industrial Marketing Management*, 35, 806–818.

Wucherer, K. 2006. Business partnering – a driving force for innovation. *Industrial Marketing Management*, 35, 91–102.

## Television Programme

Yesterday Television Channel 2010. Pornography – A Secret History of Civilisation (9 August), 11pm to 12pm.

# Appendix 3
## Additional Issues and Questions

Used for structured questionnaire input
1. Interdependencies, known and unknown
2. Nodes in the network that are at risk (external and internal penetration, and risk of duplication)
3. Interoperability
   - Current needs – company (supplier, manufacturer, and various customer organizations, governments and institutions)
   - Future needs – company (supplier, manufacturer, and various customer organizations, governments and institutions)
4. Databases to share information – holding information and shared information, risk of penetration (internal and external, companies and government agencies)
5. Automated reports – frequency, form, degree of detail
6. Management model(s) of partners
   - What organizational value system is evident?
   - What type of leadership style is evident?
   - What organizational structure is in place?
   - What extended organizational partnership structure is in place?
   - What management influence is there?
   - Who in the organization influences the management decision-making process(es)?
7. Business models of partners (offshoring, outsourcing, confidentiality agreements and after-service provision)
   - Immediate needs, tensions, conflicts
   - Future needs, tensions, conflicts
8. Privacy and access
   - Who determines this?
   - How is it determined?
   - In what form does it appear?
   - What accountability is there?
9. Governance and compliance linked to accountability via audit process (internal and external)
   - What are the key factors?
   - What are the main constraints?
   - What are the main limitations?
10. Industry and government involvement (regulations and enforcement of regulations)
    - Current, future, national, international
11. Limitations of sensors – response times, delay times, malfunctions/failures
12. Government involvement in network systems (direct and indirect – consequences of)
13. Cloud computing (control over data storage and data flow: By whom? Where? When?)
14. Computer usage and priority of data sensitivity

15. Business continuity planning and backup recovery systems: Where? In what form? Location?
16. Information technology knowledge across partners and education training updates
17. Ministry of Defence involvement and influence
18. Movement to wireless systems and remote sensing
    - Which industry is leading?
    - Which companies are leading?
    - Which nation is leading?
    - Existing technology versus future technology, the main issues.
19. Threats of hacking, cracking and industrial espionage (commercial companies and government agencies) form, type, access, penalties, frequency, opportunity costs
20. Over the horizon technology and US–UK cooperation versus the rest of the world
21. Time zones and legal accountability and responsibility worldwide
22. Information assurance countermeasures
    - What are they?
    - How effective are they?
    - Who influences them?
23. Interface variability and points of weakness
24. Type of management control system in place (more than one and integrated)
25. Interlinked management systems and variability (threats)
26. Geographical imperfections, internal connections, critical information infrastructure protection requirements and policies
27. Local government, national government and overseas government/interdependencies and areas of conflict or future cooperation
28. Audit trial requirements and planning framework
29. Inputs from senior management, middle management, junior management, marketing, finance etc.
30. User interface agents
31. User interface reports – knowledge, knowledge development, knowledge transfer, skills and training programmes
32. User needs – uniform, not uniform, priorities, backup systems, reporting formalities
33. Security management policy
    - What management structure is in place?
    - What organizational structure is in place?
    - What reporting systems are evident?
34. SWOT
    - Strength – management expertise
    - Weakness – technical knowledge
    - Opportunity – increasing market demand
    - Threat – different Internet language
35. SLEPT
    - Social – increasing crime (internal and external fraud)
    - Legal – accountability and performance against standards, regulations, move to standardization
    - Economic – possible recession (cost cutting)
    - Political – policy influenced by UK and overseas government(s)
    - Technology – existing and emerging technology, known and unknown

36. Interlinked topics
    - Technology failure
    - Pressure points
    - Solutions and compromises
    - Pull and push factors
    - Types of network configurations and their vulnerabilities
    - Man in the loop, man out of the loop (e.g. sensor self-report)
    - Overlapping loops and intersections (supply chain management issues)
37. Network failures
    - Due to infrastructure, overload of data, loss of data, ramifications as regards privacy: Who has control?
    - What are the risks?
    - Are bypass approaches evident? Is backup data system recovery satisfactory?

# 3 Organizational Strategic Governance Framework

## 3.0 Introduction

In order to design an appropriate organizational strategic governance framework, it is necessary to take into account management, organizational and structural issues, resource availability and implications, and operation specific factors. Furthermore, it is unlikely that an appropriate framework will be developed unless cooperation is facilitated among and between industry partners and also, information sharing between government agencies and other relevant organizations and other relevant bodies (NGOs) takes place. The sharing of information is necessary in order that a realistic counter-intelligence strategy is devised and implemented. What management need to remember is that the type and degree of sophistication of threat is changing and all industry partners are at risk. Hence it is necessary for audits to be undertaken from time to time to identify and fix existing and potential organizational vulnerabilities.

This chapter starts by setting the scene (Section 3.2) and progresses to look at inter-organizational development (Section 3.3). Attention then focuses on developing an organizational strategic governance framework (Section 3.3) and the chapter ends with a conclusion (Section 3.4).

## 3.1 Setting the Scene

Doz and Kosonen (2008: 17) state:

> *Strategic agility is most needed in markets characterized by fast changes and growing systemic interdependencies. In such rapidly changing and complex conditions, the usual recipes for sustained advantage do not apply. Scale and scope or traditional concepts of competitive advantage – such as bargaining power and relative concentration between customers and suppliers at various stages of a value chain – do not last. Competitive advantage is constantly being challenged by the irruption of new technology, the imagination of new business models and the clash of competitors from different origins, bringing with them diverse business patterns and corporate values creation logics. In such an environment, advantage is always precarious, and most often only transient. It needs to be constantly renewed, and regained, through innovation. Value creation and capture come from being first with innovative propositions, and from the business-building expertise required to turn ideas into reality fast.*

Senior managers need to be fully aware of the ingenuity of those that plan and orchestrate cyber attacks, and the existing and future ramifications associated with these attacks. It is clear that specialist and skilled labour is needed vis-à-vis cyber security (Baker, 2010) and attention needs to focus on hiring individuals with the following necessary skills: system forensics; network forensics; deep pocket installations; Windows; UNIX; PDA defence configurations; log analysis; script development; exploitation and penetration testing; service coding; reverse engineering; and counter-intelligence (Paller, 2010). Cyber security leadership will be provided by government and a number of cyber security initiatives will be implemented, as it has been recognized that e-business can provide a nation with the potential to leap forward within a short time span by embracing interconnectivity (Neville-Jones, 2010). This highlights the fact that government need to provide incentives for domestic companies to invest in e-business and for institutions of higher education to embrace information assurance and cyber security and link with other bodies of knowledge, thus providing a pool of highly trained and marketable graduates and specialists that can be deployed in various areas of counter-intelligence. The point highlights that industry and government need to work closely together, to share resources and skilled labour and to produce a collectivist focus for cyber security training and education (sometimes interpreted as staff development involving short courses, sponsorship on a diploma or postgraduate programme of study for example).

Being close to universities and monitoring political trends will allow managers, through the deployment of scenarios and simulations, to undertake a risk assessment that takes into account actual threats as well as future disruptive behaviour such as that carried out by activist groups. The latter is possibly less predictable than understanding patterns in existing data which may well identify the emerging actions of criminal syndicates and terrorist networks. So a key point to note is that an organizational strategic governance framework needs to incorporate a mechanism for identifying a cyber attack that is launched from anywhere in the world, at any time and via any form. Effective counter-attack measures need to be in place and they need to be active within real time. The main point to note is that the strategic leadership needed to put various counter-intelligence systems and processes in place, needs to be underpinned by a security oriented organizational cultural value system.

It is clear that security controls deployed in an information system provide valuable information with regards to protecting organizational assets, and senior management need to 'place risk mitigation within a security management framework and process' (NIST, 2009: 1). The cryptographic modules and information technology products to be tested, evaluated and validated include (NIST, 2009: 4): 'operating systems, database systems, firewalls, intrusion detection devices, Web browsers, Web applications, smart cards, biometrics devices, personal identity verification devices, network devices, and hardware platforms using national and international standards'.

Placing cyber security within an international context will ensure that an organizational strategic governance framework will encompass a centralized system for monitoring and will provide a security focus. This will allow an entire system to have real time response. As well as attacks on critical national infrastructure and critical information infrastructure in particular, power outage, terrorism, bird flu and extreme weather conditions are the main threats that have been placed within the context of risk management (EIU, 2006). Scenario planning and business continuity planning are useful aids to disaster planning and recovery, and the 'system of systems' approach outlined by Stouffer (2005: 7) is gaining acceptance as a means of understanding the complexities associated with how the interdependencies between industrial sectors need to be viewed, for example: 'Critical infrastructures are highly interconnected and mutually dependent in complex ways, both physically and through a host of information and communications technologies. What happens to one infrastructure can directly and indirectly affect other infrastructures through cascading and escalating failures.'

Stouffer (2005: 9–10) has indicated that management need to think in terms of operational and technical security controls (countermeasures), as this is a means of mitigating the risk associated with vulnerabilities identified. As regards devising a risk management strategy, senior managers need to (NIST, 2009: 13–14):

1. categorize information systems, and then select the security controls;
2. implement the security controls;
3. assess the security controls;
4. authorize the information systems; and
5. monitor the security controls, and then categorize information systems, all of which is encapsulated within a risk management framework.

The person in charge of internal security is known as the Head of Security and the person in charge of external security is the Director of Corporate Intelligence. The Head of Security reports to the Director of Corporate Intelligence and has their own department. This is to some degree supportive of the view of Fox and Epstein (2010: 3) who advocate the enterprise risk management (ERM) concept. ERM is possibly a good starting place in the sense that top management are aware of what the organization can tolerate in the way of risk, and how risk can be related to the organization's goals and objectives. The ERM model indicates how important environmental and intelligence scanning is and a formalized scanning operation can be used to identify internal organizational vulnerabilities, prioritize risks and evaluate contingency plans. Again, the importance of scenario planning (reinforced by futures research) is made clear.

Senior management need to ensure that risk is managed in a proactive manner; financial reporting is timely and accurate; governance is in place; the management controls in place are operational; and organizational learning results in greater organizational resilience. The following questions need to be answered:

- How robust is the recruitment process vis-à-vis the vetting of potential employees?
- How secure are computer systems vis-à-vis highly skilled and inquiring minds?
- How does the organizational value system embrace the aspirations of employees?
- If an employee were to engage in computer abuse, would the effects be limited only to the company/partner organization(s)? And how would this affect trust enhancement between partners?
- At what stage does the organization involve the police and/or make matters public?
- Should staff behaviour be monitored 24/7?
- How should trust based relationships with external partners be managed?

## 3.2 Inter-organizational Development

Bearing the above points in mind, it is necessary to think in terms of what constitutes a successful and sustainable partnership arrangement. Trim and Lee (2008a: 224) have addressed this issue and have produced a conceptual sustainable partnership development (SPD) model, which is outlined in Figure 3.1. The SPD model has at its core, monitoring and evaluation, and requires managers to adopt a strategic intelligence focus. In order for a manager to become a strategic thinker, it is necessary for them to work with a strategic marketing intelligence framework (Trim and Lee, 2007: 61), as this will allow them to identify information needs and gaps, and think in terms of sharing information to facilitate knowledge development (Diagram 3.1).

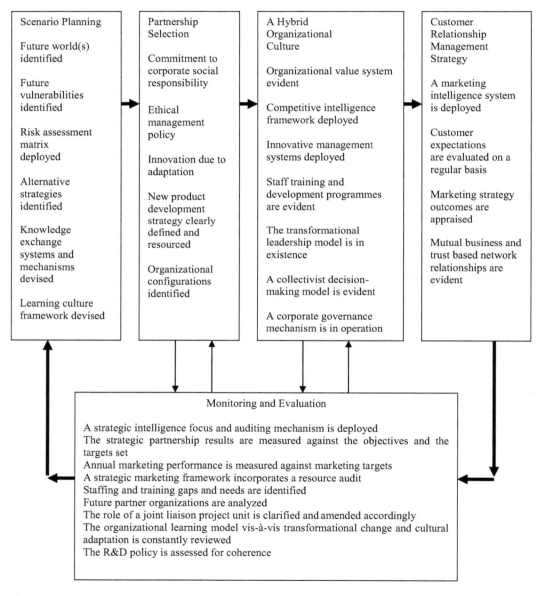

**Figure 3.1   Sustainable Partnership Development (SPD) Model**

*Source*: Trim and Lee, 2008a: 224. Reproduced with permission.

From Diagram 3.1, it is clear that the strategic thinking process is highly formalized and holistic, and there is a close link and strong working relationships among staff in marketing, corporate intelligence and corporate security. Staff based in the corporate legal department and in the information systems and technology department are also involved in intelligence and security work, and the link between marketing and counter-intelligence is strengthened as a result of the formal and informal associations between organizational members and staff employed by trade associations, various chambers of commerce and industry, and government departments and law enforcement agencies. External experts are involved in business intelligence and marketing research, and organizational strategists receive information from a variety of internal sources. The strategic marketing intelligence framework is flexible and adaptive, and strategic alliance partners can also be built into the framework.

The strategic marketing approach, coupled with the contingency management approach, should provide organizational resilience robustness in the context of cyber

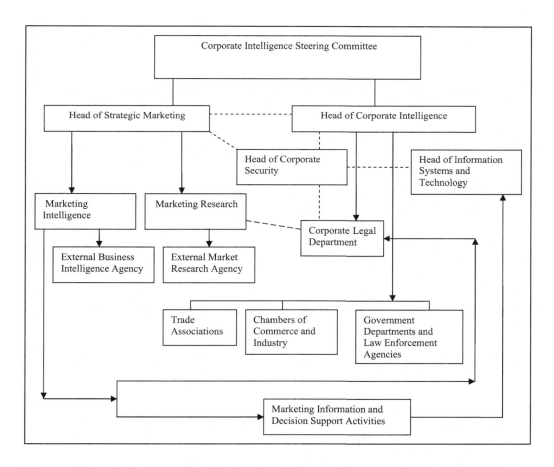

**Diagram 3.1    A Strategic Marketing Intelligence Framework**

*Source*: (Trim and Lee, 2007: 61). This figure appears in Managing Strategic Intelligence: Techniques and Technologies edited Mark Xu. Copyright 2007, IGI Global, www.igi-global.com <http://www.igi-global.com>. Reprinted by permission of the publisher.

security. The issues of operational security and situational awareness will receive attention, and the Generic Cyber Security Management Model (GCSMM) (Trim and Lee, 2010: 5) is useful with respect to placing strategic intelligence within a cyber security context. Senior managers need, therefore, to take into account the main components of an e-commerce system (e-commerce development platforms, database management systems, operating systems and infrastructure) (Someswar et al., 2002: 154) and know how the various components and tools are linked, and have a sound idea of the relationship between technologies and tools (Someswar et al., 2002: 155–156). The meaning of this becomes clear when the following definition of strategic marketing is taken into account (Trim and Lee, 2008b: 739):

> ... strategic marketing is an intelligence focused and led process that has both an internal and an external dimension, which utilises the skills of competitive intelligence officers who work with marketing managers and strategists to establish trust-based relationships throughout the partnership arrangement, which results in the organisation satisfying existing customer needs, producing innovatory products and services that are aimed at satisfying unmet customer needs, and which ultimately results in the organisation fulfilling its mission statement.

## 3.3 An Organizational Strategic Governance Framework

Drawing on the work of Sharman and Copnell, Fahy et al. (2005: 161) suggest that corporate governance needs to take into account the effectiveness of management structures, the role that the directors play, the accuracy of corporate reporting, and understand the effectiveness of risk management systems. Fahy et al. (2005: 161) suggest that corporate governance 'is the systems and processes put in place to direct and control an organisation in order to increase performance and achieve sustainable shareholder value'. The key elements are (Fahy et al., 2005: 164): strategy, stewardship, corporate culture, corporate reporting, IT systems and board operation. As regards compliance, one now needs to think in terms of 'a measurement of responsibility to the stakeholder, the environment and the community. Business leaders must be prepared to demonstrate and explain their social contribution on training, employment, income generation, wealth creation, innovation, and supply chain development' (Fahy et al., 2005: 231).

It is important at this stage to reflect and ask the question: what does an agile company need to do in order to maintain its competitive position in the market? Kim and Mauborgne (2005) have provided an answer by defining a successful company in terms of one that devises and implements a blue ocean strategy. Kim and Mauborgne (2005: 18) suggest that managers need to be aware of the difference between conventional thinking as defined by a red ocean strategy (compete in existing market space, beat the competition, exploit existing demand, make the value–cost trade-off, and align the whole system of a firm's activities with its strategic choice of differentiation or low cost) and a holistic view that incorporates the blue ocean strategy perspective (create uncontested market space, make the competition irrelevant, create and capture new demand, break the value–cost trade-off, and align the whole system of a firm's activities in pursuit of differentiation and low cost). Taking the above into account, it is possible to produce an organizational strategic governance framework (Figure 3.2). It should be pointed out that the topics cited in Appendix 4 and the questions cited in Appendix 5 were instrumental in focusing attention on a number of important factors vis-à-vis linking certain aspects of the framework.

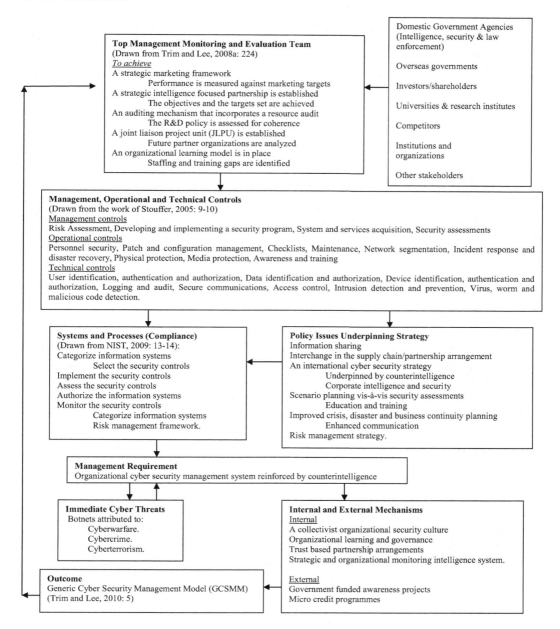

**Figure 3.2    Organizational Strategic Governance Framework**

## 3.4 Conclusion

There is no easy or straightforward way to devise and put in place an organizational strategic governance framework, although it should be added that the strategic marketing school of thought does provide guidance for doing so. The strategic marketing school of thought allows organizationalists to better understand the complexities involved and to incorporate, in a bespoke manner, essential elements that add depth as regards linking management, operational and technical controls with systems and processes. By taking into account how policy issues underpin the development and implementation of strategy, it is possible for an appropriate counter-intelligence mechanism to be put in place. Various internal and external mechanisms can be embraced to facilitate the process and ultimately a Generic Cyber Security Management Model can be developed.

## References

Baker, J. 2010. Talk at the Cyber Security Challenge UK, University College London (26 July).

Doz, Y., and Kosonen, M. 2008. *Fast Strategy: How Strategic Agility Will Help You to Stay Ahead of the Game*. Harlow: Pearson Education Ltd/Wharton School Publishing.

EIU. 2006. *Catastrophe Risk Management: Preparing for Potential Storms Ahead*. London: The Economist Intelligence Unit (EIU).

Fahy, M., Roche, J., and Weiner, A. 2005. *Beyond Governance: Creating Corporate Value Through Performance, Conformance and Responsibility*. Chichester: John Wiley & Sons Limited.

Fox, C.A., and Epstein, M.S. 2010. *Why is Enterprise Risk Management Important for Preparedness?* White Paper. New York: Risk Insurance Management Society, Inc.

Kim, C.W., and Mauborgne, R. 2005. *Blue Ocean Strategy*. Boston, MA: Harvard Business School Press.

NIST. 2009. *Recommended Security Controls for Federal Information Systems and Organizations – NIST Information Security Special Publication 800-53 Revision 3*. Gaithersburg, MD: National Institute of Standards and Technology, US Department of Commerce (August).

Neville-Jones, P. Rt Hon. 2010. Minister of Security, talk at the Cyber Security Challenge UK, University College London (26 July).

Paller, A. 2010. Talk at the Cyber Security Challenge UK, University College London (26 July).

Someswar, K., Ramanujan, S., and Sridhar, N. 2002. A framework for analyzing e-commerce security. *Information Management & Computer Security*, 10 (4), 149–158.

Stouffer, K. (2005). NIST industrial control system security activities, pp. 1–12. *Proceedings of the ISA Expo*, Chicago, IL (25–27 October).

Trim, P.R.J., and Lee, Y-I. 2007. A strategic marketing intelligence framework reinforced by corporate intelligence, in *Managing Strategic Intelligence: Techniques and Technologies*, edited by X. Xu. Hersey, PA: Information Science Reference, 55–68.

Trim, P.R.J., and Lee, Y-I. 2008a. A strategic approach to sustainable partnership development. *European Business Review*, 20 (3), 222–239.

Trim, P.R.J., and Lee, Y-I. 2008b. A strategic marketing intelligence and multi-organisational resilience framework. *European Journal of Marketing*, 42 (7/8), 731–745.

Trim, P.R.J., and Lee, Y-I. 2010. A security framework for protecting business, government and society from cyber attacks, pp. 1–6. *5th IEEE International Conference on System of Systems (SoSE): Sustainable Systems for the 21st Century*, Loughborough University (22–24 June).

# Appendix 4
## Organizational Specific Factors

A number of organizational specific factors have been identified:

1. criminals breaking into online banking networks and stealing money;
2. the time taken to trace and recover money transferred illegally;
3. the consequences associated with the amounts of money lost;
4. the role played by the law enforcement agencies and other organizations and institutions and governments;
5. password-stealing Trojan horses;
6. interdependence (associated vulnerability) and interchange (associated opportunity);
7. the interdependencies between nations, organizations and infrastructures;
8. a nation's cyber security strategy needs to be placed in the context of an international cyber security strategy;
9. the organizational, management and resource concerns relating to cyber security in the context of nuclear programmes;
10. cooperation and information sharing between governments and organizations, and other relevant bodies make it is possible for government representatives to put in place a cyber security management system and framework that counteracts illegal activities;
11. the lack of specialist and skilled cyber security personnel (especially system forensics; network forensics; deep pocket installations; Windows; UNIX; PDA defence configurations; log analysis; script development; exploitation and penetration testing; service coding; reverse engineering; and counter-intelligence);
12. distinguish between: cyber warfare, cyber crime and cyber terrorism;
13. a change in organizational culture is needed in order to ensure that staff become much more aware of such threats and also that people in positions of responsibility communicate issues or highlight problems before they become full blown problems;
14. cloud computing;
15. the risk associated with operational activities;
16. Supervisory Control and Data Acquisition (SCADA) systems and their vulnerability;
17. power outage, terrorism, bird flu and extreme weather conditions are considered the main threats;
18. the context of risk management processes;
19. scenario planning and business continuity planning;
20. management, operational and technical security controls (countermeasures) in order that they mitigate the risk associated with the vulnerabilities identified;
21. trust in the context of service provision; and
22. risk management strategy.

# Appendix 5
# Questions Arising

How are attacks communicated between organizations?

How should the data in the computer logs be made international? (For example, evidence of government orchestrated attacks, successful defences, disasters and errors all need to be made known).

How can an organization build resilience?

How does organizational learning underpin the organizational cultural value system?

How can a formal and systematic approach to environmental scanning be developed?

What constitutes an effective monitoring system?

How can international supply chains be safeguarded?

How robust is the recruitment process vis-à-vis the vetting of potential employees?

How secure are computer systems vis-à-vis highly skilled and inquiring minds?

How does the organizational value system embrace the aspirations of employees?

If an employee were to engage in computer abuse, would the effects be limited only to the company/partner organizations? And how would this affect trust enhancement between partners?

At what stage does the organization involve the police and/or make matters public?

How can a sustainable partnership be established between organizations?

What is the interrelationship between applications development platforms, database management systems, systems software and network infrastructure?

What training and staff development programmes need to be put in place?

What safeguards need to be put in place with respect to offshoring and outsourcing business models?

## Additional Questions Underpinning Governance

What organizational value system is evident?

What type of leadership style is evident?

What organizational structure is in place?

What extended organizational partnership structure is in place?

What management influence is there?

Who in the organization influences the management decision making process(es)?

Is the current overarching business model(s) (including partner organizations) (offshoring; outsourcing; confidentiality agreements; and after-service provision) adequate?

Is privacy and access an issue?

Who determines privacy and access?

How is privacy and access determined?

In what form does privacy and access manifest?

What accountability is there regarding privacy and access?

What are the key factors regarding governance and compliance linked to accountability?

How successful is the audit process (internal and external) regarding governance and compliance issues?

What are the main constraints regarding governance and compliance?

What are the main limitations regarding governance and compliance?

What is the current and future level and degree of industry and government involvement (regulations and enforcement of regulations)?

What limitations have been noted in the technology/technological process?

What is the level of government involvement in network systems (direct and indirect – consequences of)?

## Additional Questions of a Wider Nature

What are the current and future problems associated with cloud computing?

Is the business continuity planning process satisfactory?

Are the backup recovery systems satisfactory?

What information technology knowledge across partners is needed?

What are the current knowledge gaps?

What education and training is required?

What is the current and future level of Ministry of Defence involvement and influence?

What problems have been noted as regards current and future wireless systems and remote sensing facilities?

Which industry is leading?

Which companies are leading?

Which nation is leading?

Existing technology versus future technology, what are the main issues?

What are the current and future threats relating to hacking, cracking and industrial espionage (commercial companies and government agencies)?

In what form will these threats manifest?

What should the penalties be?

How will the industry be policed?

How realistic is it to think in terms of US–UK cooperation versus the rest of the world?

How will legal accountability and responsibility worldwide change?

What necessary information assurance measures will be introduced?

How effective will the information assurance measures be?

Who influences the information assurance measures?

What type of management control system needs to be put in place (more than one and integrated)?

What do managers need to think of in terms of interlinked management systems and variability (threats)?

What critical information infrastructure protection requirements and policies will need to be devised and implemented?

What local government, national government and overseas government interdependencies and areas of conflict/future cooperation are evident?

What audit trial requirements and planning frameworks are needed?

What inputs are needed from senior management, middle management, junior management, marketing, finance etc.?

What are the requirements for user interface agents ?

What is required with respect to user interface reports (e.g. knowledge, knowledge development, knowledge transfer, skills, and training programmes)?

Are user needs uniform? If not, why not?

Is the existing security management policy adequate?

What management structure(s) need to be put in place?

What organizational structure is in place?

What reporting systems are evident?

## SWOT

Strength – Is all the management expertise available?

Weakness – Is the necessary technical knowledge available?

Opportunity – Is there an increasing market demand for the product/service?

Threat – Are different Internet languages evolving?

## SLEPT

Social – Is crime increasing (internal and external fraud)?

Legal – Is there a need for more accountability and performance measured against standards?

Is there a move to standardization?

Economic – Will a recession result in cost cutting?

Political – Is policy influenced by UK and/or overseas government(s)?

Technology – Is the existing technology adequate?

Are emerging technologies evident?

Do types of network configurations increase an organization's vulnerability?

What supply chain management issues have been identified?

How will network failures affect the organization's sustainable competitive advantage?

Who controls the infrastructure?

What are the ramifications for privacy?

Who has control?

What are the risks?

Are bypass approaches evident?

Is backup data system recovery satisfactory?

# CHAPTER **4** *Business Continuity Management Planning Framework*

## 4.0 Introduction

In order to design an appropriate business continuity management planning framework, it is necessary to take into account management, organizational and structural issues, resource availability and implications, and operation specific factors. Furthermore, it is unlikely that an appropriate framework will be developed unless cooperation is facilitated among and between industry partners and also, industry partners adhere to business continuity management planning that incorporates contingency plans for business recovery should an event (possibly low probability but high impact) warrant it.

Such frameworks do not come about easily or by chance. Organizational crisis simulation workshops and computerized simulation models can be devised and deployed to assist the learning process and indeed strengthen the organizational learning approach so that training programmes can reflect reality as much as possible (Thierry et al., 2006: 143–144). Scenario planning can be used to fine-tune the detail and contingencies that are contained in a business continuity management plan and result in an appropriate framework that is company and industry specific.

This chapter starts with business continuity management (Section 4.1) and continues with dependency modelling (Section 4.2). This is followed by IT and risk management (Section 4.3) and this in turn is superseded by business continuity in the context of IT (Section 4.4) and the relevance of strategic purchasing (Section 4.5). Next, attention is given to a nine stage business continuity planning process (Section 4.6), education and training (Section 4.7) and a business continuity management planning framework (Section 4.8). A conclusion is also provided (Section 4.9).

## 4.1 Business Continuity Management

If it were proven that the crisis management model in existence did not reflect the organization's recovery situation, then it would mean that the crisis management model would have to be redefined in order that it covered appropriately three main areas (Smith, 2006: 155): crisis management, operational crisis and crisis of legitimation. As regards the issue of recovery, Upton (2007: 84–85) has looked in detail at various emergency exercises and responses, and states:

*In the absence of common standards, it is difficult to say whether and when emergency response exercises and simulations are successful. They undoubtedly serve a useful purpose. Participants often report anecdotal evidence of this. Perceived benefits include:*

- *greater familiarity with emergency response plans;*
- *ability to spot error or shortcomings in these plans or other operational procedures (... action is not always taken to rectify these problems);*
- *less tangible benefits, like getting to know 'opposite numbers' in other agencies, making cooperation faster and easier during real incidents; and*
- *improved confidence and better reactions from responders.*

Reflecting on the above, it is possible to suggest that senior managers need to think in terms of:

1. formalizing the business continuity management planning process;
2. providing adequate leadership and organizational support;
3. ensuring that training and staff development are utilized wisely using scenario planning;
4. putting in place a business continuity management planning framework that is all-embracing and which takes into account the support and assistance provided by government agencies;
5. building on the initiatives of various trade associations and other institutional advisors;
6. integrating the views of all the stakeholders in the business continuity management planning process; and
7. devising initiatives involving a number of public and private sector organizations and coordinating communication between the sectors.

Simmons (2009: 132 and 136) states that 'Business continuity management deals with keeping an organisation functioning after a period of downtime' and goes on to explain the linkage involving crisis management, business continuity, emergency planning and disaster recovery; and the process associated with building resilience which involves planning for an event, responding to an event, coping with an event and recovering from an event. Simmons (2009: 137) indicates that organizations need to be resilient and to be able to carry on even in the most difficult times. This brings us to the topic of risk management and Simmons (2009: 144) has this to say:

*The pillars on which risk management needs to be structured and utilised within a resilient organisation include:*

- *Moving business continuity from just impact assessment to plotting likelihood and mitigation of all mutating and evolving risks.*
- *The mechanism to combine crisis and risk management, information and corporate security – not just through the prism of either business continuity, risk or security, but together in absolute harmony with enterprise risk management, corporate social responsibility and environmental and ethical polices; thus maturing an holistic view of risk management. This then fully supports corporate governance too.*
- *A process predicated on corporate uncertainty vis-à-vis reputation management, rather than maintenance of an ideal status quo.*

- *A coherent and holistic business strategy that combines accountability, customer confidence, and competitive advantage.*
- *A mechanism to advance the reality of corporate uncertainty – where it is not possible to know what events will alter the competitive operating landscape for better or worse and the need to combine, not just compliment a range of existing but discrete activities.*

## 4.2 Dependency Modelling

Taking these interrelated points into account, it is possible to develop a better appreciation of what risk management is, and Hyslop (2009: 157) provides useful guidelines with respect to this:

*Understanding risk involves understanding why we depend on things we cannot control, through an understanding of Dependency Relationships. The formal part of the organization can be thought of as being under constant attack by the uncontrollable part. Risk Management is about designing the former to be maximally resilient to the latter. While we cannot control the root causes, the uncontrollables, nevertheless the effects are more under our control through management of the dependency relationships within the organization. Interdependency relationships are unique to the particular organization, and only by coming to terms with the actual relationships in that organization can anything really valuable be done to understand, manage and reduce risks.*

Hyslop (2009: 157) continues his line of argument and states:

*Dependency Modeling was developed to capture these interdependencies in a highly visual model so that the consequence of failures could be uncovered in the safe, virtual environment of the computer. Having created the model it is relatively easy to:*
- *Infer the risk to the organization implied by the model.*
- *Illustrate the risk graphically in easy-to-understand terms.*
- *Find which scenarios are the most dangerous to the organization.*
- *Find variations of the organizational structure which carry less risk.*
- *Evaluate the effectiveness of any countermeasures.*
- *Determine which factors are important and which can be ignored.*
- *Support management proposals with evidence.*
- *Avoid spending money on measures which are likely to be ineffective.*
- *Find ways of reducing risk without necessarily spending money.*

Hyslop (2009: 157–158) goes on to state that:

*Using the methodology above also allows us to create an Asymmetric Warfare or Obstructive Marketing Risk Model. The risk model, of course, would be different for each organization looking to deal with Asymmetric Warfare or Obstructive Marketing threats. This modeling is important because it has allowed the concepts of Asymmetric Warfare and Obstructive Marketing to move from an idea, to a concept, through examples, to a scientific base, to a plan to control them. Clearly, the model has developed from the who, when, where, how and why questions. This is not only a complete cycle – but completes the requirement concerning the ordering experience.*

Doz and Kosonen (2008: 17) have highlighted the need for managers to think in terms of how rapid change and growing systemic interdependencies will effect the process of managing complex organizations. Acknowledging that a cyber attack can be launched from anywhere in the world, at any time and through various routes, an organization must be robust enough to withstand such an attack and it is essential that risk mitigation is placed within a security management framework (NIST, 2010: 1). In order to do this successfully, it is necessary to take into account the linkage between IT and risk management.

## 4.3 IT and Risk Management

It is useful at this point to make reference to the concept of a Community Cyber Security Maturity Model as outlined by White and Huson (2009: 308), and to note that underpinning the use of a maturity model is the view that it can help 'an organization gain control of and improve its IT-related processes'. Maturity models can assist IT staff with respect to software development, project management and risk management, and with respect to the security environment, they can focus attention on securing a community's computer systems and networks (White and Huson, 2009: 308). In other words, maturity models can be used to help a community establish its level of preparedness, establish what steps need to be taken in order to achieve the required level of preparedness and also, establish how to measure the community's level of preparedness (White and Huson, 2009: 308). As noted by White and Huson (2009: 308), the word 'community' can be interpreted in several ways but a useful approach is to think of a 'community' in a geographical context (metropolitan area, city, town or village).

The work of Fox and Epstein (2010: 3) is useful, as it highlights the need for staff to engage in environmental and intelligence scanning. The framework focuses management's attention and should ensure that senior management view risk from a multi-dimensional perspective and thus manage risk in a proactive manner. Underpinning this is a commitment to organizational resilience and organizational sustainability. According to ENISA (2006: 7), when thinking in terms of IT security risk management, it is crucial for managers to think in terms of rating the processes from 'high' to 'low' in importance and to determine whether something has a high dependency (the disruption of information systems results in severe hindering of the dependent process) or a low dependency (the disruption of information systems results in minor hindering of the dependent process). It is acknowledged that (ENISA, 2006: 9): 'An IT security risk is composed of an asset, a threat and vulnerability: if one of these items is irrelevant, then there is no risk to encounter. Aggregation of all single IT security risk results in the total IT risk. A key step in the risk management process is risk assessment; this involved evaluating each IT risk as well as total risk, and then giving them priorities.'

The following simplified definitions can assist managers to better understand what is at stake (ENISA, 2006: 9): an asset is anything that has value to an organization; a threat can be viewed as an action/event which has the potential to cause harm; and a vulnerability is a weakness in an asset that can be exploited in terms of one or more threats. Bearing this in mind, it can be suggested that an IT security risk is 'a potential event that a threat will exploit vulnerability in an asset and thereby cause harm to the organization and its business' (ENISA, 2006: 10). In order to put this in perspective, it is necessary for senior managers, when formulating an IT security risk management policy, to think in terms of controls and risk management. For example, as regards controls, managers need to have a sound understanding of (i) logical controls (protection of data, network assets and access to applications for example); (ii) physical controls (including alarm systems, fire sensors, physical access control and surveillance for example); (iii) organizational controls (usage rules, administration procedures, process descriptions and definition of roles for example); (iv) personnel controls (such as sanctions, confidentiality clauses in contracts, and training and awareness for example); and (v) security controls, all of which link the situation to the type of control, for example, awareness training for certain managers would be associated with control of personnel type (ENISA, 2006: 12). With respect to (i) risk management, managers need to think in terms of risk assessment, which is about establishing which risks will be treated (the risks that apply to a business will be identified and then evaluated); (ii) risk treatment, the objective of which is to select and implement security controls in order to reduce risks (the different effects include mitigation, transfer, avoidance and retention of risks); (iii) risk acceptance, here the concern is that when a risk has been treated there may well be residual risks and management need to come to terms with how the risks have been treated; and (iv) risk communication, which is concerned with informing decision makers and involved stakeholders about potential risks and the various controls. Figure 4.1 outlines the relation between the different phases of risk management.

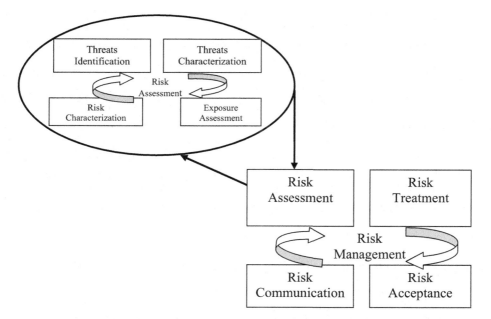

**Figure 4.1   The Relation Between the Different Phases of Risk Management**
*Source*: (ENISA, 2006: 14). Reproduced with permission.

Customers are required to keep their applications up to date and this means a patch strategy needs to be in place (ENISA, 2009: 10). As regards information assurance, senior managers need to ensure that there are clear guidelines for hiring IT personnel and that these are adhered to; and that there is also a security education programme in place (ENISA, 2009: 12). As regards subcontracting and outsourcing in particular, it is essential that provision is made on a regular basis to audit subcontractors and that third party service levels are of the right quality and are maintained, and that remote access policy is defined and that backup policies and procedures are available for scrutiny for example (ENISA, 2009: 12–13).

Referring back to service level agreements, as regards business continuity management, it is important for senior management to ensure that such a policy covers the minimum amount of time systems are available; that a documented method exists outlining the details associated with the impact of a disruption; that the recovery point objective and the recovery time objectives are linked with the criticality of the service; advice as to how information security activities are addressed in the restoration process is provided; in the event of a disruption, the lines of communication are made known to end customers; the roles and responsibilities of the teams involved with dealing with a disruption are made known; the provider also categorizes the priority for recovery and has defined the relative (low, medium or high) priority (in the case of the end user or customer) to be restored; the dependencies relevant to the restoration process (including suppliers and outsource partners) are outlined; and should a primary site be made unavailable, it is made known what the minimum separation time is for the secondary site to be operational (ENISA, 2009: 20).

Guidelines have also been provided with respect to incident management and response, which is an important aspect of business continuity management. For example, ENISA (2009: 20–21) provide direction with respect to an organization minimizing the probability of an occurrence or reducing the negative impact of an information security incident and highlight the following areas of attention by raising questions: a formal process for detecting, identifying, analysing and responding to incidents and establishing how effective the response is; a focus on how the detection capabilities are structured; how the severity levels and escalation procedures are defined; reference is made to how incidents are documented and evidence is collected; reference is made to the controls that are in place to prevent or minimize malicious activities by insiders; reference to a forensic image of the virtual machine offered to the customer and which incident reports are made public; how often are the disaster recovery and business continuity plans tested by the provider is made known; the frequency and occurrence of customer service satisfaction levels, help desk tests, penetration testing, vulnerability testing and rectifying vulnerabilities are all covered.

# 4.4 Business Continuity in the Context of IT

According to ENISA (2008: 8):

> *Business Continuity is the term applied to the series of management processes and integrated plans that maintain the continuity of the critical processes of an organisation, should a disruptive event take place which impacts the ability of the organisation to continue to provide*

*its key services. ICT systems and electronic data are crucial components of the processes and their protection and timely return is of paramount importance.*

Hence IT Service Continuity Management has developed as a separate body of knowledge and the Information Technology Service Continuity Process is outlined in Figure 4.2.

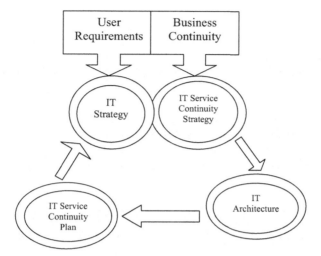

**Figure 4.2    The Information Technology Service Continuity Process**
*Source*: (ENISA, 2008: 12) Reproduced with permission.

The context is clear. Business continuity is perceived as a method of risk treatment to mitigate continuity risks in a proactive manner (agreements and systems are in place to deal with a possible disruption) and a reactive manner (business continuity plans); and a disaster recovery plan details the procedures for restoring IT components, telephony and information after a disruptive event has occurred  (ENISA, 2008: 12–13). It is at this stage important to sit back and think in terms of what corporate governance represents. For example, ENISA (2008: 17) stipulate that:

*Corporate Governance is concerned with improving the performance of companies for the benefit of shareholders, stakeholders and economic growth. It focuses on the conduct of, and relationships among, the Board of Directors, Managers and Shareholders. It generally refers to the processes by which organisations are directed, controlled and held to account. It encompasses authority, accountability, stewardship, leadership, direction and control exercised within the organisation [HB 254-2005].*

What can be deduced from this is that business continuity management is focused on managing risks so that in the event of an occurrence the organization is able to continue functioning to a 'pre-determined minimum level' (ENISA, 2008: 18). Should an impact materialize, it can be suggested that (ENISA, 2008: 19):

*Disaster Recovery Planning is concerned with the actual technical recovery of the IT components and details the procedures to be used to restore the IT components following a failure. As the plan is devised by ICT without the knowledge and understanding of business units as to their IT requirements, it is an orderly but non-prioritised recovery process. ...Information Technology Service Continuity Management (ITSCM) ensures that information technology technical and services facilities (including computer systems, networks, applications, telecommunications, technical support and service desk ...) can be recovered within required and agreed business timescales.*

Table 4.1 makes a comparison of risk management and business continuity. It is essential that senior managers understand the difference and embrace the correct tools and techniques in an appropriate manner in order to solve unique and recurring problems.

**Table 4.1    A Comparison of Risk Management and Business Continuity (Based on the BCI Good Practice Guidelines 2007)**

|  | Risk Management | Business Continuity Management |
|---|---|---|
| Key Method | Risk analysis | Business impact analysis |
| Key Parameters | Impact and probability | Availability and impact |
| Type of Incident | All types of events | Events causing significant business disruption |
| Size of Events | All events affecting the organisation | Those threatening availability of organisation's core processes |
| Scope | Focus primarily on management of risks to core business objectives, to prevent or reduce incidents | Focus mainly on incident management and recovery of critical business processes following an incident |
| Intensity | All, from gradual to sudden | Sudden or rapid events (although response may also be appropriate if a creeping incident suddenly becomes severe) |

*Source*: ENISA (2008: 17). Reproduced with permission.

It is clear from the above that Information Technology Service Continuity Management (ITSCM) is an integral and important element of business continuity planning and needs to be thought of in the context of emergency planning. It can be argued that a thorough business impact analysis is a highly important element of business continuity planning and needs to (ENISA, 2008: 22): (i) assess risks and impacts; (ii) analyse results; (iii) prioritize recovery and define critical resource requirements. Two other highly important components can be referred to: the delivery of the business continuity process and the way in which the business continuity management programme can be sustained. ENISA (2008: 22) has provided relevant insights here. The delivery of the business continuity process needs to incorporate an incident response plan, an incident management plan, a business recovery plan, a recovery support plan, a communications and media plan, an IT service continuity plan, and a business resumption plan. As regards sustaining the business continuity management programme, senior managers need to ensure that staff are adequately trained; the business continuity process is maintained and reviewed; and awareness is developed.

In order that the business continuity planning process is as effective as it should be, it is essential that a business continuity steering committee is appointed in order that 'the organisation's Business Continuity Plans are regularly considered, reviewed, tested and updated when organisational change occurs' (ENISA, 2008: 29). As well as having a business continuity steering committee in place, it is necessary to have a business continuity management team led by the business continuity manager; an incident management team (composed of the senior management team, which will incorporate business continuity steering committee members and which is referred to as the Gold team (e.g. stakeholder management, strategic decision making and media interviews); an incident management team referred to as the Silver team (management of the incident using the incident management plan, tactical decision making, communication briefings and escalation of issues); and a business unit management team known as the Bronze team (management of recovery using business recovery plans, communication with staff, escalation of issues) (ENISA, 2008: 28–31). An organization will experience an impact of some kind during its working life and because of this needs to appoint a risk manager who has responsibility for maintaining the organization's risk register. Senior management need to think in terms of maintaining three risk registers (ENISA, 2008: 56–57): (i) a corporate risk register (the main risks to the organization); (ii) a business continuity risk register (details about incidents that have occurred); and (iii) an IT risk register (the risks associated with information technology and information systems). From information provided by ENISA (2008: 93–95) (drawn from HB 292–2006), it is clear that the business continuity management planning process is composed of six main steps: (i) a definition of what business continuity management represents; (ii) a business impact analysis (e.g. risks are assessed, disruptive scenarios are developed and a business impact is conducted); (iii) business continuity planning (e.g. business continuity management strategies are developed and resource requirements are assessed and collated); (iv) the delivery of recovery plans are outlined (this covers the writing of the plan, activation and development, and the development of a communications strategy); (v) testing the business continuity plan (training and awareness, performance and assurance); and (vi) sustaining the business continuity plan (training and awareness, performance and assurance, overall it is concerned with regular maintenance to ensure the various plans fit together). In order that business continuity management planning is considered strategic and placed within the core activities of the business (business continuity management is considered an integrated business activity and not a stand alone business function for example), it is important to highlight the management and structural, organizational design issues. With this in mind, please consult Figure 4.3.

In order to engage in effective strategic business planning, senior managers need to think in terms of scenario planning and business continuity planning, if emergency and disaster situations are to be handled adequately and the necessary training and staff development programmes are put in place to ensure that those lower down the hierarchy carry out their duties in a timely and responsible manner. Business continuity planning takes into account operational factors and requires that management devise

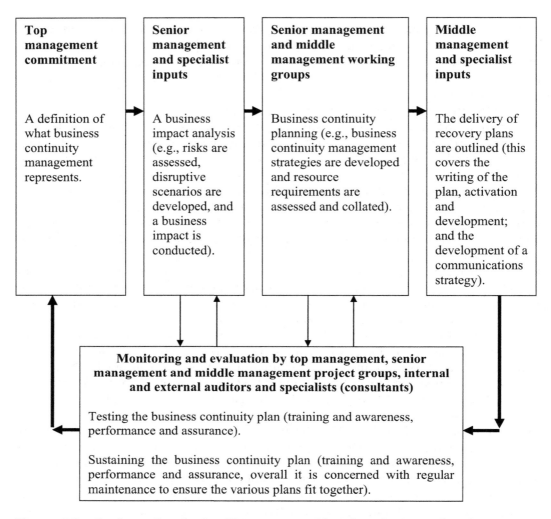

| Top management commitment | Senior management and specialist inputs | Senior management and middle management working groups | Middle management and specialist inputs |
|---|---|---|---|
| A definition of what business continuity management represents. | A business impact analysis (e.g., risks are assessed, disruptive scenarios are developed, and a business impact is conducted). | Business continuity planning (e.g., business continuity management strategies are developed and resource requirements are assessed and collated). | The delivery of recovery plans are outlined (this covers the writing of the plan, activation and development; and the development of a communications strategy). |

**Monitoring and evaluation by top management, senior management and middle management project groups, internal and external auditors and specialists (consultants)**

Testing the business continuity plan (training and awareness, performance and assurance).

Sustaining the business continuity plan (training and awareness, performance and assurance, overall it is concerned with regular maintenance to ensure the various plans fit together).

**Figure 4.3    Business Continuity Management Planning, Structural and Organizational Design Issues**

and implement relevant management models and concepts, which allow the business planning process to run smoothly and for contingency plans to be implemented when necessary.

A crisis/disaster/emergency can be used to generate new insights into management training and staff development procedures, and can result in more effective organizational learning. Effective business continuity planning takes into account the interdependencies between organizations and institutions and is influenced by government guidelines. Bearing this in mind, it can be argued that effective business continuity planning also links with critical national infrastructure and critical information infrastructure in particular.

Taking into account the issues and factors cited in the above and drawing on the conceptual interpretation of the strategic marketing intelligence framework produced by Trim and Lee (2007: 61), it is possible to develop a business continuity management planning framework. First however, an additional number of factors will be drawn on, as they will make the framework more robust. By being committed to corporate intelligence or competitive intelligence, senior managers can undertake 'intelligence gathering which leads to better visioning and more exciting scenario development' (Wright, 2005: 4). This being the case, senior managers can think in terms of making the organization less vulnerable than it is and can embrace the concept of resilience. Sutcliffe and Vogus (2003: 95) indicate that 'Resilience refers to the maintenance of positive adjustment under challenging conditions', and this is an important view as it refers to strategic intent, which according to Hamel and Prahalad (1994: 8) is about developing further the organization's capabilities and securing additional resources.

## 4.5 The Relevance of Strategic Purchasing

One reason why the concept of partnership is important is because marketing managers need to think in terms of building on the work outlined by Porter (1985)(the value chain concept), and this means embracing the concept of supply chain management and placing this within a comprehensive supplier relations programme (Sheth and Sharma, 1997) that results in continuity of supply. Creating value is a key objective and by 'managing knowledge-based strategies' (Kaplan and Norton, 2001: 2) it should be possible for managers to promote an intelligence culture within the organization (Trim and Lee, 2008b: 733). Eells and Nehemkis (1984: 75), stipulate that intelligence is:

> the product of collection, evaluation, analysis, integration, and interpretation of all available information that may affect the survival and success of the company. Well-interpreted information, provided by a properly designed intelligence function, can be immediately significant in the planning of corporate policy in all of its fields of operations. Stated in both operational and organizational terms, the main purpose of intelligence is to help the chief executive officer fulfil his wide ranging responsibilities.

Tan and Ahmed (1999: 298) suggest that intelligence is a 'continuing and interacting structure of people, equipment, and procedures to gather, sort, analyze and distribute pertinent, timely and accurate information for use by marketing decision makers to improve their marketing planning, implementation and control'. Montgomery and Weinberg (1991: 345) state that a strategic intelligence system is about identifying 'what information is relevant and actionable' and not just about the production of data. Competitive intelligence officers are involved in risk assessment and policy formulation aimed at reducing the organization's level of vulnerability, and are 'also involved in the development of resilience oriented organizational procedures and mechanisms' (Trim and Lee, 2008b: 734). The key appears to be to enhance the strategic decision making process and to improve the flow of information from line managers (Ghoshal and Westney, 1991: 23) and this can be done by turning information into intelligence (Kahaner, 1997: 280).

Trim and Lee (2008b: 735) have stated that:

> Scenario analysis and planning is used by competitive intelligence officers to develop possible future worlds, and future world typologies can reinforce the intelligence focus and ensure that marketing intelligence officers and competitive intelligence officers adopt a strategic intelligence

*approach. Marketing intelligence systems should have a practical orientation and be both adaptable and flexible.*

Ghoshal (2004: 382) is right to suggest that managers are confronted with various kinds of risks (macro-economic, policy, competitive and resource) and because managing risk is a complex affair, various levels of management expertise and knowledge are needed in order to manage change. Jones et al. (2005: 383) have linked a human relations culture orientation with a new computing system, and this raises questions about how a strategic intelligence policy can be devised that incorporates and gets the best out of technology. By linking human factors with the application of technology, and by adopting a proactive approach to risk assessment, senior managers should be in a position to devise an organizational resilience value system (Lee and Trim, 2006: 738–739) that underpins mutually beneficial working relationships with partner organizations. Hence, if an organization is to enter into a partnership arrangement with other organizations, attention needs to be given to how potential partners organize and formalize the intelligence activities and policies within the organization (Trim and Lee, 2008b: 736). Sheffi (2005: 13) is right to state: 'The events of 9/11 have brought home for many U.S. executives the dangers of a terror-based disruption, but accidents and random events such as severe weather or earthquakes can also cause significant disruptions.' Senior managers will need to take into account a wide range of threats and to look more closely at what constitutes a vulnerability. Bearing this in mind, it is essential that the findings from a risk assessment feed into the strategic marketing intelligence process of the organization, and that a robust counter-intelligence policy is in existence in order that an effective corporate security operation feeds into the organization's strategic intelligence operation (Trim and Lee, 2008b: 737).

Senior managers will need to ensure that counter-intelligence activities have a strategic marketing component (Trim, 2001b, 2004) as a wide range of threats are visible, including counterfeiting and industrial espionage. Taking into account the type and amount of damage that can be caused to an organization's brand and image, it can be argued that corporate intelligence and corporate security need to be linked more firmly with all of the organization's different activities. Trim (2001a: 54–55) defines corporate intelligence as:

> *the acquisition of knowledge using, human, electronic and other means, and the interpretation of knowledge relating to the environments, both internal and external, in which the organization operates. It provides selected staff within the organization with up-to-date and accurate information, which allows strategists to develop and implement policy so that the organization maintains and/or gains a competitive advantage in the marketplace. It also provides a mechanism for implementing counter-intelligence measures to safeguard corporate data and secrets.*

Such a definition of corporate intelligence is useful, as it provides a basis upon which a strategic marketing intelligence framework can be developed and promoted throughout the organization and its partners. To make sure that there is an ongoing link between security and intelligence work, top management can appoint a corporate intelligence steering committee to oversee, advise and regulate the work of the intelligence unit and an Executive Intelligence Alliance Policy Strategy Monitoring Group can be established that has the principal aim of monitoring the work of the intelligence unit (Trim, 2001b: 351–352).

It is clear that a better appreciation needs to be made as to what strategic marketing represents. Trim and Lee (2008b: 739) have indicated that strategic marketing is an intelligence focused process aimed at satisfying unmet customer needs. Trim and Lee (2008b: 739) reinforce their view by stating:

> *It is logical to assume that a strategic marketing intelligence and multi-organisational resilience framework will facilitate the flow of information between authorised staff in each of the partner organisations and key staff based in government agencies, chambers of commerce and industry, and trade associations. In-house marketing researchers, marketing intelligence officers, marketing strategists, competitive intelligence officers and purchasing officers can share information and data when required, and can draw on the services of external market research agencies, international business intelligence specialists and industry analysts when required. Information sharing needs to be sanctioned by both the Head of Strategic Marketing and the Head of Corporate Intelligence in order that leaks of sensitive data and information do not occur. This suggests that competitive intelligence officers can also undertake an auditing role, and monitor the situation in order to ensure that there are no leaks of sensitive data and information.*

A strategic marketing intelligence and multi-organizational resilience framework is depicted in Figure 4.4 and it can be noted that a strategic intelligence ethos permeates throughout the organization and its partners. It can be noted from Figure 4.4 that marketing and intelligence activities are closely linked, and that scenario analysis and planning are used in order to provide an intelligence focus.

The strategic marketing approach, coupled with the contingency management approach, can provide a basis for understanding how operational security and situational awareness are linked. The Generic Cyber Security Management Model (GCSMM) (Trim and Lee, 2010: 5) is useful with respect to placing strategic intelligence within a cyber security context.

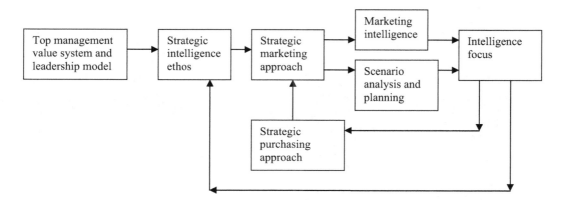

**Figure 4.4    A Strategic Marketing Intelligence and Multi-Organizational Resilience Framework**

*Source*: (Trim and Lee, 2008b: 740). Reproduced with permission.

## 4.6 A Nine Stage Business Continuity Planning Process

Baily et al. (1994: 167) have outlined a seven step multi-meeting negotiation process (the pre-negotiation stage, the introductory meeting, the preparation for discussion meeting, the discussion meeting, the preparation for agreement meeting, the agreement meeting and the post-negotiation meeting) that can be used as a basis for developing a business continuity plan. A nine stage business continuity planning (BCP) process is outlined in Figure 4.5. It incorporates the multi-meeting phases outlined by Baily et al. (1994: 167) and can be viewed as an extension of their seven step model.

It can be suggested that the business continuity planning (BCP) process outlined in Figure 4.5 is not confined or limited to an annual planning cycle but can be implemented as and when necessary. It is possible for there to be a minimum of two and a maximum of four *discussion meetings* and as a consequence there will be two or four *preparation for agreement meetings*. This should ensure that all the issues relating to business continuity planning are discussed and placed in an appropriate context, and that all the manuals/documentation drawn up are as accurate as possible. Furthermore, the various integrated computer information procedures and systems that need to be designed will undergo testing to ensure that they respond in the way that they are expected to.

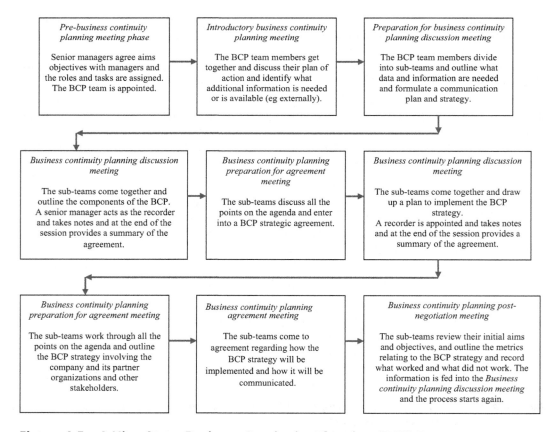

**Figure 4.5    A Nine Stage Business Continuity Planning (BCP) Process**

If the organization's business continuity plans fit well with local and national government contingency plans, then the overall effects associated a disruption should be limited (for example, the recovery system is implemented in a timely manner). Senior managers need to ensure that if the disruption occurs abroad, the organization is not isolated and that the inter-government discussions that take place are aimed at maximizing the recovery situation and that the media is kept informed about events and how the organization is responding.

## 4.7 Education and Training

A disruption of any magnitude is likely to have ramifications for both industry and government, and the growing importance of intra-firm trade (Brooks, 2005: 25) must not be underestimated. Although the concept of theory building has been associated firmly with universities, it can be suggested that a great deal of knowledge exists in the private sector relating to how business continuity planning can be made more effective. Hambrick (2007) has done much to focus on the development of theory and its applicability. Scenario planning can be used by academics and managers from commerce and industry to develop more robust business continuity plans and planning processes, Lindgren and Bandhold (2003), and Ringland (2006) have made reference, and rightly so, to the need for scenario planning to be fully utilized in order to increase educational/training capacity.

In order for the learning associated with business continuity management planning and contingency planning formulation to be effective, it is essential that simulation exercises include a debriefing element in order that the lessons learned can be logged and acted upon to improve organizational learning. Debriefing needs to take place at the end of the simulation exercise and all written and verbal feedback needs to be comprehensive, accurate and reinforce the organization's learning aims and objectives. Weaver (2006: 379) is right to suggest that feedback needs to be produced that assesses performance and results in improvements, and bearing this in mind, those conducting a simulation exercise 'can appoint an experienced observer (teacher/trainer) to monitor the actions of each person involved in the simulation' (Trim and Lee, 2008a: 56–57). Indeed, Trim and Lee (2008a: 57) follow this point through by suggesting that when individuals are placed in break-out groups to discuss data and information at various stages of the simulation, 'it should be reasonably straight forward for the observer(s) to monitor both individual and group involvement and attainment, and to establish how key decisions were reached, how plans were implemented, and how reflection resulted in a change in understanding/interactive action that resulted in a different approach/strategic objective.'

Those involved in simulation exercises need to think in terms of required outcomes and need to (Trim and Lee, 2008a: 57):

1. *develop a holistic view as to what business continuity is in the context of crisis/disaster and emergency management situations;*
2. *develop a holistic view as to what crisis management involves, from the perspectives of policy and planning;*
3. *devise new methodological approaches to study crisis/disaster and emergency situations and to model them more effectively;*

4. *encourage the development of international project teams that can use models, simulations and scenarios;*
5. *encourage the development of new management theory and insights; and*
6. *encourage the use of inter-disciplinary/multi-disciplinary approaches that place business continuity within an international security context.*

Simulation exercises can be used to compare security procedures with information management security systems, and the main advantage of this is that a comprehensive organizational security policy can be devised and put in place (Irvine and Thompson, 2003: 8–9). Trim and Lee (2008a: 54) state: 'Those involved in business continuity training exercises, need to be skilled at assessing technical, interpersonal and leadership skills, as well as assessing both an individual's and a group's teamwork and motivation level.' Ways need to be found to facilitate knowledge sharing and skill enhancement at various levels. Hyslop (2007: 198) states: 'Resilience in Critical Infrastructure and Critical Information Infrastructure Protection has implications at international, national, local, corporate, individual, and political level.' In some countries, a high percentage of critical national infrastructure is owned by organizations in the private sector, and Brear (2007) has pointed out that many of the lessons learned from business continuity have not been disseminated as widely as they should have been to those individuals occupying positions of responsibility for dealing with crises and emergencies; this is worrying as it suggests that the body of business continuity knowledge is rather fragmented.

How robust is the business continuity planning process within the organization? In order to answer this question, it is useful to reflect upon the advice of experts. For example, Turner (2006: 125) has indicated that organizational exclusivity (the disregard of non-members) can prove problematic because a mentality may exist suggesting that 'it was automatically assumed that the organization knew better than outsiders about the hazards of the situations with which it was dealing'. This further reinforces the fact that more attention needs to be given to education and training in the context of security management and intelligence.

# 4.8 A Business Continuity Management Planning Framework

From the above, it can be deduced that a business continuity management planning framework is composed of the following components:

1. A proactive leadership approach  to facilitate internal marketing (departments, subsidiaries and partner organizations) and relationship building with external organizations and stakeholders (government, trade associations, suppliers and subcontractors for example); and communication and advice (public relations and legal for example) linked with corporate social responsibility.
2. A staff development and training programme is in being that utilizes simulation exercises and scenario planning.
3. A model of crisis management linked with emergency planning and disaster recovery, and which includes details of customer satisfaction levels (as a result of trials and tests to improve recovery services and facilities).

4. A model of strategic corporate intelligence and linkage to corporate security that embraces risk assessment and management and which incorporates counter-intelligence in the context of cyber security and which is reinforced by the inputs from dependency modelling.

5. A maturity model underpinned by information assurance that incorporates stakeholder resilience and ethical policy inputs and can be viewed as partner focused and trust based.

6. A clearly defined controls and risk management policy and strategy that identifies logical controls, physical controls, organizational controls, personnel controls and security controls (ENISA, 2006: 10); and includes risk management, risk treatment, risk acceptance and risk communication (ENISA, 2006: 12).

7. An Information Technology (IT) Service Continuity Process that underpins the organization's commitment to corporate governance and ensures that should there indeed be an event of any kind, the organization can recover and be operational again in an agreed timescale (ENISA, 2008: 8–19).

8. A business continuity management department is in existence which is presided over by a business continuity manager and the business impact analyses that are undertaken feed into the strategic situation(al) analysis, and both internal events (brought about by an insider) and external events (brought about by an external computer hacker) are placed in context. Staff in the department need to undertake an incident response plan, an incident management plan, a business recovery plan, a recovery support plan, a communications and media plan, an IT service continuity plan, and a business resumption plan (ENISA, 2008: 22). An incident management team is in being (e.g. Gold, Silver and Bronze Command) (ENISA, 2008: 28–31). A nine stage business continuity planning process is in being.

9. A business continuity steering committee needs to be appointed in order to review, test and update the organization's business continuity plans (ENISA, 2008: 29). The business continuity management policy and strategy needs to be monitored through time, and certain functions and processes need to be audited.

10. A risk manager is appointed to take responsibility for maintaining the organization's risk registers (a corporate risk register, a business continuity risk register, and an IT risk register) (ENISA, 2008: 56–57).

11. The business continuity management planning process is composed of six main steps: (i) a definition of what business continuity management represents; (ii) a business impact analysis; (iii) business continuity planning; (iv) outlining the delivery of recovery plans; (v) testing the business continuity plan; and (vi) sustaining the business continuity plan (ENISA, 2008: 93–95 (drawn from HB 292-2006)).

12. The business continuity management planning framework is encompassed within a strategic marketing intelligence framework and supply chain management is a key component.

13. A security management and education and training programme is in being that is for internal staff and staff of external organizations (suppliers and outsource partners and selected organizations in the marketing channel).

The business continuity management planning framework is depicted in Figure 4.6. It can be noted that internal marketing plays a key role in fashioning internal relationships within an organization and also, the relationship building process is extended to staff in external (partner) organizations. These relationships are placed in a corporate social responsibility context and ensure that all the relevant stakeholders are incorporated.

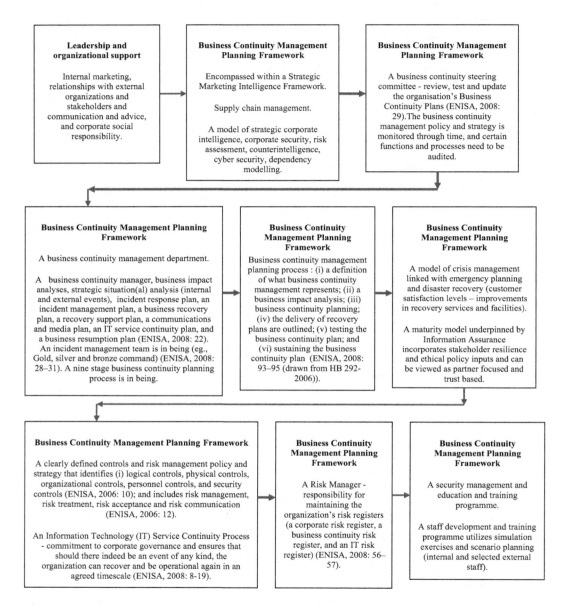

**Figure 4.6   A Business Continuity Management Planning Framework**

## 4.9 Conclusion

Business continuity management planning is a formal process that incorporates a number of frameworks and involves staff throughout the organization. In order for it to be effective, the necessary leadership is required and also, bespoke training and staff development programmes need to be developed to ensure that the contingency plans in place are realistic and can be operationalized in the time specified. The planning process can be enhanced by the commitment to strategic purchasing, as this would focus attention on supply chain activities and identify and rectify any vulnerabilities that are evident.

## References

Baily, P., Farmer, D., Jessop, D., and Jones, D. 1994. *Purchasing Principles and Management*. London: Pitman Publishing.

Brear, K. 2007. Isomorphic learning in business continuity: A review of processes employed to capture and disseminate the business continuity lessons identified, following the events which occurred in London on the 7 July, 2005, pp. 1–42. *The Third CAMIS Security Management Conference: Strategizing Resilience and Reducing Vulnerability,* Birkbeck College, University of London (5 to 7 September).

Brooks, S.G. 2005. *Producing Security: Multinational Corporations, Globalization, and the Changing Calculus of Conflict*. Princeton, NJ: Princeton University Press.

Doz, Y., and Kosonen, M. 2008. *Fast Strategy: How Strategic Agility Will Help You to Stay Ahead of the Game*. Harlow: Pearson Education Limited/Wharton School Publishing.

Eells, R. and Nehemkis, P. 1984. *Corporate Intelligence and Espionage: A Blueprint for Executive Decision Making*. New York: Macmillan Publishing Company.

ENISA. 2006. *Risk Assessment and Risk Management Methods: Information Packages for Small and Medium Sized Enterprises (SMEs)*. European Network and Information Security Agency (30 March), 1–20. Athens: Greece.

ENISA. 2008. *Business and IT Continuity: Overview and Implementation Principles*. European Network and Information Security Agency (February), 1–179. Athens: Greece.

ENISA. 2009. *Cloud Computing: Information Assurance Framework*. European Network and Information Security Agency (November), 1–24. Athens: Greece.

Fox, C.A., and Epstein, M.S. 2010. *Why is Enterprise Risk Management Important for Preparedness?* White Paper. New York: Risk Insurance Management Society, Inc.

Ghoshal, S. 2004. Global strategy: An organizing framework, in *The Strategy Reader*, edited by S. Segal-Horn. Oxford: Blackwell Publishing, 377–394.

Ghoshal, S. and Westney, D.E. 1991. Organizing competitor analysis systems. *Strategic Management Journal*, Volume 12, 17–31.

Hambrick, D.C. 2007. The field of management's devotion to theory: too much of a good thing? *The Academy of Management Journal*, 50 (6), 1346–1352.

Hamel, G. and Prahalad, C.K. 1994. Strategic intent, in *Global Strategies: Insights from the World's Leading Thinkers*, edited by P. Barnevik, and R.M. Kanter. Boston, MA: Harvard Business School Press, 3–28.

HB 254-2005. *Governance, Risk Management and Control Assurance Handbook*. Standards Australia/Standards New Zealand. Sydney: Australia.

HB 292-2006. *A Practitioners Guide to Business Continuity Management*. Standards Australia/Standards New Zealand. Sydney: Australia.

Hyslop, M. 2007. *Critical Information Infrastructures: Resilience and Protection*. New York: Springer.

Hyslop, M. 2009. Towards the hardened organization, in *Strategizing Resilience and Reducing Vulnerability*, edited by P.R.J. Trim and J. Caravelli. New York: Nova Science Publishers. Inc., 149–163.

Irvine, C.E., and Thompson, M. 2003. Teaching objectives of a simulation game for computer security, pp. 1–15. *Proceedings of the Informing Science and Information Technology Joint Conference*, Pori, Finland (24–27 June). http://cisr.nps.navy.mil/cyberciege/papers.html [accessed 22 January 2008].

Jones, R.A., Jimmieson, N.L. and Griffiths, A. 2005. The impact of organizational culture and reshaping capabilities on change implementation success: The mediating role of readiness for change. *Journal of Management Studies, 42* (2), 361–386.

Kahaner, L. 1997. *Competitive Intelligence*. New York: Touchstone.

Kaplan, R.S. and Norton, D.P. 2001. *The Strategy-Focused Organization: How Balanced Scorecard Companies Thrive in the New Business Environment*. Boston, MA: Harvard Business Review.

Lee, Y-I. and Trim, P.R.J. 2006. Retail marketing strategy: The role of marketing intelligence, relationship marketing and trust. *Marketing Intelligence & Planning, 24* (7), 730–745.

Lindgren, M., and Bandhold, H. 2003. *Scenario Planning: The Link between Future and Strategy*. Basingstoke: Palgrave Macmillan.

Montgomery, D.B. and Weinberg, C.B. 1991. Toward strategic intelligence systems, in *Marketing Classics: A Selection of Influential Articles*, edited by B.N. Enis and K.K. Cox. Boston, MA: Allyn and Bacon, 341–358.

NIST. 2010. *Guide for Assessing the Security Controls in Federal Information Systems and Organizations: Building Effective Security Assessment Plans – Information Security Special Publication 800-53A Revision 1*. Gaithersburg, MD: National Institute of Standards and Technology, US Department of Commerce (June).

Porter, M. 1985. *Competitive Advantage: Creating and Sustaining Superior Performance*. New York: The Free Press.

Ringland, G. 2006. *Scenario Planning*. Chichester: John Wiley & Sons.

Sheffi, Y. 2005. *The Resilient Enterprise: Overcoming Vulnerability for Competitive Advantage*, Cambridge, Massachusetts: The MIT Press.

Sheth, J.N. and Sharma, A. 1997. Supplier relationships: Emerging issues and challenges. *Industrial Marketing Management, 26*, 91–100.

Simmons, A.C. 2009. A journey towards resilience: Lessons from the British experience, in *Strategizing Resilience and Reducing Vulnerability*, edited by P.R.J. Trim and J. Caravelli. New York: Nova Science Publishers, Inc., 130–148.

Smith, D. 2006. Beyond contingency planning: Towards a model of crisis management, in *Key Readings in Crisis Management: Systems and Structures for Prevention and Recovery*, edited by D. Smith and D. Elliott. London: Routledge, 147–158.

Sutcliffe, K.M., and Vogus, T.J. 2003. Organizing for resilience, in *Positive Organizational Scholarship*, edited by K.S. Cameron, J.E. Dutton and R.E. Quinn. San Francisco, CA: Berrett-Koehler Publishers, Inc., 94–110.

Tan, T.T.W. and Ahmed, Z.U. 1999. Managing market intelligence: An Asian marketing research perspective. *Marketing Intelligence & Planning, 17* (6), 298–306.

Thierry, T., Pauchant, C., and Mitroff, I.I. 2006. Crisis prone versus crisis avoiding organizations: Is your company's culture its own worst enemy in creating crises? in *Key Readings in Crisis*

*Management: Systems and Structures for Prevention and Recovery*, edited by D. Smith and D. Elliott. London: Routledge, 136–146.

Trim, P.R.J. 2001a. Public-private partnerships in the defence industry and the extended corporate intelligence and national security model. *Strategic Change*, 10 (1), 49–58.

Trim, P.R.J. 2001b. A framework for establishing and implementing corporate intelligence. *Strategic Change*, 10 (6), 349–357.

Trim, P.R.J. 2004. The strategic corporate intelligence and transformational marketing (SATELLITE) model. *Marketing Intelligence & Planning*, 22 (2), 240–256.

Trim, P.R.J., and Lee, Y-I. 2007. A strategic marketing intelligence framework reinforced by corporate intelligence, in *Managing Strategic Intelligence: Techniques and Technologies*, edited by M. Xu. Hersey, PA: Information Science Reference, 55–68.

Trim, P.R.J., and Lee, Y-I. 2008a. An explanation of how case study research and simulation can be used to teach negotiation exercises relating to international security, in *The International Simulation and Gaming Research Yearbook: Teaching and Learning Through Gaming and Simulation, Volume 17*, edited by K. Tan, L. Muyldermans and P. Johal. Edinburgh: SAGSET, 49–62.

Trim, P.R.J., and Lee, Y-I. 2008b. A strategic marketing intelligence and multi-organizational resilience framework. *European Journal of Marketing*, 42 (7/8), 731–745.

Trim, P.R.J., and Lee, Y-I. 2010. A security framework for protecting business, government and society from cyber attacks, pages 1–6. *5th IEEE International Conference on System of Systems (SoSE): Sustainable Systems for the 21st Century*, Loughborough University (22–24 June).

Turner, B.A. 2006. The organizational and interorganizational development of disasters, in *Key Readings in Crisis Management: Systems and Structures for Prevention and Recovery*, D. Smith and D. Elliott. London: Routledge, 115–135.

Upton, D. 2007. Official crisis simulations in the UK and elsewhere, in *The International Simulation and Gaming Research Yearbook. Volume 15, Effective Learning from Games and Simulations*, edited by P.R.J. Trim and Y-I. Lee. Edinburgh: SAGSET, 70–88.

Weaver, M.R. 2006. Do students value feedback? Student perceptions of tutor' written responses. *Assessment & Evaluation in Higher Education*, 31 (3), 379–394.

White, G.B., and Huson, M.L. 2009. An overview of the community cyber security maturity model, in *Global Security and Global Information Assurance: Threat Analysis and Response Solutions*, edited by K. J. Knapp. Hershey, New York: Information Science Reference, 306–317.

Wright, S. 2005. The CI marketing interface. *Journal of Competitive Intelligence and Management*, 3 (2), 3–7.

# 5 *Communication Risk Management Strategy*

## 5.0 Introduction

The strategic marketing concept has a strategic management dimension and can be considered all-embracing from a company–industry point of view. The strategic marketing approach requires that marketing managers think in terms of developing and maintaining a sustainable competitive advantage (Aaker, 1984; Cady, 1984), hence the planning and strategy formulation approach as advocated by Baker (1996: 3339) is very much at the heart of the approach. This said, it is important to note that a communication(s) component of any strategy needs to be grounded in a marketing context or embrace a strong marketing element.

This chapter is composed of the following sections: culture and communication (Section 5.1); business continuity management planning revisited (Section 5.2); communication risk management strategy (Section 5.3); and a conclusion (Section 5.4).

## 5.1 Culture and Communication

The availability of communications services is a key consideration because during an emergency situation (caused by a natural disaster or a man-made terrorist attack for example), local telephone networks can be swamped with activity and this may have knock-on effects (Sommer and Brown, 2011: 78). Indeed, Sommer and Brown (2011: 79) state:

> Localised but significant failure of Internet service in all or part of their territory, possibly occasioned by failure at a major Internet Exchange in turn caused by fire, flood, bomb, failure of electricity supply. Such a failure would disconnect the population as a whole from online government guidance and information and would also inhibit the role of emergency responders.

It is clear from the above that an organization's risk management strategy (ENISA, 2011: 3) needs to take into account the entire risk management and the communication channels, and the communications policy is embedded within the management of risks. In order to be effective and have a coordinated communication policy, it is essential that there is an internally oriented risk communication strategy and an externally oriented risk communication strategy. In order to be effective, risk management needs to become part of the organization's culture, hence creating awareness about risk is very important, as ENISA (2011: 3) have indicated:

*External communication and consulting by specialized consultants, as well as exchange of information and cooperation with other organizations, should also be planned and implemented on a regular basis. The exchange of this knowledge and experience can prove extremely helpful for addressing issues related to both the risks and the process to manage these risks, leading thus to a view on risks that is free from subjective estimations. Furthermore, involving external personnel in such activities contributes towards the renewal of available know-how and risk perception.*

As regards knowing who to communicate with in the external environment, it is useful to think in terms of the local market, the business itself, the competitors and their actions; the broader financial and political environment,; the law and regulatory environment; the social and cultural conditions that prevail; and the external stakeholders (ENISA, 2011: 4). Of importance are matters such as perception, image and reputation management, and this requires that top management take ownership of the risk management process. As regards the internal environment, a number of areas need scrutiny (ENISA, 2011: 5): these include key business drivers (market indicators, competitive advances and product attractiveness for example); the organization's strengths and weaknesses, and also the opportunities and threats; the internal stakeholders; the organization's culture and structure; the assets of the organization(s) from the perspective of resources (people, systems, processes and capital for example); and the goals and objectives, and the strategies that are in place to assist management to achieve those goals and objectives.

At this point in the proceedings it is useful to reflect on how an organization's value system can be developed and embrace the human factors concept (experience of staff, ambition, commitment, motivation, consciousness) and how this links with possible risk mitigation (actions to be taken if a disgruntled employee sabotages the computer system or network) or plants malware. It can be argued that effective organizational learning requires a high absorptive capacity which has two major elements – prior knowledge base and intensity of effort (Kim, 1998: 506). If one accepts this view, it should be possible to better understand what organizational learning is about. For example, Duncan and Weiss (Kim, 1998: 507) state that organizational learning 'is the process whereby knowledge is created, is distributed across the organization, is communicated among organization members, has consensual validity, and is integrated into the strategy and management of the organization'. The word 'communication' is evident and it is clear that top management need to ensure that communication procedures cover external relationships as well as internal relationships.

By evaluating the type of threats posed, it is possible to establish the consequences (impacts for example); the likelihood that such events will have an impact; and the cumulative impact of a series of events that may occur at the same time (ENISA, 2011: 12). Top management need to put in place a security policy and a security education policy that incorporates risk assessment, and link the outcome with the likelihood that threats may/will result in events/impacts in the short term, the medium term and the long term. As regards communication with external stakeholders, it is essential to prioritize and rank information sharing and exchange activities, as this will help to establish management hierarchies and organizational structures.

Trim and Lee (2007: 110) suggest that:

*in the case of a disaster (both man made and natural), a number of emergency staff (including firemen and medical staff) work and liaise with a range of scientists and technical people, and staff from the media, the general public and various government departments. Issues such as working practices, communicating with the general public, and utilizing the assistance of both domestic and overseas based disaster and emergency experts is key.*

During a disaster, government-to-government relations play a significant and influential role, and international institutions collaborate in order to ensure that the recovery period does not take longer than expected and all operational matters are handled as smoothly as possible. This raises the question, how do those responsible for dealing with a crisis/emergency/disaster prepare staff to work effectively in such situations? The use of simulation exercises proves most helpful with respect to this. However, another question surfaces. How can those involved in designing simulation exercises develop communication models that outline how a range of experts and their organizations can produce more relevant inputs relating to a disaster? Those that are engaged in research (Trim and Lee, 2007: 108):

*do need to focus on inter-government co-operation and inter-agency interaction, and develop simulation exercises that are viewed as holistic. Simulation designers and those providing the training are required to think carefully about learning outcomes and how the learning process can increase the skill base/knowledge of those participating in simulation exercises. Those involved in simulation exercises need to think of using relevant methodological approaches and need also to link the learning process firmly to forward thinking, and scenario analysis and planning.*

When considering how individuals relate to and communicate with each other, it is important to think in terms of cultural differences, and this means having an appreciation of the 'concepts of the self and others (as assumptions located *within* persons) as well as to a model of interaction *between* people' (Usunier and Lee, 2009: 43). Taking this a stage further, it is possible to suggest that societies with an *individualistic* value system are likely to be self-sufficient and less dependent in their outlook, while those from a collectivist society are highly influenced by the norms and duties emanating from the in-group (Usunier and Lee, 2009: 43–44). Drawing on this knowledge is important because it will assist managers to better understand and explain how cultural value systems influence the communication process and the communication procedures.

The interactionist communication model, which focuses attention on how views are recreated and interpreted and the 'self' is an active participant vis-à-vis the creation of meaning (Schiffman et al., 2001: 159) and this is important for understanding the psychological factors that are embedded in communication processes. It can be noted that the 'self' is an object (a 'me') (consciousness) and 'subject' ('I') of action. The term *cultural embeddedness* is important and symbols and other communicative symbols in the communication process are to be placed in a cultural context (Schiffman et al., 2001: 160), and this suggests that both verbal and non-verbal forms of communication play a part and influence the communication process.

The elaboration likelihood model of persuasion is known to outline the two ways a consumer can think of acting once he/she has received a message and decoded it. The model is relevant in the context of communication more generally as it can be used to explain how an individual makes a complex decision and how the sender of a message can influence their desire to purchase a product/service. This is useful with respect to information technology service continuity management. For example, the message content, the arguments and counterarguments put forward, and the supporting arguments will all be taken into account when an individual's beliefs are formed and evaluated (Schiffman et al., 2001: 179–180).

## 5.2 Business Continuity Management Planning Revisited

It is important that managers understand the relationship between the different phases of risk management and it is important to stand back and rethink what the model is telling us. Risk communication is clearly outlined and a key element appears to be the risk acceptance dynamic. Senior management need to be aware and justify how risk acceptance is interpreted from the stance of risk appetite and this may change from time to time as the threats in the external environment place additional pressure on the organization and its staff, and security and intelligence gain momentum and are better synchronized.

At this juncture, we can reflect on some key issues relating to business continuity management planning. As regards service level agreements, senior management need to ensure that the overarching policy covers the minimum amount of time systems are available; that a documented method is in being outlining the details associated with the impact of a disruption; that the recovery point objective and the recovery time objectives are linked with the criticality of the service; advice as to how information security activities are addressed in the restoration process is provided; that in the event of a disruption, the lines of communication are made known to end customers; that the roles and responsibilities of the teams involved with dealing with a disruption are made known; the provider also categorizes the priority for recovery and has defined the relative (low, medium or high) priority (in the case of the end user/customer) to be restored; that the dependencies relevant to the restoration process (including suppliers and outsource partners) are outlined; and should a primary site be made unavailable, it is made known what the minimum separation time is for the secondary site to be operational (ENISA, 2009: 20).

With respect to incident management and response, ENISA (2009: 20–21) provide direction with respect to an organization minimizing the probability of an occurrence or reducing the negative impact of an information security incident. ENISA highlight the following areas: a formal process for detecting, identifying, analysing and responding to incidents and establishing how effective the response is; a focus on how the detection capabilities are structured; how the severity levels and escalation procedures are defined; reference is made to how incidents are documented and evidence is collected; reference is made to the controls that are in place to prevent or minimize malicious activities by insiders; reference to a forensic image of the virtual machine offered to the customer and which incident reports are made public; how often the disaster recovery and business continuity plans are tested by the provider is made known; the frequency and occurrence of customer service satisfaction levels, help desk tests, penetration testing, vulnerability testing and rectifying vulnerabilities are all covered.

A risk communication strategy must therefore be grounded in the business continuity management planning framework and if an impact does occur, the recovery process can be as rapid as possible owing to the fact that the procedures are adequately documented and those in charge or associated with the recovery process are competent to ensure that it goes ahead as planned. It is important at this point to stress the fact that a situation(al) analysis must be undertaken on a regular basis or the results from a business impact analysis are fed into the business continuity management planning process so that the data and information available are accurate and can be acted upon. It can be argued that a thorough business impact analysis is a highly important element of business continuity planning and needs to (ENISA, 2008: 22): (i) assess risks and impacts; (ii) analyse results; (iii) prioritize recovery and define critical resource requirements. Two other highly important components can be referred to: the delivery of the business continuity process and the way in which the business continuity management programme can be sustained.

## 5.3 Communication Risk Management Strategy

According to Rouse and Rouse (2002: ix–xx), culture can be considered a framework that enables communication and also a framework for interpreting communication, and strategy draws business communications together. Building on the work of Mitchell et al. (1997) relating to relevant stakeholders, Rouse and Rouse (2002: 246–248) extend the concepts of *power* (defined as 'the ability of one person or group to influence or force change in another's behaviour'); *legitimacy* (defined as 'the behaviour or status of individuals, groups or other organizations that are socially accepted as being proper or appropriate'); and *urgency* (which 'refers to the idea that stakeholders have variable degrees of urgent claim on some of the value being generated by an organization'). Indeed, it can be noted from this line of thought that the stakeholders have been mapped and are clearly identifiable, which means that it is possible for management to identify the attributes and the interests of each stakeholder and in so doing communicate with each stakeholder as effectively as possible through the kinds of information transmitted, the quality of the communication, the frequency of the communication and by associating this with an originating hierarchical level (Rouse and Rouse, 2002: 250).

Bearing the above in mind, it is possible to construct a communication risk management strategy that can be considered generic in nature and which can be reconfigured depending upon the actual company and the industry or the segment of the industry that it competes in (Figure 5.1).

## 5.4 Conclusion

A crisis/disaster/emergency can be used to generate new insights into management training and staff development procedures, and can result in more effective organizational learning. Effective business continuity planning takes into account the interdependencies between organizations and institutions and is influenced by government guidelines. Hence in order to be effective, a risk communication strategy needs to be grounded in and form an integral component of the business continuity management planning framework. The appointment of a risk manager with clearly defined responsibility and accountability will help the organization to develop a strategic corporate intelligence capability and this will raise the profile of the corporate security function.

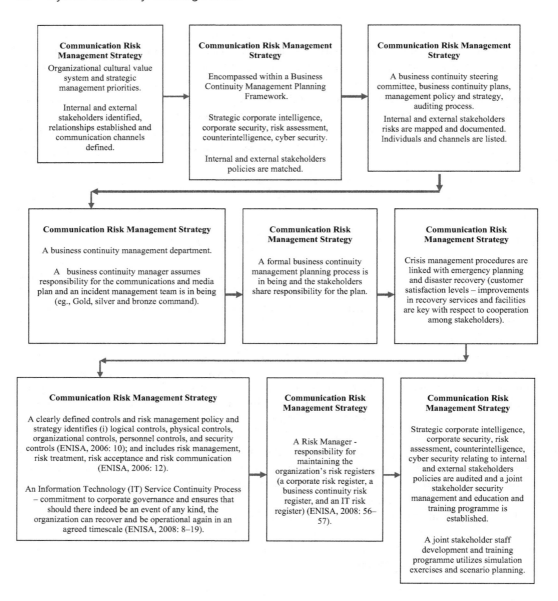

**Figure 5.1    Communication Risk Management Strategy**

# References

Aaker, D.A. 1984. *Strategic Market Management.* Chichester: John Wiley & Sons Limited.

Baker, M. 1996. Marketing strategy, in *International Encyclopaedia of Business and Management,* edited by M. Warner. London: Routledge, 3333–3347.

Cady, J.F. 1984. *Strategic Marketing Management: The Course,* Harvard Business School Paper Number 9-584-076. Boston, MA: Harvard Business School Publishing.

ENISA 2006. *Risk Assessment and Risk Management Methods: Information Packages for Small and Medium Sized Enterprises (SMEs)*. European Network and Information Security Agency (30 March), 1–20. Athens: Greece.

ENISA 2008. *Business and IT Continuity: Overview and Implementation Principles* (February), European Network and Information Security Agency, 1–179. Athens: Greece.

ENISA 2009. *Cloud Computing: Information Assurance Framework* (November), European Network and Information Security Agency, 1–24. Athens: Greece.

ENISA 2011. *Risk Management*. European Network and Information Security Agency, pp. 1–108. http://www.enisa.europa.eu/act/rm/cr/risk-management-inventory/rm-process [accessed 27 February 2011].

Kim, L. 1998. Crisis construction and organizational learning: Capability building in catching-up at Hyundai Motor. *Organization Science*, 9 (4), 506–521.

Mitchell, R., Agle, B., and Wood, D. 1997. Toward a theory of stakeholder identification and salience: Defining the principle of who and what really counts. *Academy of Management Review*, 22, 853–886.

Rouse, M.J., and Rouse, S. 2002. *Business Communications: A Cultural and Strategic Approach*. London: South-Western, Cengage Learning.

Schiffman, L., Bednall, D., Cowley, E., O'Cass, A., Watson, J., and Kanuk, L. 2001. *Consumer Behaviour*. Frenchs Forest: Pearson Education Australia Pty Limited.

Sommer, P., and Brown, I. 2011. *Reducing Systematic Cybersecurity Risk*. Paris: OECD.

Trim, P.R.J., and Lee, Y-I. 2007. An extended multi-cultural communication model for use in disaster and emergency simulation exercises, in *The International Simulation and Gaming Research Yearbook Volume 15, Effective Learning from Games and Simulations*, edited by P.R.J. Trim and Y-I. Lee. Edinburgh: SAGSET, 108–118.

Usunier, J-C., and Lee, J.A. 2009. *Marketing Across Cultures*. Harlow: Pearson Education Limited.

# CHAPTER 6

# Risk Assessment Policy and its Strategic Context

## 6.0 Introduction

Mont and Brown (2011: 1) make a number of relevant points when stating that:

> *Security decision-makers need to assess the risks their companies are exposed to (due to current and foreseeable threat environments) and how current security policies effectively address them; the priorities of various stakeholders and business objectives need to be taken into account; they need to understand the implications, at the operational level, of mandating or changing specific policies; they need to decide which investments (e.g., automation, education, better monitoring/ compliance, etc.) are necessary and most suitable in order to support these policies.*

This chapter starts with understanding what risk involves (Section 6.1) and continues with defining the term *vulnerability* (Section 6.2). Reference is then made to risk assessment policy (Section 6.3) and a strategic management framework is included (Section 6.4). Cyber security strategy (Section 6.5) is given prominence and this is followed by cloud computing (Section 6.6). A conclusion is provided (Section 6.7).

## 6.1 Understanding what Risk Involves

There are different methods of risk assessment and some may be more suitable than others. Some involve mathematical formulas and some are more qualitative and involve the use of score cards for example. In order to better understand the complications associated with risk, it is important for senior management to know what type of business model is in place and what type of exposure the organization is confronted with; more importantly the size and complexity of the organization itself; management's attitude to change and innovation; a consideration of the non-human factors and human factors (both internal and external); and an appreciation of the fact that those who might launch an attack on the organization have the resources to do so. They should also have an overall appreciation of the complexity of the IT resources, the internal and external use of the Internet, the access that the organization's partners (outsourced service providers) have to the organization's IT networks and resources, the extent to which employees engage in home working and remote working, and other considerations such as legal and regulatory requirements and possible breaches; the consequences of an organization not being able to access business critical information from the organization's information systems, changes being made to business critical information on an organization's information systems without the knowledge of staff or authorisation, and the likely impact on the organization should, for example, the confidentiality of the business critical information on the organization's systems be compromised (ENISA, 2007–2008: 4–8). Other considerations that top management need to take into account are the significance of the organization's information systems with respect to it achieving its business objectives and what the impact on various stakeholders might be should a disaster occur with the organization's information systems (ENISA, 2007–2008: 8).

## 6.2 Defining the Term Vulnerability

Before discussing the general subject of risk assessment policy, it is important to outline what we mean by the term *vulnerability*. Sheffi (2005: 20) indicates that 'A firm's "vulnerability" to a disruptive event can be viewed as a combination of the *likelihood* of disruption and its potential severity'. Management need to think in terms of something going wrong, the likelihood it will go wrong and the consequences associated with it going wrong (Sheffi, 2005: 20). McGill and Ayyub (2007: 39) have enhanced our understanding by providing a useful definition of what is termed overall vulnerability:

> *Overall vulnerability is a multidimensional property of a system that describes the degree to which it is susceptible to realizing a specified degree of loss following the occurrence of an initiating threat event.*

## 6.3 Risk Assessment Policy

Strategic risk analysis has been given increased attention in recent years and attention seems to be focusing on what is known as evidence based analysis. French (2007: 16) has stipulated that in order to be useful, strategic threat assessment 'must communicate distinct threat levels for multiple scenarios and it must allow managers to understand what evidence was considered and how it affects the results'. Following on from this, it is possible to deploy event tree analysis and threat severity analysis, both of which are based on detailed data and information, and the deployment of complex scenarios (French, 2007: 16). Other approaches exist and top management need to decide which technique is appropriate for the organization.

The US Department of Homeland Security's definition of risk is well accepted (HSSAI, 2010: 3): 'The potential for an unwanted outcome resulting from an incident, event, or occurrence as determined by its likelihood and the associated consequences.' Taking this into account, it can be suggested that the enterprise risk management model is limited and that risk needs to be viewed from a holistic stance but related clearly to each functioning component of the organization. Should this be the case, it will be possible for top management to more adequately establish what risks exist and which risks are likely to become more pronounced, for each business function of the organization. In other words, a risk associated with critical information infrastructure is not to be viewed as IT related only; this is because of secondary effects but also because it needs to be viewed from an operational perspective and include supply chain, distribution and transport issues, and warehousing, goods inward and outward, and hence payment systems are all part of the equation. The risk of non-supply or a breakdown in continuity of supply (raw material and components) may also prove serious, as this may affect final delivery of the product and a breakdown in customer relations, which may in turn affect the organization's profitability and require reputation management of some kind. The fact that supply chains are international in orientation and customers are increasingly becoming dominant, suggests that a breach of security or penetration of the organization's computer system(s) may result in a number of outcomes such as the loss of financial data and/or intellectual property rights and the organization losing competitive advantage to a competitor.

There is a need for managers to review how risk is assessed and to think in terms of what controls exist and how these controls can be used/developed to explain more adequately what corporate risk management is and how risk assessment can be more widely interpreted to underpin an organization's security policy so that it avoids the silo mentality way of thinking. Risk needs to be re-evaluated from an organizational perspective (e.g. IT, financial, marketing), and linked more firmly with compliance and governance. This requires that risk needs to be viewed at different levels: national and international, as governance requirements differ depending upon the industry and the geographical location. A key issue to emerge is that companies need to increase their understanding of and sophistication of what the chief information officer (CIO) is required to do and have a better appreciation of what enterprise risk management entails. For example, an organization may have a number of security products in place but IT staff do not understand what enterprise risk management is and how contingency management and business continuity planning can be used in a strategic context. Furthermore, management need to understand better what risk assessment involves and how to engage in effective risk communication. This requires that risk is also addressed from a conceptual perspective and that managers devise conceptual risk management models in order to convey a range of messages including emergency management in the context of business continuity planning, actionable policies and programmes during periods of financial disruption, which may then result in preventing operational disruptions from cascading into real problems.

Business continuity as a process needs to be viewed from the perspective of impact criticality and what needs to be done in terms of strategic recovery, and this needs to be placed in the context of managing assets. So the terms *risk*, *criticality*, *value of the asset* (impact on the asset), *risk profile* (e.g. risk related to individual assets), *critical business requirements* and *business continuity* are all linked and can be portrayed in a conceptual risk model.

Human resource staff need to ensure that employees have the necessary skills to ensure that a strategic approach to risk assessment is undertaken, and that staff responsible for setting financial targets are aware of what risk management is and how risk at the functional level is translated into an overarching enterprise risk management model. Managers also need to be aware of contract risk and project risk, and customer relationship management (CRM) and enterprise resource planning for example.

Top management are concerned with enterprise risk management (Fox and Epstein, 2010) but enterprise risk management is not linked to a standard. Furthermore, as regards the controls, management need to know the value of the assets and how the assets are to be protected. As regards financial controls, managers need to ask 'How much of the revenue is protected?' So how much revenue is protected? And how much is at risk?

Underlying this is the concept of countermeasures against risks and how important and relevant the financial controls are in terms of security and business continuity, and in relation to brand reputation. What also has to be borne in mind is if a company's brand loses value then how does this affect the company's share price? If an organization has a problem but management deny that a problem exists, then consumers may stop buying the company's product, hence reputation risk may be key.

Senior management also need to think in terms of the opportunity costs associated with doing business and this may necessitate a better understanding of political risk. An organizational approach to risk assessment will involve senior management thinking in terms of business continuity planning and devising a resilience model, which incorporates disaster and emergency management, and this means that senior managers need to prioritize risk, identify threats and take action to reduce the effect of a potential impact, assuming that if something occurs, an impact is likely. If a number of impacts occur simultaneously or in quick succession, then the consequences may be severe.

As regards the supply chain, management need to understand that there are risks/vulnerabilities evident and that it is not possible to transfer risk because it is not possible to transfer the ownership of risk, and risk needs to be managed. Countermeasures need to be in place to reduce risk or the effects of an impact, and one of the arguments against adopting an enterprise risk management model is that companies in different industries need different models. Devising a generic model of risk is appropriate, but the detail required is different depending on the industry in question.

An adequate risk assessment requires managers to take into account the technological, human and related organizational vulnerabilities in an integrated and focused manner. The human factor element is particularly pronounced because organizational staff/specialists are required to judge or score the various threats identified and to develop countermeasures. Integrated governance, risk and compliance (iGRC) improves the information flow within the decision making process, and creates value by identifying future problems/problem areas and providing a holistic approach to holding people within the organization accountable for formulating realistic and timely contingency plans.

Risk assessment takes into account the various views of experts, based in different industries and representing different professional groups, who are skilled enough to provide judgements underpinned by knowledge and expertise. However, different methodological approaches exist with respect to developing and explaining how risk can be measured/interpreted, and it is for this reason that managers working in the same industry may approach the risk assessment exercise from a different perspective depending upon whether the organization is a leader or follower, or whether it is publicly owned or privately owed, or whether it is domestic or global in its operations. For example, there may be similarities between organizations in different sectors (e.g. banking and insurance) but they have different drivers; differ in context (large or small or medium sized companies); and have a similar but different customer base. It can also be suggested that some customer organizations are operating in a risky way, or are competing in a more risk intense industry or a riskier part of the world.

As regards outsourcing and offshoring, there may be a case for undertaking due diligence exercises in order to identify hidden risks, and one risk which is not always visible is the human resources element. Outsourcing and service provision in the context of supporting services may be financially viable but quality of work and continuity of supply, and the loss of intellectual property rights, may not be so immediately visible. To this can be added health and safety risks, and in the case of the oil industry, health and safety and non-financial return (e.g. barren oil fields) work together in order to increase the level of risk and non-return on investment. To this can be added energy supply and power and a lack of it or a breakdown in power provision and the possibility that an oil rig may become non-functional. If the argument is expanded to include sabotage, or unexpected acts by terrorists, or appropriation of assets by an overseas government, then the complexity increases. And one can also add factors such as the fall in the price of a barrel of oil and the effect on world markets; breakthroughs in other forms of energy production such as wind power which may affect the way in which national governments view the supply of energy; and the role of government agencies and increased regulation after oil spills.

Senior managers need to think in terms of adapting the enterprise risk management model to their particular organization and develop a matrix model which becomes a generic model of risk. Deciding how much complexity to build into the process is important and care has to be taken that the generic model does not become too specialized and too rigid. The grounded theory approach can be used to develop and build an enterprise risk management model that takes into account risk at various levels (tactical, operational and strategic) and links with a customer relationship strategy. Possibly senior management need to define more clearly what the organization's risk strategy is supposed to cover and ensure that the organization's cultural value system views risk from a business-to-business (B2B) and business-to-customer (B2C) perspective. It can also be argued that enterprise resource planning is important as it identifies various supporting services which may or may not be viewed as essential and at risk. The issue of interoperability is another important consideration in the context of a partnership arrangement, and any holistic model of risk needs to include supply chain activity, and in the case of B2B and B2C, the nodes evident in the marketing channels need to be identified from a risk perspective.

It seems possible that senior management would ask the question: 'What does a holistic model of risk look like?' Ultimately, senior management need to decide who within the organization and/or partnership arrangement has responsibility for network security beyond the organization's boundaries. Although government organizations such as the UK's CPNI can and does offer specific advice to companies in the UK, it is the responsibility of senior management to develop a risk strategy that embraces and deploys appropriate technology and at the same time does not erode the human factor element, which draws upon the insights of organizational staff and their external advisors. External advisors have independent knowledge about the utilization of international standards, and various experts can be consulted regarding how enterprise resource planning can more adequately embrace risk management. Focusing on cloud computing, it is clear that different models exist and each cloud computing model may require a different or a broader view of what risk is.

In addition to the above question, senior management are also likely to ask: 'How can a holistic model of risk adequately take into account the unknown factors associated with cloud computing?' Senior management need to bear in mind that as the nature of the threat(s) changes through time, a new approach to risk management or a new way of assessing the risks confronting an organization needs to be found. But more is required. A new approach to risk assessment is needed in the face of changing cyber developments and it is not just a question of adding additional threats to a 'new' threat list. One way forward is for management to produce a generic model of risk, which could stem from a cyber security analysis, and then link with the cyber security IT systems/tools deployed; however, what needs to be borne in mind is that the same risk may be triggered by different actors (people) or events and the impacts may occur at different times.

Risk has a direct impact on cost. For example, risk management requires that an impact, which could be deemed operational (e.g. financial) or technological (e.g. production), and its consequences is studied with cost in mind to produce a more robust/resilient organization; however, the additional financial costs of making the organization more resilient maybe inhibitive. Senior management need to realize that implementing countermeasures and controls to nullify risk may not be the full answer in the sense that the controls in place do not give 100 per cent cover, and therefore what is known as *residual risk* in financial terms has to be taken into consideration.

The weighting factors need to be clarified so that the impacts associated with the event are changed through time. Impacts and their effects need to be linked with acceptable, projected losses and/or a compromise needs to be agreed between functional heads that these are the most severe risks in the risk matrix. The risk matrix needs to be made available to all senior managers, the degree of risk, how it is estimated and the appendix listing scenarios underpinning the possible risk outcomes, all need to be made available for consultation and future discussion about risk management policy.

Senior management will need to agree upon a common definition of risk and identify different types of risk, and establish the commonality between different industry risk models. Furthermore, attention will need to be given to which risk analysis technique on an industry-by-industry basis is more relevant than others and can help managers to mitigate against risk, and how they can devise a risk communication strategy.

It seems possible, that senior management would ask the question: 'What would a conceptual generic model of risk, based on a cyber security analysis, look like?' As outlined by BSI (2010: 17–18), risk assessment is 'the overall process of risk identification, risk analysis and risk evaluation'. At the risk identification stage, managers need to identify and list the sources of risk, and make reference to their causes and potential consequences. It is important that management are aware of the potential cascade effects and also the cumulative effects, and scenario analysis can be used to make the consequences of an impact more obvious than might be the case, and various experts can be called upon to add depth to how the impacts and their consequences can be interpreted (BSI, 2010: 17). With respect to risk analysis, it is crucial that managers develop an understanding and an appreciation of risk, the causes and sources of risk, and the consequences and the interdependence of the various risks and their sources. Understanding the level of risk involved, how the level of risk can be communicated, and the likely impacts should the risk materialize are important considerations, and modelling can be used to explain the intricacies involved (BSI, 2010: 18). With respect to risk evaluation, managers are concerned that the outcomes associated with risk analysis aid the decision making process and in particular, they need to establish which of the risks identified need treatment and what the priorities are for treatment implementation (BSI, 2010: 18). It is important to highlight the need for accuracy and detail, as risk evaluation paves the way for risk treatment and this may warrant additional resources being deployed to provide more robust countermeasures.

Maintaining a sustainable competitive advantage needs to be viewed from the context of how able an organization is to withstand a number of impacts. It has been established that an appropriate definition of resilience is (HSSAI, 2010: 9):

*the ability of a system to attain the objectives of resisting, absorbing, and recovering from the impact of an adverse event, before, during, and after its occurrence. It is also a dynamic process that seeks to learn from incidents to strengthen capabilities of the system in meeting future challenges. The goals are to maintain continuity of function, degrading gracefully, and recover system functionality to a pre-designated level, as rapidly as desired and feasible.*

Following through the logic of Kahan et al. (2009: 29–30), for example, resilience principles need to be mapped against resilience objectives, it is clear that by building appropriate organizational defences, management can ensure that the threats identified will have a limited impact on the organization should they materialize or if they do they will not affect the operational capability of the organization, as appropriate recovery systems and procedures are in place. By being able to absorb impacts the organization will increase its robustness through time and this will act as a beacon for other less robust organizations in the industry. It has often been argued that organizations need to be agile/ dynamic and by being flexible, they are able to devise relevant and timely policies that translate into risk mitigation strategies, and this will further strengthen the organization's ability to become adaptable and for management to engage in risk-informed planning and strategy implementation. In other words, risk assessment will be integrated within the strategic management process and managers in each functional area of activity will engage in risk analysis. A risk expert will be placed in overall charge of the process and report directly or via a senior manager to the board or a board representative. In the context of a partnership arrangement, it can be noted that the risk assessment process in one organization will be replicated in partner organizations and as a consequence there will be a strategic risk assessment partnership process in being. This will add depth to the risk decision making process, as it will continually be updated from a number of internal and external sources, and will as a consequence help senior management to make informed strategic decisions.

Because the level of complexity is increasing, it can be argued that senior managers in the private sector will need to work more closely with senior managers in the public sector, if the strategic risk assessment partnership process that is established is going to adequately take into account what is happening in the areas of critical national infrastructure and critical information infrastructure. By implementing a collectivist decision making approach, it will be possible to work with government representatives in a much more open manner than is the case at present. Both the private sector and indeed government are keen to ensure that adequate investment is maintained in updating and improving a nation's critical national infrastructure and critical information infrastructure; however, unforeseen impacts will result in a reassessment of investment needs and will possibly place stress on overstretched financial sources, which ultimately places pressure both on individual organizations and the government to invest additional sums of money in infrastructure in times of uncertainty.

Taking this a step further, it can be argued that senior managers in the private sector need to work with government policy advisors and think in terms of identifying and making sense of the four resilience domains highlighted by HSSAI (2010: 6–7): infrastructure, organizations, communities and ecosystems. This would ensure that critical information infrastructure is viewed as a whole and that all the interlinked systems and networks, all associated supply chains, all business related and non-business related activities, and the links between a community and the physical environment are known and are protected.

This suggests that risk assessment is wider than merely assessing the likely impacts on an organization should an event materialize, as it brings into focus how organizations relate to the wider environment. The wider environment includes where workers live and how they interact with each other when not at work, and also, how corporate social responsibility programmes integrate with local community activities.

Soo Hoo (2000: 3) has provided a useful insight into risk and states that risk assessment 'is the process for identifying, characterizing, and understanding risk; that is, studying, analyzing, and describing the set of outcomes and likelihoods for a given endeavour'. Soo Hoo (2000: 3) goes on to state: 'Risk management is a policy process wherein alternative strategies for dealing with risk are weighed and decisions about acceptable risks are made. The strategies consist of policy options that have varying effects on risk, including the reduction, removal, or reallocation of risk'.

Taylor et al. (2002: 3) talk in terms of the survivability of computer systems and how they are able to recover from an attack. Furthermore, Taylor et al. (2002: 3) outline the probability risk assessment approach, which is composed of three stages: (i) risk identification, (ii) risk quantification and (iii) risk evaluation and acceptance. With respect to risk identification, of key importance is knowing what can go wrong and this requires that the source of a risk is identified. As regards risk quantification, managers are keen to establish the likelihood that something will go wrong and what the consequences will be. This demands that the probability is assessed and the causal relationships and impacts are modelled. Finally, risk evaluation and acceptance challenges management to establish what can be done and establish the options available and the necessary trade-offs. The emphasis here is on creating policy options and making trade-offs vis-à-vis risks and the cost/benefit of mitigation. The relationships between the risk management principles, framework and process are outlined in Figure 6.1.

## 6.4 Strategic Management Framework

What are senior managers in the private sector required to do in order to prepare the organization to protect itself from impending threats? They need to appraise the organization so that any internal threat is identified and eradicated and also, any external threat or threat on the horizon is eradicated before it can do damage. The strategic marketing management framework outlined by Aaker (1992: 23) is useful with respect to this because it can be expanded to include (in the internal and external dimensions) both partner organizations and branches of government. Customers include end users (consumers) and those that buy for resale, and government departments and institutions for example. A thorough market analysis will include trends and key success factors, and a thorough internal analysis will identify organizational capabilities and constraints. As regards an environmental analysis, of key concern to senior managers and policy advisers are: technological advances and government support mechanisms, and a wide and available skill base to draw on. Aaker and McLoughlin (2010: 93) have indicated that strategists need to think broadly and establish: (i) what a strategic uncertainty is related to (trends or events impacting a business), the importance of the business and the number of businesses likely to be affected; and (ii) the immediacy of a strategic uncertainty and what it is related to (the probability that something will occur), the time frame involved and the reaction time necessary to develop and implement an appropriate strategy.

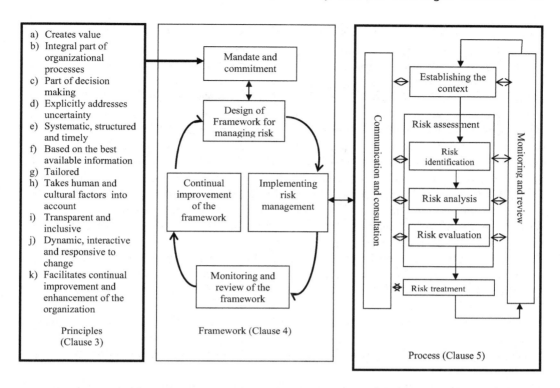

**Figure 6.1   Relationships Between the Risk Management Principles, Framework and Process**

*Source*: (ENISA, 2007–2008: vii). Reproduced with permission.

Emergencies will occur from time to time and the US Homeland Security Studies and Analysis Institute (HSSAI, 2010: 15–16) is right to suggest that a *situational awareness* (people, organizations and technology during an emergency maintain communications and develop a common operating picture that allows leaders to make appropriate and timely decisions vis-à-vis priorities and objectives) as it is known, is a key activity that needs concerted attention. Furthermore, the organizational culture in place needs to stimulate people to be *resourceful* (the capability to improvise and innovate after or during an adverse event); and also, the organization itself needs to exhibit a *learning capacity* (the capability to learn from events and the lessons learned are used to improve future performance during adverse conditions).

Some critics argue that enterprise risk management is perceived to be not as relevant an approach as some would like. Kendrick (2010: 14–17) focuses on three types of principal risks associated with Internet technologies: (i) technology risk, (ii) legal and compliance risk and (iii) operational risk. A number of questions emerge here which senior management are required to address. For example, technology risk may not just be associated with computer viruses and encryption and may not always be the answer for a number of reasons. In-house computer security awareness programmes and staff development programmes relating to enterprise security and intelligence issues may prove beneficial with respect to developing a security culture within the organization, and highlight and reinforce the risk management process.

As regards legal and compliance risk, the practicalities associated with complying with the various statutory and regulatory provisions that are in place to govern Internet technologies need to be fully thought through and it has to be said that the legal issues involved are not as obvious or indeed as interpretable as managers would like or expect. With respect to operational risk, there is no doubt that managers within organizations are devoting resources to devising and implementing workable systems and procedures, and that increased attention is being given to ensuring that employee behaviour in the work environment is monitored more closely than was the case in the past. Employee behaviour in the work environment will be governed more closely in the future. Training employees how to handle and safeguard data is key because this is where some organizations are most vulnerable. Protecting an organization's reputation can prove costly and if mishandled, may see the organization exiting the market/industry.

Alternatively, it may be possible, because of the resource base of the organization, for a chief information officer (CIO) to be appointed who (Swanson et al., 2010: 8):

> is responsible for the organization's information system planning, budgeting, investment, performance, and acquisition. As such, the CIO provides advice and assistance to senior organizational personnel in acquiring the most efficient and effective information system to minimize supply chain risks within the organization's enterprise architecture.

The system-of-systems approach can be used as a methodological process and framework for bringing together various stakeholders to produce a strategic security framework encompassing risk assessment. It can be used to defend the organization against the growing number of cyber attacks. Trust is key and it has to be said that both internally developed relationships as well as externally oriented relationships need to be nurtured in an evolutionary and cautionary manner, as the risk from penetration is high. Industry–government relations, government–society relations and company–society relations, all need to be viewed in the context of the international environment and not just the home country. The fact that a number of governments are now talking about actively cooperating is important both in terms of raising awareness throughout society and stopping cyber attacks escalating and being concentrated on or launched from countries with dysfunctional governments. As well as warning people in society about the dangers associated with giving out passwords and sharing data with people they do not know (mostly through social websites), it needs to be remembered that the essence of strategic marketing is to include an unmet needs element (Aaker and McLoughlin, 2010: 35–38). It is this unmet needs element that is security. As Aaker and McLoughlin (2010: 35) state: 'An unmet need is a customer need that is not being met by the existing product offering.'

As well as external threats there is a growing threat from internally orchestrated attacks (Trim, 2008; Koo, 2011). An unmet need is normally interpreted from the stance of a latent/hidden need associated with the customer, however, as regards cyber space, it can be interpreted in several ways: the customer requires security to be built into the product/system and the threats evident are far beyond what the customer can do or think of doing to protect themselves; social networking is embedded in lifestyle and the threats evident need to be defined and explained; and additional products and services need to be placed in the context of a community resilience model so that a wider society security approach can be adopted to provide a security mindset to make people more aware of the threats and vulnerabilities that are in existence.

## 6.5 Cyber Security Strategy

Integrating security with intelligence is key and needs to be viewed as such. A multi-disciplinary approach is needed in order to counteract the threats posed by cyber attackers and to ensure that the issue of organizational resilience is addressed by all senior and junior managers, and is not just left to the organization's risk manager. The GISES (Global Intelligence and Security Environmental Sustainability) Model outlined by Trim (2005) can be used to develop a security–intelligence interface and also, the SATELLITE (Strategic Corporate Intelligence and Transformational Marketing) Model (Trim, 2004) can be deployed to link more firmly the various environmental issues with business intelligence planning. The multi-disciplinary approach to security embedded in these models should enable the risk manager and his/her colleagues to link security with intelligence, and to provide a focus of momentum that results in a security culture being established within the partnership arrangement. According to Trim and Lee (2010: 4):

> It can also be stated that by integrating security more firmly into the organization's structure, it should be possible to reduce the organization's level of risk and facilitate information sharing. Information sharing should enhance co-operation between partner organizations and add to the defensive capability vis-à-vis establishing effective counter-cyber attack measures.

Samani (2011) suggests that when considering various business propositions, it is necessary for managers to view information risk management from a multitude of perspectives, but most importantly, managers need to pose a number of questions:

- *How is risk adequately assessed?*
- *What metrics are needed in order to establish the actual level of an organization's vulnerability?*
- *How can the identifiable threats be prioritized?*

## 6.6 Cloud Computing

It has to be remembered that the cloud will 'revolutionise traditional outsourcing models' (Quillinan, 2010: 32). Geographical proximity (reduced travel time and costs associated with managing a contract) and the fact that the country where the work is outsourced to may possess highly skilled IT workers (Quillinan, 2010: 32) are important from the point of adding value. For example, the company that outsources to a local supplier may be required by the government in that country to help develop a supplier base (provide training support and additional investment in the form of investing in partnership arrangements) and may be required to engage in some sort of buy-back agreement. So outsourcing, as an umbrella term, needs to be looked at more strategically because a company may be developing, long term, a relationship with what may become a major competitor. Another point that needs to be noted is that if an outsourcing arrangement is terminated for whatever reason, the previous outsource company may hold a certain amount of sensitive data on the company and this data may be used in a way that is unforeseen. With respect to this, it can be suggested that precautions are taken from the outset. At the pre-screening and pre-selection stages, senior managers need to evaluate the risk posed by an outsourcer if confidential data is used in business decision making. Issues of compliance and knowing where data is, and the risks associated with losing it (Quillinan, 2010: 33) are key considerations and so is the degree of interoperability, which reflects the way in which user behaviour creates security issues within partner arrangements with virtualisation specialists (Adams, 2010: 49). Information assurance and breaches in security that result in leaks of data require that managers think through what they are safeguarding and who they are accountable to, and if a leak does occur, a damage limitation policy may fail to stop financial losses and/or the identities of individuals being stolen. What has to be remembered is that a data breach may result in the identity of staff being revealed and also, their intellectual property rights or the intellectual property rights of the organization. This may have tremendous ramifications for the organization: staff may resign; staff may have to be redeployed; relationships with partnership companies may be terminated as trust breaks down; and the share value of the company may fall as investors lose confidence in the way that the organization is managed and sell their shares in the company.

The above has highlighted the fact that there are still many unknowns as regards issues such as devising an effective strategic policy for cloud computing and that, as new ways of doing business unfold, there will be additional or different pressures exerted on senior management. New working practices that are evolving, such as remote working for example, need to be viewed from the perspective of how a holistic security policy that incorporates counter-intelligence will reduce the threats associated with industrial espionage for example. Remote working may have wider benefits than those relating only to the organization and its partnership arrangements. For example, Rosch (2010: 35) has reported: 'Barclays plans to cut its energy consumption further too, by replacing standard desktops with thin client terminals connected virtually to a remotely located server. BGRB is also virtualising a lot of its servers, 550 in its Gloucester data centre alone, allowing it to make further significant energy savings.'

Taylor et al. (2002: 5) indicate that risk assessment requires that attack scenarios be used in order to highlight which system components will be affected should an attack be launched on a computer system and this is a constructive way of looking for vulnerabilities in the system. Managers in small and medium sized companies tend to rely on scenario-analysis to establish how a computer security system is likely to be compromised; however, although scenarios are considered appropriate for highlighting the vulnerabilities of an organization should a certain attack manifest, and can be used in order to stimulate brainstorming activities relating to computer security, they have limited scope (Soo Hoo, 2000: 11).

There are other types of risk that need to be acknowledged. For example, when analysing vulnerabilities in the supply chain, it is essential that management pay attention to such issues as the obsolescence of systems and in particular, how parts, subsystems and technologies that make up a system, become outdated or discontinued (Swanson et al., 2010: 15). It has to be remembered that the supply chain includes all aspects of the product life cycle from design, development and acquisition of custom or what is known as commercial off-the-shelf (COTS) products, as well as system integration and system operation, and ultimately disposal (Swanson et al., 2010: 3). To this can be added people and processes, and services and products (Swanson et al., 2010: 3). Hence senior management need to understand that: 'Supply chain attacks may involve manipulating computing, system hardware, software, or services at any point during the life cycle' (Swanson et al., 2010: 1). An attack may originate via an individual or an organization, and may take various forms such as data being stolen or the corruption of the system/infrastructure or the disabling of mission critical operations (Swanson et al., 2010: 1).

## 6.7 Conclusion

Senior management will need to put in place a risk manager and indeed a set of assistant risk managers (based in the organization's various functions) and these will constitute a risk committee, presided over by a senior/top manager. By having a structure in place, it should be possible to develop a security culture that embraces risk assessment, and this is important for establishing which controls are going to be used and how much they are likely to cost – the objectives being to reduce the level of controls, extend risk coverage and eradicate duplication. By having in place a workable communication mechanism, the risk manager and his/her colleagues (assistant risk managers) are well able to track the threats pending at a high level of detail, and back up their risk management framework with a governance framework and/or mechanism. This is important because of the problems associated with compliance and the fines imposed and also, should an organization be fined, the damage to the organization's image and the extra costs associated with reputation management could prove damaging. So the picture that emerges is that risk assessment needs to be addressed from a 'what-if' perspective, but also from a cost perspective and a structural perspective (the appointment of a risk manager and assistant risk managers).

Information sharing is something that senior management need to consider and also, over the horizon scanning is necessary, as changes in government policy and emerging policy issues may result in conflicts of interest, which result in a move away from offshoring to near shoring and the development of a new business model. A business model may change as a consequence of a new shareholder joining and the business model may be extended to incorporate suppliers (which need to be ISO 27 000 compliant and this would provide ISO 27 000 end-to-end coverage). It may be the case that not all the suppliers are incorporated as such and management need to decide which controls are relevant and if a supplier is to be included, audited and certified, the criteria for certification must be explicit. This goes right across the partnership arrangement and cascades down through the value chain.

Although there are various interpretations of risk and there are different risk models, managers do need to prioritize risks, and identify current and future threats in the short, medium and long term, and deploy enterprise risk management to provide situational analysis (senior and junior managers need to understand the threats identified in the internal and external environments). A PESTLE (Political, Economic, Social, Technological, Legal and Environment) analysis can be used to identify threats, and business continuity management used to integrate a set of sub-areas. By placing risk assessment at the centre of the strategy process, it should be possible to connect with all the other areas of business activity. In order to engage adequately in risk assessment, it is possible that top management will ask staff lower down the hierarchy to benchmark against competitors or industry guidelines, but this may not always be the most appropriate way forward, however it may be a start.

Senior management will need to quantify the organization's risk exposure, plan for the unexpected, implement contingency plans quickly when necessary, and ensure that the organizational value system is receptive to devising and implementing risk policy initiatives. This should ensure that resources are utilized and if necessary the key stakeholders can be integrated into the decision making process.

By focusing on cyber space, it should be possible to place IT security risk management at the centre of a risk assessment policy and this will, if this is the case, integrate the organization's risk management model with the external environment (e.g. supporting infrastructure). The key point to note is that enterprise risk management can only be successful if risk is broken down and a response can be in real time, and this means that technology and managers must work together.

What has to be acknowledged is that management need to be aware that: 'risk management in alliances is a complex endeavour that is related to specific types of trust and control' (Das and Teng, 2001: 277). For this reason, it is import to review again the relationship between the different phases of risk management and for top management to sanction a communication risk management strategy that can be used to integrate more clearly a risk assessment policy in the context of a partnership arrangement.

# References

Aaker, D.A. 1992. *Strategic Market Management*. Chichester: John Wiley & Sons Limited.

Aaker, D.A., and McLoughlin, D. 2010. *Strategic Market Management*. Chichester: John Wiley & Sons Limited.

Adams, D. 2010. Virtual reality. *Financial Sector Technology*, 16 (4), 48–50.

BSI. 2010. *Risk Management – Principles and Guidelines*. BS ISO 31000: 2009. London: British Standards Institute.

Das, T.K., and Teng, B-S. 2001. Trust, control, and risk in strategic alliances: An integrated framework. *Organization Studies*, 22 (2), 251–283.

ENISA. 2007–2008. *Determining Your Organization's Information Risk Assessment and Management Requirements and Selecting Appropriate Methodologies*. Ad Hoc Working Group on Risk Assessment/ Risk Management. Crete: European Network and Information Security Agency (September).

Fox, C.A., and Epstein, M.S. 2010. *Why is Enterprise Risk Management Important for Preparedness?* White Paper. New York: Risk Insurance Management Society, Inc.

French, G.S. 2007. Intelligence analysis for strategic risk assessments. *Critical Infrastructure Protection: Elements of Risk*. Arlington, VA: School of Law, George Mason University, 12–24.

HSSAI. 2010. *Risk and Resilience: Exploring the Relationship*. Arlington, VA: Homeland Security Studies and Analysis Institute, Department of Homeland Security, Science and Technology Directorate (22 November).

Kahan, J.H., Allen, A.C., and George, J.K. 2009. An operational framework for resilience. *Journal of Homeland Security and Emergency Management*, 6 (1), 1–48.

Kendrick, R. 2010. *Cyber Risks for Business Professionals*. Ely: IT Governance Publishing.

Koo, M. 2011. An information war? Balancing national security, trade secrets and the rights of the individual. The Strand, London: Australia House (19 May).

McGill, W.L., and Ayyub, B.M. 2007. The meaning of vulnerability in the context of critical infrastructure protection. *Critical Infrastructure Protection: Elements of Risk*. Arlington, VA: School of Law, George Mason University, 25–48.

Mont, M.C., and Brown, R. 2011. *Risk Assessment and Decision Support for Security Policies and Related Enterprise Operational Processes*. HPL-2011-12. Bristol: HP Laboratories, pp. 1–10. http://www.hpl. hp.com/techreports/2011/HPL-2011-12.html [accessed 14 September 2011].

Quillinan, J. 2010. Austerity rules. *Financial Sector Technology*, 16 (4), 32–33.

Rosch, V. 2010. Living the dream. *Financial Sector Technology*, 16 (4), 34–36.

Samani, R. 2011. Is it possible to control security in any cloud service? *Second International Secure Systems Development Conference: Designing In Security*, Hilton London Olympia Hotel, London (18–19 May).

Sheffi, Y. 2005. *The Resilient Enterprise: Overcoming Vulnerability for Competitive Advantage*. Cambridge, MA: The MIT Press.

Soo Hoo, K.J. 2000. *How Much is Enough? A Risk Management Approach to Computer Security*. Stanford, CA: Consortium for Research on Information Security and Policy Working Paper, Stanford University (June). http://iis-db.stanford.edu/pubs/11900/soohoo.pdf [accessed 14 September 2011].

Swanson, M., Bartol, N., and Moorthy, R. 2010. *Piloting Supply Chain Risk Management: Practices for Federal Information Systems*. Draft NISTIR 7622. US Department of Commerce, Gaithersburg, MD: NIST (National Institute of Standards and Technology) (June).

Taylor, C., Krings, A., and Alves-Foss, J. 2002. Risk analysis and probabilistic survivability assessment (RAPSA): An assessment approach for power substation hardening. Moscow, ID: University of Idaho, pp. 1–10. http://www2.csuidaho.edu/-krings/publications/SACT-2002-T [accessed 14 September 2011].

Trim, P.R.J. 2004. The strategic corporate intelligence and transformational marketing model. *Marketing Intelligence and Planning*, 22 (2), 240–256.

Trim, P.R.J. 2005. The GISES model for counteracting organized crime and international terrorism. *International Journal of Intelligence and CounterIntelligence*, 18 (3), 451–472.

Trim, P.R.J. 2008. Effective communication and persuasion for behaviour change. *Master Class session, The Malicious Exploitation of Information Systems Conference*, University College London (7 November).

Trim, P.R.J., and Lee, Y-I. 2010. A security framework for protecting business, government and society from cyber attacks, pp. 1–6. *5th IEEE International Conference on System of Systems Conference (SoSE): Sustainable Systems for the 21st Century*, Loughborough University (22–24 June).

# 7 *Resilience Policy and Strategy Mapping*

## 7.0 Introduction

The aim of this chapter is to provide insights into the current needs and evolving complexities associated with cyber security issues from the perspective of corporate security and resilience. The term *corporate security* needs to be revisited and placed in a broader context, for example (Trim, 2009: 213):

> *... a robust stakeholder security architecture requires that attention is given to intra-government and inter-government working arrangements based on information sharing. It also requires that trust-based relationships between companies that provide disaster relief services and institutions that coordinate disaster relief operations are solidified through time ... a more robust global disaster and emergency management policy and strategy [will] emerge and be implemented ... [and will] reinforce the fact that a more pro-active approach is needed with respect to dealing with disaster and emergency situations and [furthermore] the international community needs to view disaster and emergency management from the perspective of stakeholder security.*

This chapter starts with risk and resilience defined (Section 7.1) and continues with examples underpinning the need for resilience (Section 7.2). Attention is given to resilience policy (Section 7.3) and promoting resilience (Section 7.4). Reference is made to resilience domains and features (Section 7.5) and a conclusion (Section 7.6) is provided.

## 7.1 Risk and Resilience Defined

From an organizational perspective, a resilience policy needs to be viewed as wide ranging and holistic. For example, every security and intelligence related activity undertaken in order to produce competitive positioning strategies involves counter-intelligence to safeguard the organization against the continuing threats that it is confronted with. The threats originate from existing and future competitors, government regulators, activists and lobbyists, overseas governments that are undertaking industrial espionage activities in order to gain intellectual property rights across industry sectors, criminal concerns and in particular organized crime syndicates and terrorist networks. Should an organization's countermeasures be ineffective, then it is possible that the damage caused to the organization will be measured in thousands or millions of pounds. Should this be the case, a damage limitation programme will be implemented to restore faith in the organization. It is for this reason that management need to understand what resilience is and how an organization can become more resilient.

The US Homeland Security Studies and Analysis Institute (HSSAI, 2010) explored the link between risk and resilience and added to the body of knowledge and our understanding of what risk is and what resilience is. For example, the US Department of Homeland Security definition of risk has been adopted widely (HSSAI, 2010: 3): 'The potential for an unwanted outcome resulting from an incident, event, or occurrence as determined by its likelihood and the associated consequences.'

The following definition of resilience has been deemed appropriate (HSSAI, 2010: 9):

*Resilience is the ability of a system to attain the objectives of resisting, absorbing, and recovering from the impact of an adverse event, before, during, and after its occurrence. It is also a dynamic process that seeks to learn from incidents to strengthen capabilities of the system in meeting future challenges. The goals are to maintain continuity of function, degrading gracefully, and recover system functionality to a pre-designated level, as rapidly as desired and feasible.*

## 7.2 Examples Underpinning the Need for Resilience

Bearing in mind the current economic climate, it is important to point out that in some countries, where critical national infrastructure and critical information infrastructure are owned by the private sector, the private sector will, in times of limited resources, be required to invest large sums of money not only to bring the services on offer up to public expectation but also, to invest in additional security to protect what is in being and at the same time outwit those who are attempting to exploit the vulnerabilities in the system (organized crime syndicates and terrorists for example).

It is necessary, at this juncture, to cite a few examples of evidence. Kendrick (2010: 11), referring to the PriceWaterhouseCoopers *Information Security Breaches Survey 2010*, indicates that the cost of a breach is between £27,500 and £690,000. Kendrick (2010: 14–17) goes on to state that there are three types of principal risk associated with Internet technologies: (i) technology risk, (ii) legal and compliance risk and (iii) operational risk. Associated with technology risk are computer viruses and their ability to affect the performance of a system and ultimately to cause it to fail. Furthermore, the transfer of sensitive and confidential information is an issue, and encryption and educating staff vis-à-vis its use and application is important with respect to enhancing security. As regards legal and compliance risk, organizations that fail to comply with the various statutory and regulatory provisions will be subject heavy fines. With respect to operational risk, of key importance here are the systems and procedures in place for governing employee behaviour in relation to the production of goods and services, and the fact that new policies need to be devised and implemented. Issues of information security vis-à-vis implementing security solutions, legal compliance and training employees how to handle data are all important considerations with respect to safeguarding against reputational damage and managing relationships with customers (Kendrick, 2010: 17).

The board of directors are responsible for corporate governance, which has been defined by Kendrick (2010: 20–21) as 'a business strategy based upon transparent decision making; the establishment of lines of accountability and responsibility; securing shareholder and stakeholder value; and the adoption of sound risk management strategies, including information security'. Kendrick (2010: 21–22) goes on to state that:

*IT governance is a subset of corporate governance....IT governance is essentially a framework within which IT is designed, deployed and managed in such a way as to ensure that its employment and application remain aligned to the organisation's business objectives.....Project governance may be regarded as a subset of corporate governance...[and] .is a set of principles that addresses the development, management and conclusion of projects.*

Outsourcing is an area of increased attention and one that offers potential savings but also has risks associated with it. Owing to the fact that an organization faces many risks it is logical to suggest that a risk manager be appointed that heads a risk management team (Kendrick, 2010: 25), and ultimately the risk manager is accountable to the board of directors or a senior manager.

As organizations embrace, cautiously at times, cloud computing, it can be stated that as regards the consumerization of information technology, the issues of (i) availability, (ii) integrity, (iii) authentication, (iv) confidentiality and (v) non-repudiation (Singh et al., 2009: 294–295) have, at least to the non-specialist, been overlooked in the past. Ownership, control and all-round resilience of a system or organization to cope with threats and ensure that any damage created will be dealt with speedily and with limited cost to the end user, underpins the concept of a resilience policy. The power of governments to regulate at a time when competition between industry innovators is intense and technological transformation is viewed as essential for an organization's survival, are key issues that need to be recognized by strategic decision makers within organizations.

During the St George's House Annual Lecture 2010, Lord Winston (2011: 7), talking on the theme of 'Scientists & Citizens', stated:

*In our digital economy, government can be remarkably careless about the information it stores on our behalf. Unbelievably, the UK government lost the national insurance numbers of 17,000 citizens in 2008. In retrospect, it seems farcical that this digitally stored data was sent by routine post. If that were not enough, the Ministry of Justice lost information affecting more than 45,000 people, in some cases revealing their criminal records and credit histories. Details of 25 million child benefits claimants vanished last year, and the Home Office lost the personal details of 3,000 agricultural workers –including passport numbers when two CDs went missing in an envelope. In five separate cases, the Foreign Office mislaid information affecting about 190,000 people. And the Department for Transport misplaced personal data on six separate occasions, including 3 million records of driving test candidates in May 2007. One might reasonably expect that where national security is involved, officials would encourage particular care – yet the Ministry of Defence lost an unencrypted laptop computer containing 620,000 personal records, including bank account and national insurance numbers and information on 450,000 people named as referees or next of kin by would-be servicemen and women.*

*These breaches do not necessarily mean that these data will be used by unauthorised persons. But the potential for damage to the individuals concerned is substantial and long-lasting, ranging from financial losses to loss of reputation. Moreover, if when using a personal computer we have our identity stolen we may even be accused of crimes we didn't commit. Other risks undoubtedly include threats to personal safety and the potential for physical or psychological harm. One high profile threat is that posed to children.*

Lord Winston (2011: 12) has provided a number of conclusions and recommendations, which include:

*… every society needs to ensure that the scientific education provided is of the highest quality. Governments need to reflect on a current trend and question whether investing in science education simply because it is valuable to the economy is sound policy. Rather, they should consider investment in science education vital because it is the best way of ensuring that we, our children and grandchildren will live in a safer and healthier society.*

*In being more science-literate, we might consider that the announcement of a new discovery is almost [always] heralded by exaggerated claims for its immediate value, that many technological advances have a threatening aspect which is not usually recognised at the time of the invention, that most human advances have beneficial applications which are not envisaged when the discovery is first made and that many really important discoveries are arrived at by serendipity …*

*Communication is a two-way process. Good engagement with the public involves not merely imparting information, but listening to and responding to the ideas, questions, and concerns of the public …*

*We should consider the ethical problems raised by the application of our work …*

*Commercial interests so often promoted by governments and universities cannot be disregarded if technology is to be exploited for public good. But scientists need to be aware of the dangers of conflicts of interest. The history of science shows that the pursuit of commercial interests can lead to the loss of public confidence.*

The issues and challenges associated with changes in working practices also need attention. For example, remote working cannot be considered without paying adequate attention to security and counter-intelligence work. Intelligence work is likely to be given a higher platform within an organization as it becomes increasingly obvious that those intent on gaining an advantage from industrial espionage will carry on using illegal business practices to do so. Remote working is also considered to have economic and environmental benefits. For example, Rosch (2010: 35) has reported that Barclays plans to reduce the use of desktops with client terminals that are connected to a remotely located server. Initiatives such as this can be expected to occur through time as developments in technology facilitate new business model configurations.

Talking at the governmental level, President Obama stated in 2009 that a resilient nation is (HSSAI, 2010: 4) 'one in which individuals, communities, and our economy can adapt to changing conditions as well as withstand and rapidly recover from disruption due to emergencies'. UK Foreign Secretary William Hague (2011), speaking on the theme 'Security and freedom in the Cyber Age – Seeking the rules of the road', stated:

Many government services are now delivered via the internet, as is education in many classrooms. In the UK 70% of younger internet users bank online and two thirds of all adults shop on the internet. This is not a phenomenon confined to any one part of the world. In less than 15 years the number of web users has exploded from 16 million in 1995 to more than 1.7 billion today, more than half of whom are in developing countries. By 2015, it is said that there will be more interconnected devices on the planet than humans.

Along with its numerous benefits, cyberspace has created new means of repression, enabling undemocratic governments to violate the human rights of their citizens.

It has opened up new channels for hostile governments to probe our defences and attempt to steal our confidential information or intellectual property.

It has promoted fears of future 'cyber war'.

It has enabled terrorist networks to plan atrocities, flood internet chat rooms with their ideology and prey on the vulnerable from thousands of miles away.

And it provides rich pickings for criminals. On-line criminals steal the identities of ordinary citizens. They empty bank-accounts, extort money from firms and defraud government departments, and cost the global economy as much as $1 trillion annually...

Cyber-security is on the agendas of some thirty multilateral organisations, from the UN to the OCSE and the G8. NATO's Lisbon Summit in November launched a new programme to defend NATO's communication systems from cyber attack. But much of this debate is fragmented and lacks focus.

We believe there is a need for a more comprehensive, structured dialogue to begin to build consensus among like-minded countries and to lay the basis for agreement on a set of standards on how countries should act in cyberspace. How this dialogue is organised is up for discussion. But we need to get the ball rolling faster...

So in Britain's view, seven principles should underpin future international norms about the use of cyberspace:

1. The need for governments to act proportionately in cyberspace and in accordance with national and international law;
2. The need for everyone to have the ability – in terms of skills, technology, confidence and opportunity – to access cyberspace;
3. The need for users of cyberspace to show tolerance and respect for diversity of language, culture and ideas;
4. Ensuring that cyberspace remains open to innovation and the free flow of ideas, information and expression;
5. The need to respect individual rights of privacy and to provide proper protection to intellectual property;
6. The need for us all to work collectively to tackle the threat from criminals acting online;
7. And the promotion of a competitive environment which ensures a fair return on investment in network, services and content.

We are open to the ideas of others and we have already begun to discuss cyber with our allies in Washington, Paris, Berlin, Canberra and elsewhere. We must widen the debate over the coming year. We have a major opportunity to promote the Budapest Convention on Cyber Crime, which the UK will look to do when we chair the Council of Europe from November. Here, as in every *debate about how to fashion collective responses to the security challenges of our time, Britain is ready to play its part.*

As regards the benefits of cloud computing, Clapperton (2010: 17) has stated:

*In general, though, cloud specialists provide more efficient environments than their customers could achieve in-house, Craig-Wood says, not just through virtualisation improvements, but also through investing in mass automation of data centres, which results in reduced power and hardware requirements. Companies should consider outsourcing to the cloud via two routes, she advises: IaaS (infrastructure as a service), which involves renting servers that reside in the cloud; and SaaS (software as a service), where email hosting and other applications are provided as a cloud-based service.*

This raises a number of interesting and linked topics: data storage and the use of a data centre, and the energy savings that can be made, which translate into carbon savings. For example, Bray (2010: 19) states:

*Within the data centre, organisations need to consider two aspects: the IT equipment itself (servers, storage, networking equipment, etc), and the infrastructure that supports it (cooling, ventilation, humidification, power supply etc). As a rule of thumb, for every pound you spend buying a server you can reckon to spend another pound to manage it and two pounds to power and cool it, so energy considerations should be an important part of the procurement decision.*

The process of virtualisation is, according to Hamilton (2010: 41) 'a technology that allows firms to abstract IT services from an underlying infrastructure' and 'in simple terms, offer[s] a trustworthy path to slashing energy costs and reducing data centre space', and needs to be placed in the context of an organization's long–term IT strategy. More generally, Hamilton (2010: 41) has explained this by stating that:

*Boards understand cost, but they also understand that in today's world you need to be more responsive and that means having the ability to release new financial products that meet rapidly changing market demands. To enable these core demands to be met, other key elements in the migration to the cloud will be critical. These include refreshing older applications, some of which can't handle the demands of cloud computing, and equally important, ensuring that, for example, IT operational processes are optimised to reflect the importance of on-demand computing in the private cloud.*

*What are some practical actions you can take to start achieving these objectives? Assessing the readiness of your IT infrastructure and processes to deliver cloud-based services is a good place to begin. Many firms are also developing financial models and business cases to determine the feasibility of cloud for their operations. Workshops with application and business stakeholders can establish priorities for cloud-enabling applications, align business requirements to IT service levels, and clarify compliance and security requirements.*

Speaking on the topic of controlling security in the cloud, at the Second International Secure Systems Development Conference, Raj Samani (2011) made it known that there are five key challenges:

1. Assure the multitude of third party conditions in a scaleable manner.
2. Be able to objectively and reliably measure the risk management maturity of third parties.
3. Ensure that all risk management requirements are reflected in contracts (and will be applicable in the future).
4. Perform the due diligence required within current resourcing constraints.
5. Find an approach that leverages existing investment and will be adopted by suppliers.

Following on from these points Samani (2011) made it known that managers need to devise an approach that allows information risk management to be incorporated objectively into the tender process; and also establish a way in which to compare risk maturity between different suppliers. Following on from this it can be argued that full transparency is needed with respect to auditing and should this be the case, any partnership arrangement entered into will be based on mutuality and viewed as trustworthy. Key questions that emerge are:

• How is risk adequately assessed?
• What metrics are needed in order to establish the actual level of an organization's vulnerability?
• How can the identifiable threats be prioritized?

A point to note that emerged from the Second International Secure Systems Development Conference, was that mobile computing will drive cloud services and as a result security problems will increase. Harper (2011), speaking at the same conference, indicated that in access of US$288 billion is spent worldwide each year on information security and that 75 per cent of the attacks are on the application layer. It is believed that 10 to 100 vulnerabilities are evident in core applications and although the case can be made for more penetration testing, penetration testing is not a solution in itself. For example, penetration testing normally occurs at the stage of pre-introduction and it should take place at the start of the software development life cycle (Harper, 2011).

Although networks are considered reasonably secure and the main threat appears to be via the application layer, it has to be remembered that Stuxnet infiltrated networks and became a worm (Barnell, 2011). To avoid this happening, it is recommended that managers take the following into account (Barnell, 2011):

1. Carry out continual monitoring in order to identify suspicious behaviour.
2. Implement an adequate information assurance programme.
3. Use file level encryption.
4. Check advice offered on the security response websites.
5. Investigate contractors to ensure that they are reputable and that they will share responsibility for risk.
6. Ensure that contractors are not using stolen software (this is how Stuxnet penetrated the network).

With respect to the traditional System Development Life Cycle (SDLC), Virgona (2011: 6) states:

*Disaster recovery is dependent on the SDLC for ensuring disaster recovery planning is integrated throughout the technology development process: the requirements for the system's recovery are defined in the analysis phase, the system is designed to provide service during a disaster within the specified timeframes and testing the recovery capabilities is part of the creation of the project, thus ensuring continued use during a disaster.*

## 7.3 Resilience Policy

Monitoring employees is a controversial subject and some authors associate it with a lack of trust (Cialdini et al., 2004: 71). Trust based relationships need to be developed through time and it is accepted that 'Organisational politics, combined with apathy and distrust, can militate against the formation and development of trust based relationships' (Trim et al., 2009: 350). According to Dawson (1996: 268–269), a number of issues and factors need to be taken into account by managers when analysing an organization:

1. *Organisations are interactive systems, with change in one aspect having repercussions for others, sometimes in an unintended or unanticipated way.*
2. *Organisations are highly complex systems in which there is a great deal of uncertainty.*
3. *There is no one best way to act in organisations: an appropriate path should be taken through paradox and contradiction in a manner appropriate to the context.*
4. *Resources are always scarce, and any action is likely to have financial or social costs as well as benefits.*
5. *Organisations are arenas for the activities of different interest groups which are linked through patterns of conflict, consensus and indifference.*
6. *People in organisations perceive varying sources of opportunities for, and constraints on, possible action.*
7. *Activities in, and outcomes from, organisations can be analysed in terms of the level of the individual, group, organisation or society; it is very important to identify the levels that are appropriate to the problems, issues or opportunities with which any practitioner or analyst is concerned.*

It also has to be remembered that organizational learning or a commitment to it is an essential aspect of an organization's development (Lee, 2009: 181–196). Because senior managers need to manage inter-organizational as well as intra-organizational relationships, it is essential to note that they will need to pay attention to devising and deploying an adapted leadership style, which becomes more obvious a task when managing internationally and experiencing different cultural groups (Lee, 2009: 192). Possibly it is important to reflect on the work of Barak and Suler (2008: 1–12) who have written about psychology and cyberspace. Understanding people's behaviour in cyber space is necessary from both the stance of how customers engage with information about products and services, and how workers many thousands of miles away can be managed and motivated.

## 7.4 Promoting Resilience

According to the US Homeland Security Studies and Analysis Institute (HSSAI, 2010: 18):

*Promoting resilience can help achieve the fundamental goal of reducing and managing risk, while risk assessments can inform resilience policies ... Risk and resilience both involve operationalized planning and allocation of resources. Risk-informed resource allocation seeks to lower risk in cost effective ways. Likewise, resilience ways and means seek to allocate resources that increase resilience in cost effective ways.*

*Resilience planning can provide a framework for risk reduction that can be applied to risk assessment and management ...*

*... risk assessments can inform operational planning for system resilience by providing an understanding of the likelihood and consequences of the dangers facing those assets....*

It is useful at this point to reflect on the US government's approach to resilience. It can be noted from the work of Kahan et al. (2009: 29) that resilience principles can be mapped against resilience objectives. From the relationships noted, the following can be deduced (Kahan et al., 2009: 29–30):

- Threat and hazard limitation is principally associated with the resistance objective.
- Robustness is principally associated with the absorption objective.
- Consequence mitigation is principally associated with the restoration objective.
- Adaptability, risk informed planning, risk informed investment, harmonization of purposes, and comprehensiveness of scope are critical considerations for all three resilience objectives.
- The resistance objective is inherently linked to prevent and protect missions.
- The absorption objective is inherently linked to protect and respond missions.
- The restoration objective is inherently linked to respond and recover missions.

Bearing the above in mind, senior management can promote the concept of resilience throughout the organization and partner organizations in various ways. In order to do this effectively, both the means and key success factors need to be identified (Table 7.1).

### Table 7.1    Promoting Resilience

| Means | A Resilience Charter is in place.<br>Transparent communication exists at all levels.<br>In-house seminars and workshops (e.g. talks, table top exercises and complex scenarios) |
|---|---|
| Key factors | An appropriate leadership model is in place.<br>The risk mitigation policy is appropriate.<br>Contingency planning is across all functions.<br>The recovery process is logical and documented.<br>There is an appropriate allocation of resources or access to resources. |

## 7.5 Resilience Domains and Features

The US Homeland Security Studies and Analysis Institute (HSSAI, 2010: 6–7) has identified four resilience domains: (1) Infrastructure: engineered assets, systems, networks, both physical and cyber; including interconnected nodes – telecommunications or power stations, known as systems of systems; (2) Organizations: a range of public sector and private sector organizations are included with functional subcomponents and defined objectives, and which have associated supply chains; (3) Communities: all aspects of society are included – a city where people live, community groups, businesses, buildings, facilities and social capital for example; (4) Ecosystems: living organisms, the physical environment where people live and the interrelations they have.

The US Homeland Security Studies and Analysis Institute (HSSAI, 2010: 15–16) has identified 11 resilience features: (1) Pre-event Activity (individuals, organizations, communities and certain systems anticipate challenges and plan and prepare to deal with threats and hazards); (2) Situational Awareness (people, organizations and technology during an emergency maintain communications and develop a common operating picture that allows those in leadership positions to make appropriate and timely decisions vis-à-vis priorities and objectives); (3) Resistance (various countermeasures 'to actively redirect, thwart, or attenuate a threat, hazard, or other disruption before or at time of arrival'); (4) Cushionability (the ability of a system to absorb a blow and degrade slowly); (5) Robustness (when internal or external stress is placed on a system, this reflects the capability of the system to maintain its critical functions); (6) Redundancy (alternative options exist and critical assets and resources can be substituted, hence there is no complete dependence on a subsystem); (7) Resourcefulness (the capability to improvise and innovate after or during an adverse event); (8) Restoration (this reflects how well a system can perform its functions after an event and also, at what level it can perform this functionality); (9) Rapidity (the time taken for a system to recover after an event and perform at certain levels); (10) Learning Capacity (the capability to learn from events and the lessons learned are used to improve future performance during adverse conditions); and (11) Affordability (fiscal feasibility and practicality associated with the capabilities designed into systems that ensure that they cope with adversity).

Writing on resilience, McCreight (2009: 4–5) states that:

*Resilience and recovery are very similar, both focusing on the same objectives and outcome. Their shared goal: a survivable and viable community that has withstood disaster and emerges from it wounded, but fully capable of conducting governmental and commercial operations. The main distinction is the emphasis on planning and strategic mitigation, which is embedded in the notion of resilience. It assumes a community committed to every conceivable and robust pre-disaster activity aimed at assuring its survival and continuation. Recovery, by contrast, tends to focus more on the immediate operational, logistical, sociological, and commercial aspects of bringing a damaged community back to life in the aftermath of a disaster. Here the emphasis is on what specific tasks must be performed to restore essential community institutions, neighbourhoods, and related environments. Resilience aims to thwart, diminish, or curtail a disaster's worst effects well in advance of calamity, while recovery attempts to restore to 'nearly normal' as quickly as possible. One is short term, immediate, and temporary. The other is deliberate, strategic, and enduring for the affected community.*

There seems to be at least five dimensions to resilience:

1. personal and familial socio-psychological well-being
2. organizational and institutional restoration
3. economic and commercial resumption of services and productivity
4. restoring infrastructural systems integrity
5. operational regularity of public safety and government.

These disparate elements must be assessed independently, and then recombined in a comprehensive manner to resemble a unified strategy. Resilience is the result of a deliberative process with built-in assumptions and intentions reflecting a community's firm commitment to its own survival and restoration.

McCreight (2009: 5) defines further the five points cited and states:

*The socio-psychological aspect deals with the public's emotional consciousness, its attachment to (and influence by) the disaster itself, along with the human spirit of grit, determination, and survival. Organizational and institutional restoration deals with social and mediating institutions like schools and influential community groups. Commercial and economic activity is resumed to offer those services and commodities that the disaster nullified. Key infrastructures in power, water, sewer, communications, and related functions are demonstrably back in operation. Finally, government services and public safety must be restored. This raises the fair and urgent question of how a community achieves resilience both as a goal and a yardstick for enhancing its survivability and continuation in facing future disasters.*

A resilience policy and strategy mapping process is outlined in Figure 7.1. The reader will note that resilience policy incorporates a strategic marketing dimension and a business continuity management dimension. However, in order for the organization's resilience policy to be successful, the organization's value system must be receptive to

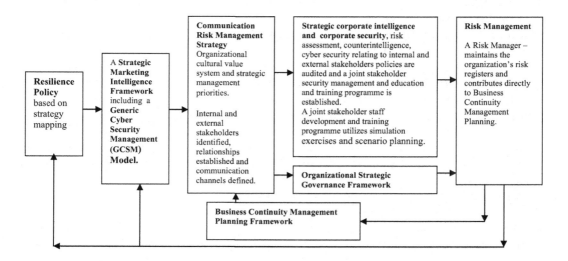

**Figure 7.1   Resilience Policy Including Strategy Mapping**

ideas and be flexible enough to allow staff to communicate with each other in an open and informal manner.

## 7.6 Conclusion

In order that management put in place an adequate resilience policy and strategy, it is important for managers throughout the organization to understand the role that information assurance plays in safeguarding the organization from potential breaches. In addition, staff need to think through how impacts, which are likely to be both industry related and non-industry related, effect the organization's operational capability, and its technological capability, and its legal and compliance capability. Changes in organizational capability are likely to result in rapid transformational change and the development of a new business model. This will place staff under new levels of stress and will result in structural changes and new, untried management systems.

## References

Barak, A., and Suler, J. 2008. Reflections on the psychology and social science of cyberspace, in *Psychological Aspects of Cyberspace: Theory, Research, Applications,* edited by A. Barak. Cambridge: Cambridge University Press, 1–12.

Barnell, D. 2011. Stuxnet – Rethink security, right across the supply chain. *Second International Secure Systems Development Conference: Designing In Security*, Hilton London Olympia Hotel, London (18–19 May).

Bray, P. 2010. Getting down to brass tacks. *The True Cost of Your IT: A Guide to Environmentally Friendly Computing*. London: Lyonsdown Media Group, 18–20.

Cialdini, R.B., Petrova, P.K., and Goldstein, N.J. 2004. The hidden costs of organizational dishonesty. *MIT Sloan Management Review* (Spring), 67–73.

Clapperton, G. 2010. Clouds, not smoke. *The True Cost of Your IT: A Guide to Environmentally Friendly Computing*. London: Lyonsdown Media Group, 16–17.

Dawson, S. 1996. *Analysing Organisations*. Basingstoke: Palgrave.

Hague, W. 2011. Security and freedom in the Cyber Age – Seeking the rules of the road. *Munich Security Conference*, Munich, Germany (4 February). http://www.fco.gov.uk/en/news/latest-news/?view=Speech&id=544853682 [accessed 1 July].

Hamilton, S. 2010. Private clouds. *Financial Sector Technology,* 16 (4), 41.

Harper, D. 2011. Building security into software. *Second International Secure Systems Development Conference: Designing In Security*, Hilton London Olympia Hotel, London (18–19 May).

HSSAI. 2010. *Risk and Resilience: Exploring the Relationship*. Arlington, VA: Department of Homeland Security, Science and Technology Directorate (22 November).

Kahan, J.H., Allen, A.C., and George, J.K. 2009. An operational framework for resilience. *Journal of Homeland Security and Emergency Management,* 6 (1), 1–48.

Kendrick, R. 2010. *Cyber Risks for Business Professionals*. Ely: IT Governance Publishing.

Lee, Y-I. 2009. Strategic transformational management in the context of inter-organizational and intra-organizational partnership development, in *Strategizing Resilience and Reducing Vulnerability*, edited by P.R.J. Trim and J. Caravelli. New York: Nova Science Publishers, Inc., 181–196.

McCreight, R. 2009. Resilience as a goal and standard in emergency management. *Journal of Homeland Security and Emergency Management*, 7 (1), 1–7.

Rosch, V. 2010. Living the dream. *Financial Sector Technology*, 16 (4), 34–36.

Samani, R. 2011. Is it possible to control security in any cloud service? *Second International Secure Systems Development Conference: Designing In Security*, Hilton London Olympia Hotel, London (18–19 May).

Singh, P., Singh, P., Park, I., Lee, J-K., and Rao, H.R. 2009. Information sharing: A study of information attributes and their relative significance during catastrophic events, in *Cyber Security and Global Information Assurance: Threat Analysis and Response Solution* edited by K.J. Knapp. Hershey, PA: Information Science Reference, 283–305.

Trim, P. 2009. Placing disaster management policies and practices within a stakeholder security architecture, in *Strategizing Resilience and Reducing Vulnerability* edited by P.R.J. Trim and J. Caravelli. New York: Nova Science Publishers, Inc., 213–227.

Trim, P.R.J., Jones, N.A., and Brear, K. 2009. Building organisational resilience through a designed-in security management approach. *Journal of Business Continuity & Emergency Planning*, 3 (4), 345–355.

Virgona, T. 2011. A decade on, what business continuity and information security lessons have been learned? *The Business Continuity Journal*, 4 (3), 1–15.

Winston, Lord. 2011. Scientists & Citizens. St George's House Annual lecture 2010. *St George's House Annual Review, 2009–2010*. Windsor: St George's House, Windsor Castle, 4–11.

# 8 *Integrated Resilience Management Model*

## 8.0 Introduction

From an organizational perspective, a resilience policy is to be viewed from a wide based and holistic perspective. This requires that security and intelligence related activity involves both externally focused competitive positioning strategy formulation and a well structured counter-intelligence operation that has as its objective to safeguard the organization's assets (however defined) from current and future threats (especially the work of organized crime syndicates, those engaged in industrial espionage, terrorist networks and activists for example, as well as fraudulent insiders). It is because those engaged in acts of industrial espionage are so expert at what they do that the topic of information assurance needs to be given attention. By having a sound appreciation of information assurance, it should be possible to devise robust organizational countermeasures that decrease the risk and resulting ramifications associated with a damaging attack/penetration. Inadequate organizational countermeasures can result in expensive damage limitation and a hastily constructed reputation management programme, and in a severe situation, a fall in the organization's share price.

This chapter starts with setting the scene (Section 8.1) and continues with formulating a resilience policy (Section 8.2). Security awareness and organizational learning (Section 8.3) is dealt with next and this is followed by working with the workforce (Section 8.4). A conclusion is provided (Section 8.5).

## 8.1 Setting the Scene

Rid and McBurney (2012) have looked closely at the challenge posed by cyber threats and have taken the argument a stage further by discussing what a cyber weapon is. What emerges from their paper is that cyber weapons have been around since the early 1980s and are deployed today. Cyber weapons can be grouped according to their potential to cause damage. The damage inflicted can be viewed from a psychological perspective as well as a physical perspective. Rid and McBurney (2012: 10) have this to say about current and future cyber weaponry: 'It would be surprising if an intelligent coded weapon capable of learning had not been developed yet. A learning weapon could observe and evaluate the specifics of an isolated environment autonomously, analyse available courses of action and take action.' This quotation not only calls into question how senior management can safeguard the organization through making it more resilient to attack, but more fundamentally it focuses attention on adaptive capacity and the need for appropriate leadership.

Longstaff et al. (2010: 7) are right to suggest that leadership can be viewed as a 'vital community resource' and used to produce innovation and learning. Longstaff et al. (2010: 9) suggest that: 'When a community possesses a high level of all three traits – institutional memory, innovative learning, and connectedness – it, in turn, possesses a high capacity to adapt to changes in the environment.' The reason why an organization needs a robust resilience policy in place is because of the 'complex consideration of threatening events, interdependencies with other infrastructures, and impact of human behaviour on systems performance' (Steinberg, 2011: 28). Furthermore, top management need to ensure that they adapt the security policies of the organization in accordance with threat information received and that they are able to mitigate threats in real time (Anand et al., 2012: 51).

The recently published Chartered Institute of Management (CIM, 2011) survey entitled *Managing Threats in a Dangerous World* incorporated cyber security. The quotation below is taken from the section entitled 'Cyber and Information Security Threats' (CIM, 2011: 13):

> *Managers were asked whether their organisation had suffered a range of IT related disruptions. Nearly a third of organisations' IT systems have been infected by a virus or malicious software in the past 12 months. Given that many viruses go undetected, the number to have been infected is likely to have been higher. In around one in ten organisations staff have lost confidential information and a similar number also suffered a significant attempt to break into their network.*

## 8.2 Formulating a Resilience Policy

There is no doubt that monitoring employees is considered controversial and is associated with a lack of trust (Cialdini et al., 2004: 71), however, trust based relationships need to be developed through time (Trim et al., 2009: 350). In order to develop trust, more attention needs to be given to the value associated with the concept of organizational learning and how the commitment of top management can result in organizational development in the context of inter-organizational and intra-organizational relationships in different cultural settings (Lee, 2009: 192). In other words, resilience is not to be viewed as only organization specific, it is a concept to be applied to all the organizations in the partnership arrangement (suppliers, manufacturer, wholesalers, retailers and other stakeholders).

Humphrey (2012) has suggested that organizations adopt a selective approach to sharing information and Humphrey et al. (2012: 1) have provided a glimpse of how organized criminals share information and how they collaborate. The insider threat is considered a major risk and Hoskins (2012), in a talk entitled 'Regulation problems resulting from an EU directive', has suggested that there are two to three breaches each week and they are reported to the customer and the relevant authorities. A CPNI Representative (2012), in a talk entitled 'Potential impact upon critical infrastructures: Data leakage and consumerisation', indicated that data leakage can occur via storage sites, social media sites, printers and photocopiers (as they possess memories), smartphones and tablets, mobile phones, laptops, anything portable that has a storage or write facility for example.

According to Humphrey et al. (2012: 4), 'The need exists for more appropriate advice to be given to people concerning practical steps to be taken to prevent data breaches and to implement corrective action if a breach has occurred.' It is possible that if a device is lost, company policy demands that the data is automatically wiped. If an employee is in breach of protocols, then it is possible that company policy will dictate that all the files on the computer are erased (Humphrey et al., 2012: 4). In order that the company has a robust security policy in place, employees may be required to sign a document that protects the company itself and other employees working for the company.

According to Hadfield (cited in Trim et al., 2012a: 1), remote working is now receiving a great deal of attention and will no doubt be in the spotlight in the years ahead. Hadfield (cited in Trim et al., 2012a: 1) is clear that the cost of a breach, both in monetary terms and psychological terms, needs to be better understood than it is at present. There are many reasons for this but one of the main reasons relates to reputational damage and how the image of a company may be tarnished. New business models that are developing are providing insights into online customer experience (Hsu and Tsou, 2011) and the subject of online community promotion has been covered by Casalo et al. (2010). Those producing innovative products will need to take into account purchase intentions and especially brand and utility, and social or hedonic utility (Arruda-Filho et al., 2010: 480).

Garlati (cited in Trim et al., 2012a: 2) states that employees do not understand the implications of using their personal devices at work and a formal security awareness programme can do much to change this. This appears sound advice. The lack of understanding can to some degree be attributed to insufficient education and training in security awareness. Hence a formal and continually reinforced educational and training security programme can do much to inform employees how best to approach the concept of BYOD (Bring Your Own Device) to work.

## 8.3 Security Awareness and Organizational Learning

Garlati (cited in Trim et al., 2012a: 2) is right to link behaviour with legal matters and also organizational culture. This point of view rightly links security awareness with organizational learning, and brings attention firmly to the issue of managing organizational cultural change.

Smith (cited in Trim et al., 2012a: 3) has suggested the insider threat is very real, and often management are focused on external issues and vulnerabilities and not on inappropriate behaviour of internal staff. Managers need to be more aware of how security systems are circumvented and how computer systems can be sabotaged.

Smith (cited in Trim et al., 2012b: 3) has also suggested that it is not surprising to learn that acts of fraud and unintentional behavioural patterns (writing down passwords on Post-it Notes, leaving computer files open while employees are not at their work station, and passing out information to unknown individuals via social networks) is common practice that can and does result in security breaches. This suggests that the main security threat to an organization is from humans as opposed to technology (Davis, 2007: 185). It is because of this that Smith (cited in Trim et al., 2012a: 4) argues that security needs also to be placed in a wider context, and that means embracing the human resource aspect more fully than is the case at present, a view that has been gaining support through time.

## 8.4 Working with the Workforce

Trim et al. (2012b) in their paper 'Understanding, explaining and counteracting inappropriate user behaviour: Insights and recommendations', drew their information from the IAAC research workshop entitled 'Understanding, Explaining and Counteracting Inappropriate User Behaviour', which was held in London at BCS, The Chartered Institute for IT on 13 March 2012. The workshop was the sixth in the series and addressed six questions:

1. What measures can be put in place to prevent individuals engaging in inappropriate behaviour?
2. How can policy be formulated that takes into account the challenges and threats posed by BYOD (Bring Your Own Device), as IT processes are simply not designed for this?
3. How can the attitudes of employees be influenced in order to change behaviour so that the necessary security procedures are embraced?
4. How useful is it to incorporate litigation based case studies in order to teach risk management and ensure that the IT policies in place are workable?
5. How can management ensure that the behaviour of employees conforms to what is classified as 'secure behaviour'?
6. If the behaviour of employees is deemed inappropriate, how can management begin the process of influencing staff attitudes towards information assurance and cyber security?

Prior to the round-table discussion, three papers were presented. Rob Hadfield (2012) talked about 'Rapidly changing patterns of work behaviour and their consequences'; Cesare Garlati (2012) provided insights into 'Education, training and organizational learning: Issues and challenges'; and Martin Smith (2012) highlighted many important issues associated with 'Implementing a security awareness programme'. Reference is made here to the key points emanating from the workshop and starts with a summary of each of the papers presented on the day. Next, reference is made to the outcome of the workshop. It is pleasing to report that 31 people attended and of this total, seven were academics and one was a postgraduate student. It can also be pointed out that one of the industry representatives present was also a visiting lecturer at a university and this is evidence that the subject was given academic input.

Hadfield (2012), in his talk entitled 'Rapidly changing patterns of work behaviour and their consequences', made reference to the fact that solutions could be found to the increasing number of problems that were arising. What was important, was that a business case was found so that user support was forthcoming. Garlati (2012), in his talk entitled 'Education, training and organizational learning: Issues and challenges', suggested that the consumerization of IT was more about the trends in consumer technology as opposed to consumer products themselves. Smith (2012), in his talk entitled 'Implementing a security awareness programme', put forward a proposition for tackling the insider threat.

Basically speaking, an insider can bypass security. There is a need to address the human factor. Management must stop focusing on obscure solutions to obscure problems. The IT security industry is not engaged in the human factor area and if management do not engage with employees, the company will be vulnerable. In most organizations, security operations are in a silo. There is a need for management to make staff aware of the risks associated with BYOD and by making staff aware of the threats (through training and staff development programmes) it is possible to reduce the risk profile of the organization and reduce the number of breaches that occur. It can be suggested that security awareness is not expensive. When raising awareness it is important not to highlight the negative aspects and also to look at the whole range of risks. Management are limited by the knowledge they have available and if things are going wrong, matters need to be tracked back to identify simple human error if that is the root cause of the problem.

A number of key points have been reiterated and new dimensions added in order to produce an integrated resilience management model (Figure 8.1), which is in fact a synthesis of the main components and elements contained in Figure 7.1, the resilience policy including strategy mapping framework. The reader will note from Figure 8.1 that a Resilience Charter is in place to outline what all the organizations in the partnership arrangement need to do in order to ensure that the reputation management programme in place is as informative as it should be. The adapted leadership style ensures that management pay adequate attention to risk management, security and intelligence work, and that they adhere to governance and compliance issues, and engage adequately in business continuity management.

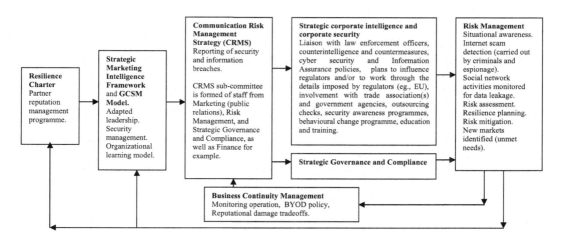

**Figure 8.1 The Integrated Resilience Management Model**

## 8.5 Conclusion

An organization needs a robust resilience policy in place in order for it to withstand the various and continual cyber attacks upon it. As well as cyber attacks, there are other challenges for management to confront and address, and it is clear that a commitment to organizational learning will provide the necessary platform from which policy and strategy can be developed that are aimed at making the organization sustainable. Formulating a resilience policy is not easy and time and resources need to be committed to ensuring that the appropriate members of staff are involved in it. Issues such as BYOD to work will continue to receive attention and will focus on what is deemed appropriate behaviour. This will, it can be assumed, result in agreements being drawn up and entered into regarding what is appropriate behaviour at work and what sanctions may be enforced should the actual behaviour deviate from what is expected.

## References

Anand, V., Sanije, J., and Oruklu, E. 2012. Security policy management process within Six Sigma Framework. *Journal of Information Security*, 3, 49–58.

Arruda-Filho, E.J.M., Cabusas, J.A., and Dholakia, N. 2010. Social behavior and brand devotion among iPhone innovators. *International Journal of Information Management*, 30, 475–480.

Casalo, L.V., Flavian, C., and Guinaliu, M. 2010. Relationship quality, community promotion and brand loyalty in virtual communities: Evidence from free software communities. *International Journal of Information Management*, 30, 357–367.

Cialdini, R.B., Petrova, P.K., and Goldstein, N.J. 2004. The hidden costs of organizational dishonesty. *MIT Sloan Management Review* (Spring), 71.

CIM. 2011. *Managing Threats in a Dangerous World*. London: Chartered Institute of Management.

CPNI Representative 2012. Potential impact upon critical infrastructures: Data leakage and consumerisation. *IAAC Consumerisation and Information Sharing Workshop*, BCS, The Chartered Institute for IT, London (17 January).

Davis, B.J. 2007. Situational prevention and penetration testing: A proactive approach to social engineering organizations, in *Terrorism Issues: Threat Assessment, Consequences and Prevention*, edited by A.W. Merkidze. New York: Nova Science Publishers, Inc., 175–188.

Garlati, C. 2012. Education, training and organizational learning: Issues and challenges. *IAAC Understanding, Explaining and Counteracting Inappropriate User Behaviour Workshop*, BCS, The Chartered Institute for IT, London (13 March).

Hadfield, R. 2012. Rapidly changing patterns of work behaviour and their consequences. *IAAC Understanding, Explaining and Counteracting Inappropriate User Behaviour*, BCS, The Chartered Institute for IT, London (13 March).

Hoskins, M. 2012. Regulation problems resulting from an EU directive. *IAAC Consumerisation and Information Sharing Workshop*, BCS, The Chartered Institute for IT, London (17 January).

Humphrey, M. 2012. The current challenges for information sharing. *IAAC Consumerisation and Information Sharing Workshop*, BCS, The Chartered Institute for IT, London (17 January).

Humphrey, M., Hoskins, M., CPNI Representative and Trim, P. (2012). *Information Assurance Advisory Council Consumerisation of IT Research Workshop Report: Questioning Existing Policy and Setting the Scene to Avoid Predictable Pitfalls: A Call to Action and the Way Forward*. London: Information Assurance Advisory Council (January).

Hsu, H.Y., and Tsou, H-T. 2011. Understanding customer experiences in online blog environments. *International Journal of Information Management*, 31, 510–523.

Lee, Y-I. 2009. Strategic transformational management in the context of inter-organizational and intra-organizational partnership development, in *Strategizing Resilience and Reducing Vulnerability*, edited by P.R.J. Trim and J. Caravelli. New York: Nova Science Publishers, Inc., 181–196.

Longstaff, P.H., Armstrong, N.J., Perrin, K., Parker, W.M., and Hidek, M.A. 2010. Building resilient communities: A preliminary framework for assessment. *Homeland Security Affairs*, 6 (September), 1–23.

Rid, T., and McBurney, P. 2012. Cyber-weapons. *RUSI Journal*, 157 (1), 6–13.

Smith, M. (2012). Implementing a security awareness programme, *IAAC Understanding, Explaining and Counteracting Inappropriate User Behaviour Workshop*, BCS, The Chartered Institute for IT, London (13 March).

Sternberg, L.J., Santella, N., and Zoli, C.B. 2011. Baton Rouge post-Katrina: The role of critical infrastructure modelling in promoting resilience. *Homeland Security Affairs*, 7 (February), 1–34.

Trim, P.R.J., Jones, N.A., and Brear, K. 2009. Building organisational resilience through a designed-in security management approach. *Journal of Business Continuity & Emergency Planning*, 3 (4), 345–355.

Trim, P., Hadfield, R., Garlati, C., Smith, M., Austin, J., and Lee, Y-I. 2012a. Understanding, explaining and counteracting inappropriate user behaviour. *IAAC Consumerisation of IT Positioning Paper*. London: Information Assurance Advisory Council (March).

Trim, P., Hadfield, R., Garlati, C., Smith, M., Austin, J., and Lee, Y-I. 2012b. Understanding, explaining and counteracting inappropriate user behaviour: Insights and recommendations. *IAAC Consumerisation of IT Workshop Report*. London: Information Assurance Advisory Council.

# 9 *Integrated Management Model and System*

## 9.0 Introduction

In order to provide insights into what management need to do to develop an integrated management model and system to ensure that the cyber security issues are dealt with adequately in the context of a corporate security and resilience policy, it is necessary to revisit what corporate security is (Trim, 2009: 213):

> ...*a robust stakeholder security architecture requires that attention is given to intra-government and inter-government working arrangements based on information sharing. It also requires that trust-based relationships between companies that provide disaster relief services and institutions that coordinate disaster relief operations are solidified through time...a more robust global disaster and emergency management policy and strategy [will] emerge and be implemented... [and will] reinforce the fact that a more pro-active approach is needed with respect to dealing with disaster and emergency situations and [furthermore] the international community needs to view disaster and emergency management from the perspective of stakeholder security.*

This chapter starts with placing the material in a security context (Section 9.1) and continues with security management (Section 9.2). A conclusion is provided (Section 9.3).

## 9.1 Placing the Material in a Security Context

Kendrick (2010: 14–17) has argued that as regards, technology risk, management need to be aware of how computer viruses affect the performance of a system and with respect to the transfer of sensitive and confidential information, encryption and educating staff about its use and application is important for enhancing security. As regards legal and compliance risk, management do need to consider how the organization is going to comply with the various statutory and regulatory provisions governing Internet technologies even if it is not easy/practical to apply them. With respect to operational risk, this is a key concern, as the systems and procedures in place for governing employee behaviour in relation to the production of goods and services need to be reinforced via new polices. Information security, generally, is about implementing effective security solutions and legal compliance, and involves training employees how to handle data.

As regards the board of directors, Kendrick (2010: 21–22) suggests that 'IT governance is a subset of corporate governance'. Outsourcing is an area of increased attention and because an organization faces many risks, a risk manager needs to be appointed to head a risk management team (Kendrick, 2010: 25). Ultimately, the risk manager is accountable to the board of directors or a senior manager. As regards controlling security in the cloud, Raj Samani (2011) is clear that all risk management requirements are covered in the contracts entered into.

The above draws on material that is highly relevant and can be considered useful for providing an appropriate context. With this in mind, it can be noted that Stuxnet has been referred to as a cyber weapon (Barnell, 2011). To guard against such forms of attack on a network, Barnell (2011) suggests continual monitoring is undertaken; an adequate information assurance programme is put in place; file level encryption is used; advice provided on security response websites is checked; contractors are checked to ensure that they are reputable; responsibility for risk is shared; and checks are made to ensure that contractors are not using stolen software.

If an attack does get through the organization's defences, it may be necessary to implement a disaster recovery programme and a reputation management programme at the same time. As has been noted previously, as organizations engage in multiple relationships, both inter-organizational and intra-organizational, management need to pay attention to how trust based relationships are maintained through time (Trim et al., 2009: 350). However, as Dawson (1996: 268–269) indicated, 'Organisations are arenas for the activities of different interest groups which are linked through patterns of conflict, consensus and indifference.' Again, it becomes evident for management to introduce an organizational learning policy and process to ensure that inter-organizational and intra-organizational relationships are governed and influenced by an adapted leadership style (Lee, 2009: 192). As regards managing the product development process, marketers in particular need to, in the case of software technology, understand what customers need, in what form it is needed, when it is needed, and how often it is expected to perform.

## 9.2 Security Management

This section draws on past work and includes the research findings from a number of Information Assurance Advisory Council (IAAC) workshops. The issues highlighted during the IAAC research workshops covered a number of points relating to security management.

The IAAC (2012a) Academic Liaison Panel meeting, which was held in London on 25 January 2012, discussed a number of issues relating to Objective 4 of the UK's Cyber Security Strategy (Cabinet Office, 2011) and the main points that emerged related to the development of skills needed to strengthen the nation's cyber security and defence capability; and in particular the supply of skilled students at all levels so that an integrated approach to developing a sustainable cyber security skill base could be developed. It was considered important that a promotional campaign was developed to reinforce the message that people needed to be more aware and cautious about the threats involved. However, a distinction needed to be made between education and training in the area of information assurance and in order to give the matter immediate attention, universities needed to take the lead and this could be done by the funding of research studentships. But it was generally accepted that cooperation and involvement of the private sector was needed.

A key recommendation to emerge from the discussions was that involvement of university business and management schools (especially modules relating to project and risk management) and schools of education was to be encouraged. It was suggested that various MSc/MA/MBA programmes could be developed and the main advantage would be that such programmes of study would bring together the academic and theory dimension and involve practising managers.

By drawing on the UK Cyber Security Strategy (Cabinet Office, 2011), the objective of the meeting was to produce inputs to the implementation of the UK government's Cyber Security Strategy (CSS) Objective 4. The vision set out in the report, which aims to achieve a 'resilient and secure cyberspace' by 2015, is based upon four objectives being achieved (Cabinet Office, 2011: 8 and 21):

- Objective 1   The UK to tackle cyber crime and be one of the most secure places in the world to do business in cyberspace.
- Objective 2   The UK to be more resilient to cyber attacks and better able to protect our interests in cyberspace.
- Objective 3   The UK to have helped shape an open, stable and vibrant cyberspace which the UK public can use safely and that supports open societies.
- Objective 4   The UK to have the cross-cutting knowledge, skills and capability it needs to underpin all cyber security objectives.

As regards CSS objective 4, the Academic Liaison Panel members (IAAC, 2012a) considered that academic staff in particular needed to focus on increasing the number of appropriately skilled cyber security students at various levels (from school to university and post-experience/practitioner level); cooperate more with government and industry; work with interested parties to produce relevant practical models for business and academia to cooperate fully; work with various stakeholders to develop and distinguish education and training provision in the fields of cyber security and information assurance; and engage more with professional groups and associations.

At an IAAC (2012b) workshop, which was held jointly with the Cabinet Office in London on 31 January 2012 to discuss the implementation of the UK government's Cyber Security Strategy CSS objective 4, three papers were presented, and the breakout discussions that followed took up the points raised by the speakers. It can be reported that training and education in the field of cyber security needs to be expanded so that those going into management positions can manage risks more effectively than is the case at present. Furthermore, there needs to be better integration between companies and universities as regards educational and training provision, although it was not realistic to suggest that universities would undertake company training. Bearing this in mind, more attention needed to be given to how policy could be more embracing with respect to making managers in the private and public sectors more accountable vis-à-vis the statements they included in the audited annual accounts. By increasing the nation's cyber knowledge base and skill level, it should be possible to better protect SMEs and to create a culture of good behaviour among people in society and to link more closely individual and organizational behaviour. It was considered that the cyber security knowledge gap that had emerged needed to be closed and young people needed to be informed about possible career opportunities in the area of cyber security. A whole range of issues were discussed ranging from the information assurance maturity model to changes in the national curriculum that were needed to promote a cultural change and a change in behaviour that witnessed better governance within organizations. It was felt that training in the area needed to be viewed more holistically and that the government needed to promote, through an awareness programme, more information about how people could gain cyber security skills. Trim (IAAC, 2012b) suggested that:

> *Those marketing the company's products and services need to be fully aware of what product liability involves and if a product/service is deficient, management need to think carefully about how unmet needs can be satisfied and a coordinated strategy can in part be complemented with a corporate social responsibility programme that is reinforced through tax incentives and which allows a company to meet a number of objectives and avoid reputational damage associated with action linked to product/service failings.*

It was clear from the deliberations that risk managers need to think in terms of identifying and satisfying unmet needs and identifying what the key success factors were. They also need to be aware of how a security management programme of study could be developed to promote cyber security. For example, resilience is a topic that has been discussed and one that is bringing together a range of experts from different fields of study. As well as universities taking the initiative to provide cyber security and information assurance related programmes of study, it is generally agreed that government need to be more actively involved in promoting such initiatives, and this is why various stakeholders (information security professionals, government representatives, academics, senior managers and various other interested parties) need to work together to devise a range of courses and programmes of study that can be delivered to different users.

A portion of this section draws on the outcome of the IAAC (2012c) Governance and Consumerisation Workshop held in London on 15 February 2012, entitled 'Who Should do What?' The speakers included Andrea Simmons (2012a) and Matthew Hogg (2012). In total 27 people attended and during the round-table discussions following the presentations answers were found to four questions (Simmons 2012a, 2012b: 2):

1. *What should government do for the public sector?*
2. *What should private sector/Centres of Excellence do for their 'parishes'?*
3. *What other solutions/controls are available to assist in delivering governance?*
4. *What is academia's role here – how can they provide inputs that would be fast-to-market regarding BYOD (Bring Your Own Device)?*

The logic underpinning and relating to the concept of Bring Your Own Device to work is not as clear cut as some would argue. For example, BYOD does relate to an individual user/employee having the right or opportunity to 'choose their own working conditions and operating environment' (Simmons, 2012b: 1) and asks that management consider a number of ownership and responsibility relevant points. These points are (Simmons, 2012b: 1):

- *Data storage, including emails, spreadsheets, documents, presentations etc., which will cause problems for 'legal discovery' identifying what has been done on behalf of the organisation.*

- *Information classification – in order to be able to identify what is personal information, and how it is to be excluded from storage, transfer, usage etc.; other data types including GPS tracks, photos etc., may also be subject to discovery.*
- *The growing integration of devices and services needs to be understood and scoped. Smartphones and other personal mobile devices may be synchronized with a home PC; users may be utilizing services such as Dropbox etc.; they may also, in the mid term be using their TV for remote access. Their phone may have been plugged in to an in-car display system. All of these situations will make it hard for organisations to know where their information has gone, even if the user is still working for them, and, of course, produces a very large attack surface. There are implications for both the individual and the organisation with regard to managing this future.*

Andrea Simmons (2012a) in her talk stressed the fact that bearing in mind the changes taking place in BYOD to work, it is essential that management identify the potential risks and impacts, as there is and will continue to be a momentum resulting in an explosion of data. It was pointed out that IT personnel do not always think in terms of security or what needs to be done to make something secure, and in some cases what needs to be done to make people think deeply about the threats posed by employees using their own devices for work. It is evident that management need to put in place a well-crafted policy to ensure that data breaches do not occur. The policy may include a £500 subsidy to employees so that they can purchase their own device and then it will be managed by the company. If an employee breaches company policy it will be dealt with in an appropriate way and it is appropriate for such a policy to be principles specific as opposed to technology specific. The issue of behaviour and how behaviour can be changed is crucial, and linked to identity theft. By placing data in the public cloud, it has to be recognized that issues will arise that need to be addressed. Are the risks associated with file sharing publicized enough? As well as data leakage, other issues need to be addressed as potentially, there are concerns regarding loss of control and access to data, security outages, architectural weaknesses that create security vulnerabilities, and regulatory and legislative concerns. Another question that arises is: 'In an economic downturn, are companies able to invest adequately in security?' The latter can be substantiated, however, the point being made is that attitudes to remote working are changing and so too is usage behaviour. It is not surprising to note, therefore, that governance is key and that as well as good governance at board level, operational governance is also needed. To be included in the policy elements are ethical and unethical decisions about usage and user behaviour; and how to manage access and dynamic risk management in particular.

Matthew Hogg (2012), in his talk entitled 'Cyber insurance: What is it about?', provided a certain amount of detail including reference to the control of risks, the role of the risk manager and the need for a risk register, and covered an often neglected topic – reputational risk. It is clear that risk assurance managers are looking at these issues and that when assessing risk exposure, it is important for managers to think in terms of risk to networks and in particular the data stored on networks, the physical damage that may result from an attack and the financial and emotional harm caused. Thinking comprehensively, management were required to address the following: costs (forensic costs in particular), risk mitigation costs, physical costs, and a range of issues linked with flexible manufacturing systems.

Matthew Hogg (2012) went on to explain that most of the costs are non-physical and customer lists needed to be guarded as do intellectual property rights. Physical injury claims would include emotional distress/damage, as well as personal injury and damage. The issue of privacy liability was important and so too were security liability and contractual liability. In particular, extortion, fraud and the bad behaviour of employees were noted. Again the issue of reputational damage surfaced and so did liability associated with the media and content on websites, and more generally the insider threat.

The cyber market covers non-physical risks, liability for data/privacy, first party damage, loss or damage to digital assets, non-physical business interruption; and management need to know the value of the company's assets, its R&D and trade secrets. Additional issues are: if the software is faulty how will this affect the management controls that are in place?

The discussion that followed the presentations covered a range of topics such as the value of an asset and first party involvement and fines imposed for losing of data. Software design issues, and in particular cover against faulty software, surfaced – product recall insurance covers a faulty product and product liability. Attention was given to a cloud provider and insurance risk cover; and the fact that an insurance policy is a negotiated contract, i.e. it covers what you want it to cover. However, do cloud users have enough knowledge about the service on offer from the cloud provider? Cloud providers need to meet certain standards: incentivization, better rates and better practices. Those that control the balance sheet have power and need to think of managing risk appropriately. For example, insurers need a business model and a company's risk register needs to contain information that a risk insurer needs to know and possibly only one-third of the claim will be covered in a pay-out. The risk manager needs to have matters joined up and be aware of what is covered and by whom. Knowing the organization's risk appetite is important and communicating risk adequately is key. Better threat modelling is required and the decision making process needs to incorporate better the chief information officer, the chief technology officer, and various others including the risk manager. The risk manager, it has been suggested, will need to know about the personal liability of employees and more generally about criminal liability. Figure 9.1 is the integrated management model and system derived from the above.

## 9.3 Conclusion

An organization's resilience policy and corporate governance policy cannot be viewed as distinct but should be viewed as integrated and will include IT governance. A risk manager assumes a pivotal role as regards the day-to-day operations of the organization and is involved in formulating and implementing various security management policies and strategies. Furthermore, he/she is also involved in reporting matters to stakeholders when required. The risk manager works closely with the IT manager and other managers, and reports at board level either directly or through a senior manager. It can be assumed that together with his/her peers, the risk manager has a high involvement in all aspects of human resource management policy relating to the development of the organization's cyber security skill base.

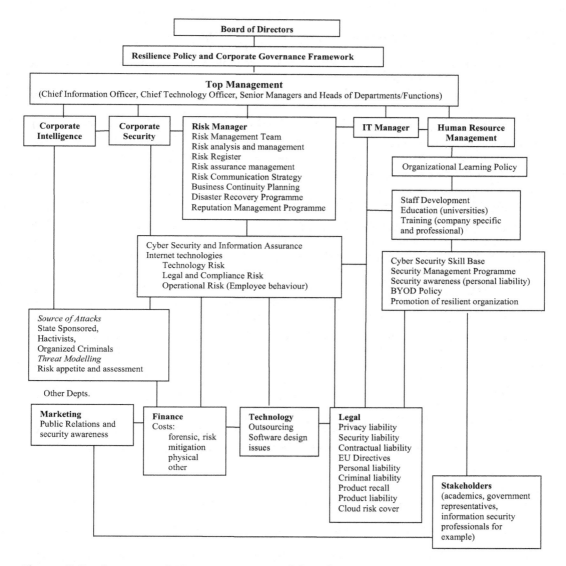

**Figure 9.1 Integrated Management Model and System**

*Note*: The interactions outlined in Figure 9.1 represent the main interactions only. There are a number of additional direct and indirect, formal and informal interactions but these have been omitted in order to simplify matters.

# References

Barnell, D. 2011. Stuxnet – Rethink security, right across the supply chain. *Second International Secure Systems Development Conference: Designing In Security*, Hilton London Olympia Hotel, London (18–19 May).

Cabinet Office. 2011. *The UK Cyber Security Strategy: Protecting and Promoting the UK in a Digital World.* London: Cabinet Office (November).

Dawson, S. 1996. *Analysing Organisations*. Basingstoke: Palgrave.

Hogg, M. 2012. Cyber insurance: What is it about? *Governance and Consumerisation Workshop. Who Should do What?* BCS, The Chartered Institute for Technology, London: Information Assurance Advisory Council (15 February).

IAAC. 2012a. Academic Liaison Panel. BCS, The Chartered Institute for Technology, London (25 January).

IAAC. 2012b. *The UK Government's Cyber Security Strategy Key Issues, Joint IAAC and Cabinet Office Workshop*. BCS, The Chartered Institute for Technology, London (31 January).

IAAC. 2012c. *Governance and Consumerisation Workshop. Who Should do What?* BCS, The Chartered Institute for Technology, London (15 February).

Kendrick, R. 2010. *Cyber Risks for Business Professionals*. Ely: IT Governance Publishing.

Lee, Y-I. 2009. Strategic transformational management in the context of inter-organizational and intra-organizational partnership development, in *Strategizing Resilience and Reducing Vulnerability*, edited by P.R.J. Trim and J. Caravelli. New York: Nova Science Publishers, 181–196.

Samani, R. 2011. Is it possible to control security in any cloud service? *Second International Secure Systems Development Conference: Designing In Security*, Hilton London Olympia Hotel, London (18–19 May).

Simmons, S. 2012a. Governance requirements for addressing consumerisation. *Governance and Consumerisation Workshop. Who Should do What?* BCS, The Chartered Institute for Technology, London: Information Assurance Advisory Council (15 February).

Simmons, S. 2012b. *Governance and Consumerisation Positioning Paper*. London: Information Assurance Advisory Council.

Trim, P. 2009. Placing disaster management policies and practices within a stakeholder security architecture, in *Strategizing Resilience and Reducing Vulnerability*, edited by P.R.J. Trim and J. Caravelli. New York: Nova Science Publishers, 213–227.

Trim, P.R.J., Jones, N.A., and Brear, K. 2009. Building organisational resilience through a designed-in security management approach. *Journal of Business Continuity & Emergency Planning*, 3 (4), 345–355.

# **10** *Integrated Governance Mechanism*

## 10.0 Introduction

The strategic marketing management framework outlined by Aaker (1992: 23) can be regarded as a useful strategic framework for analysing an organization's position in the industry in which it competes. If utilized well, the framework can be used to aid situational awareness. The US Homeland Security Studies and Analysis Institute (HSSAI, 2010: 15–16) has indicated that situational awareness (people, organizations and technology during an emergency maintain communications and develop a common operating picture that allows leaders to make appropriate and timely decisions *vis-à-vis* priorities and objectives) is a necessary activity and Kendrick (2010: 14–17) has focused attention on various types of risk associated with Internet technologies, and it can be deduced that encryption is only part of the solution. Whether the enterprise risk management model is deployed or not depends upon management's understanding, appreciation and commitment to complying with the various statutory and regulatory provisions in place to govern Internet technologies, although management still need to assume responsibility for ensuring that the organization has a security awareness programme in place. The security awareness programme aims to provide staff at all levels within the organization (and partner organizations) with up-to-date training in cyber security and also, custom designed management development programmes can be used to focus on ways in which to safeguard data and information from all sorts of internal and external threats, including fraudulent behaviour, entrapment through social networking activities and externally orchestrated hacking.

This chapter is composed of a number of headings: placing corporate governance in context (Section 10.1); harnessing appropriate technology (Section 10.2); organizational commitment to corporate governance (Section 10.3); corporate governance revisited (Section 10.4); and a conclusion (Section 10.5).

## 10.1 Placing Corporate Governance in Context

Kendrick (2010: 20–21) suggests that corporate governance represents 'a business strategy based upon transparent decision making; the establishment of lines of accountability and responsibility; securing shareholder and stakeholder value; and the adoption of sound risk management strategies, including information security'. Kendrick (2010: 21–22) continues by saying that 'IT governance is a subset of corporate governance'. Hence the argument that risk needs to be more widely interpreted than is the case at present (issues and problems associated with outsourcing and offshoring), and as a result senior management need to appoint a risk manager to head a risk management team (Kendrick, 2010: 25), which is accountable to a board member or senior manager.

Fahy et al. (2005: 2) suggest that 'Enterprise Governance is based on the principle that good governance alone cannot make an organisation successful'. Bearing this in mind, the SATELLITE (Strategic Corporate Intelligence and Transformational Marketing) Model developed by Trim (2004) is useful with respect to providing senior managers with a means to link security more firmly into the strategic management process of an organization. The Generic Cyber Security Management Model (GCSMM) (Trim and Lee, 2010: 5) has merit as it represents a useful extension of this argument and facilitates:

> *greater linkage between commerce and industry, government and academia, it is hoped that a more pro-active approach to cyber security will be established. This being the case, it can be argued that a hands-on approach to making an organization resilient will be needed, in the sense that resilient management systems and processes will provide greater protection against multi-dimensional attacks.*

The issue of linking organizational resilience to corporate governance is key, and there are various models and frameworks that can be drawn on to help managers do this. Figure 10.1 represents an extension of earlier work undertaken by Trim and Lee (2010: 5) and places the development of an organization's cyber security strategy within the context of three interlinked circles representing (i) the external environment, (ii) risk assessment which is embedded within the organization's strategic value system and (iii) the integration of security within the organization's functions and an emerging security culture within the organization.

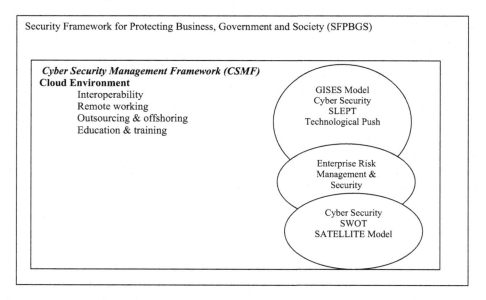

**Figure 10.1 A Generic Cyber Security Management Model (GCSMM)**
*Source*: (Trim and Lee, 2011)

The GCSMM allows senior management to improve and refine the linkage between a company's cyber security strategy and the company's ability to attract and maintain cyber security specialists. By integrating security with intelligence, and other functional areas, it is possible to embrace more effectively the GISES (Global Intelligence and Security Environmental Sustainability) Model (Trim, 2005) and to link the GISES Model with the SATELLITE Model (Trim, 2004). The intelligence oriented and multi-disciplinary security approach embedded in these models should enable the risk manager and his/ her colleagues (assistant risk managers) to link corporate security with strategic corporate intelligence, and to provide the necessary stimulation for the development of a security culture within the partnership arrangement. Trim and Lee (2010: 4) suggest that:

*by integrating security more firmly into the organization's structure, it should be possible to reduce the organization's level of risk and facilitate information sharing. Information sharing should enhance co-operation between partner organizations and add to the defensive capability vis-à-vis establishing effective counter-cyber attack measures.*

As regards new business models, management approaches and ways in which to improve corporate governance, it has to be remembered that although networks are reasonably secure, the main vulnerability is in the application layer (Barnell, 2011). Reflecting on the fact that top management need to deliver value to shareholders, they can do this by adopting what is known as the enterprise governance model, which incorporates three dimensions: *performance, conformance* and *corporate responsibility* (Fahy et al., 2005: 2–10). Fahy et al. (2005: 3–5) suggest that performance is measured in terms of how well an organization does in terms of systems, people and processes, in creating value for shareholders. As regards conformance, of key interest here is corporate accountability and how well management do in terms of regulatory codes, corporate legislation and accounting standards (Fahy et al., 2005: 5–7). According to Fahy et al. (2005: 5), corporate governance addresses five main areas: risk management and internal controls; corporate culture; stewardship and accountability; board operations and composition; and monitoring and evaluation of activities. Corporate responsibility has received a lot of coverage over the years and has often been fiercely debated in terms of what a company *should* do as opposed to what a company *might* do, as costs will be incurred which may aggravate shareholders. Notwithstanding, corporate responsibility is known to address six main areas (Fahy et al., 2005: 7–8): managing/reducing environmental, societal and cultural impact; protecting intangible assets such as reputation; promoting best practice in corporate ethics and governance; engaging in risk management; establishing traceability in supply chain management and procurement; and enhancing employee motivation and productivity.

Because cloud computing is expected to 'revolutionise traditional outsourcing models' (Quillinan, 2010: 32), senior management need to be aware of what security awareness programmes contain and put in place a continual programme of security awareness so that the various types of cyber threat are made clear. A good security awareness programme will also inform staff what needs to be done to prevent such threats materializing, and if they do, what needs to be done to limit the harm to the organization and its partners. Partner organizations normally are given sensitive data belonging to the other organizations in the partnership arrangement, and because of this senior managers need to consider compliance in the context of all the partner organizations. Adequate information assurance is necessary if breaches in security are to be avoided. However, when a data loss does occur, it is essential that working practices and the behaviour of employees are evaluated in order to assess whether future innovations (remote working for example) need to be better thought through in order to prevent acts of industrial espionage for example.

## 10.2 Harnessing Appropriate Technology

Senior management are it would seem concerned with three questions:

1. What does a holistic model of risk look like?
2. How can a holistic model of risk adequately take into account the unknown factors associated with cloud computing?
3. What would a conceptual generic model of risk, based on a cyber security analysis, look like?

A useful starting point is to look at what technology exists and how it can be used with respect to reinforcing corporate governance. Fahy et al. (2005: 163) state that 'in its simplest form, corporate governance is the systems and processes put in place to direct and control an organisation in order to increase performance and achieve sustainable shareholder value'. Attention will now be given to Proteus Enterprise™, which has a number of capabilities, as described in the following quotation:

> *Proteus Enterprise™ is a fully integrated web based 'Information Risk Management, Compliance and Security' solution that is fully scaleable....Using Proteus Enterprise™, companies can perform any number of online compliance audits against any standard and compare between them. They can then assess how deficient compliance controls affect the company both financially and operationally by mapping them on to its critical business processes. Proteus® then identifies risks and mitigates those risks by formulating a work plan, maintains a current and demonstrable compliance status to the regulators and senior management alike. The system works with the company's existing infrastructure and uses RiskView™ to bridge the gap between the technical/regulatory community and senior management by presenting the distilled information in a graphical 'dashboard' placed on their desktop.*
> *Source*: http://www.infogov.co.uk/proteus_enterprise/index.php [assessed on 11 May 2011]

As well as having the capabilities outlined in the quotation above, Proteus Enterprise™ facilitates strategic management thinking within an organization by forcing managers to think in terms of how the organization's customers view information assurance and cooperate to solve computer network problems, and introduce patches where necessary. It also allows managers to think in terms of constructing their organization's risk model, and this means paying attention to such issues as impact management and managing an asset and feedback from suppliers. In order to have an effective risk model in place, managers need to interpret risk from the company's perspective only (enterprise risk management model), or from an interlinked perspective, and this means working with a number of linked risk models, which may be viewed as dynamic as opposed to static and which are equally dependent upon human inputs as well as technical data inputs. Because there are several risk management models and approaches in existence, it has to be remembered that there is no one best approach to risk analysis. Whatever approach is adopted, managers will be required to have some way of telling how a risk is related to other risks and how a risk is linked with a control. A number of additional questions emerge:

- What are the costs associated with the controls that are in place?
- What are the likely consequences of an impact should an insider trigger what might be termed a 'low probability, high impact event'?
- How are various aspects of financial, operational and strategic risk related to the strategic functioning of the organization?
- Who in the organization (individuals/groups/departments) or externally (e.g. consultants) has responsibility for determining the parameters associated with integrating information security policy with an enterprise risk management strategy?
- How is business continuity planning aligned with security management policy?
- What is the level of risk associated with each internal and external stakeholder?
- Who in the organization is required to manage the risk assessment process?
- What trade-offs are made involving risk assessment by various departmental/ functional managers?
- How will governance, risk and compliance be integrated with sensor technology so that the sensors that detect intrusions and violations inform management in real time?
- Who in the organization validates the risk assessment process that is in place?
- Who in the organization is responsible for ensuring that the organization is compliant?
- What are the resource implications for introducing a set of controls that are judged to be absent?
- Who will be responsible for ensuring that the integrated dynamic risk management and protection system that is in place is as robust as it should be?
- How useful is it for senior management to produce a Sequence-of-Events Model that is linked with Proteus?
- Can a generic countermeasures model be used to identify threat motivations?

Bearing the above questions in mind, it is possible to focus on Proteus and to look specifically at how it relates to integrated governance, risk and compliance and sensor technologies. For example (http://www.infogov.co.uk/proteus_enterprise/index.php [assessed on 11 May 2011]):

> The novelty of the iGRC capability is an open standard to enable the integration of governance, risk and compliance technology with complementary network sensor technologies to produce an integrated model for the management of the complexity, risk and resilience of secure information infrastructure. A wide range of sensors are involved such as:
> - host based intrusion detection, vulnerability assessment, configuration and policy compliance, database logs, website logs, file accesses
> - hosts for penetration testing, email scanning, spam filters
> - network intrusion detection and prevention, netflow, firewall/router/other network devices logs

- *access and identity for successful or failed logins, new users, deleted users, privilege escalation, bio-metric identities*
- *website vulnerability detection (cross site scripting, SQL injection etc), pages visited, referred from*
- *end-point monitoring such as permitted user activity, not permitted user activity, data leakage monitoring, USB usage monitoring and reporting anti-virus, anti-phishing, malware detection*
- *applications – most keep audit logs of activity, and*
- *others such as event and audit log collection for operating systems, infrastructure and applications*

*All of these sensor types feed the GRC management suite that includes utility such as online compliance and gap analysis, business impact analysis, risk assessment, business continuity, incident management, asset management, organization roles, action plans, document repository and document dissemination, all from a risk management perspective.*

*Supporting any standard, the GRC management suite typically compliance manages BS ISO/ IEC 27001, PCI DSS, ISF SOGP, CobiT, BS ISO 38500, Sarbanes Oxley, HIPAA, BS 10012, Data Protection Act, Freedom of Information Act, Caldicott, BS25999, and Civil Contingency Act. So, as smart networks (or smart grids in electricity) are created, the incoming regulatory frameworks will be fully supported, and enhanced.*

The sensors undertake a number of tasks including highlighting attacks on the network. They detect various types of intrusion, scan for vulnerability, engage in log-file monitoring and incident monitoring, and identify unauthorized access and usage. Proteus can be used to provide answers to a range of questions including where sensitive data should be stored and in what form it should be stored. This means that an effective intellectual property rights (IPR) policy can be developed. This in itself is important from the point of view of trust being incorporated into the business model that stratifies the partnership arrangement. As regards cloud computing, it is necessary for senior management to identify the vulnerabilities of each of the partner organizations, and to ensure that the necessary protective measures are in place to counteract the actions of insiders and external hackers. Devising and implementing trusted services is now being given attention, and this raises a number of 'what-if' questions relating to information assurance, conflict between subcontractors, how reliable existing and alternative infrastructure is, privacy and who has access to personal data and when is it destroyed, the use of biometrics and its practicality, and the use of computer forensics. There will be continuing discussions involving what trust means to different parties and how many controls, and what types of controls and countermeasures should be put in place.

## 10.3 Organizational Commitment to Corporate Governance

Proteus is a risk, compliance and governance tool, which is integrated within an organization's operating system, and which can be set up and implemented within one to three days and which links into every operational activity of the organization. Risk assessments are turned into business impacts and this results in an improved situational analysis as various managers within the organization (risk managers and compliance managers in particular) are informed, by email, what they are required to do and when they are required to do it. Specific tasks may be identified and timetabled, and these become assets, for example: building a database and maintaining the database. In every case, a threat level (on a scale of 1 to 5) and a vulnerability level (on a scale of 1 to 4) are assigned to each asset, and the necessary countermeasures are identified and implemented via an action plan. Each activity identified and requested is, once it has been undertaken to the standard required, signed off by the appropriate manager/ executive and if it is felt that a further risk assessment needs to be undertaken, further action may involve a cost-benefit analysis. Three important points need to be noted regarding Proteus. First, the logic underpinning the software tool is drawn from standards that incorporate and are based on best practice. Second, the outcome of the decisions made by managers is ultimately related to the quality of the in-house knowledge capability of the organization. Third, risk management occurs in real time and this enhances the security operation by allowing managers to identify and prevent further hostile action. Furthermore, Proteus places controls on people to undertake tasks and this ensures staff are held accountable for their actions. Proteus also places an emphasis on staff to be more knowledgeable about their business function and other functions within the organization and this facilities situational analysis; it links with sensors in the network to detect incidents and this can result, through detection and appropriate action, in a reduction in the level of incident activity, which in turn reduces recovery time and the cost of the recovery; and it leads to greater efficiency through new service level contracts. Figure 10.2 outlines the linkage between an incident, an asset and a control.

Proteus is supported by a network of sensors that detect incidents (attacks and malfunctions for example) and records the level of threat activity. It assists managers by enabling them to identify and put in motion recovery activities. Another important point to note is that by identifying threats in real time, managers are well placed to prevent further attacks in real time. It can also be suggested that the software tool can reduce significantly the cost of an attack. The monitoring capability manifests in reminders being sent to staff to undertake duties they have not done and emails are stored for control and audit purposes. Safeguards are in place to ensure that only certain people have access to data and the data that is stored is placed in separate and/or linked databases, all of which are under the control of senior management. Proteus is linked to emergency planning and recovery, and this can be considered a major advantage.

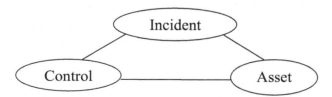

**Figure 10.2 Protecting Organizational Assets**

## 10.4 Corporate Governance Revisited

Fahy et al. (2005) are right to suggest that corporate governance needs to take into account the effectiveness of management structures, the role that the directors play, the accuracy of corporate reporting, and the understanding of the effectiveness of risk management systems. By being accountable to shareholders, it is true that management will think carefully about a whole range of issues relating to the running of the organization and as regards compliance, it is important that senior management think in terms of 'a measurement of responsibility to the stakeholder, the environment and the community. Business leaders must be prepared to demonstrate and explain their social contribution on training, employment, income generation, wealth creation, innovation, and supply chain development' (Fahy et al., 2005: 231).

## 10.5 Conclusion

The type of management model in place will be determined by both company specific and industry specific factors. Companies that operate in cyber space need to ensure that knowledge possessed by senior managers is made available to managers lower down the hierarchy, and in the context of a partnership arrangement, individual managers need to communicate with their opposite numbers in a logical and timely manner. It is important that skill gaps are identified and relevant training programmes authorized. Because it is not always possible to determine what type of attack will manifest and what form the attack will take, it is important that managers possess the skills necessary to manage change in a proactive manner. Proteus can help organizations do this, as it can trigger behavioural change and ensure that once an action has been authorized it is implemented.

## References

Aaker, D.A. 1992. *Strategic Market Management*. Chichester: John Wiley & Sons Limited.

Barnell, D. 2011. Stuxnet – Rethink security, right across the supply chain. *Second International Secure Systems Development Conference: Designing In Security*, Hilton London Olympia Hotel, London (18–19 May).

Fahy, M., Roche, J., and Weiner, A. 2005. *Beyond Governance: Creating Corporate Value Through Performance, Conformance and Responsibility*. Chichester: John Wiley & Sons Limited.

HSSAI. 2010. *Risk and Resilience: Exploring the Relationship*. Arlington, Virginia: Homeland Security Studies and Analysis Institute, Department of Homeland Security, Science and Technology Directorate (22 November).

Kendrick, R. 2010. *Cyber Risks for Business Professionals*. Ely: IT Governance Publishing.

Quillinan, J. 2010. Austerity rules. *Financial Sector Technology*, 16 (4), 32–33.

Trim, P.R.J. 2004. The strategic corporate intelligence and transformational marketing (SATELLITE) model. *Marketing Intelligence and Planning*, 22 (2), 240–256.

Trim, P.R.J. 2005. The GISES model for counteracting organized crime and international terrorism. *International Journal of Intelligence and CounterIntelligence*, 18 (3), 451–472.

Trim, P.R.J., and Lee, Y-I. 2010. A security framework for protecting business, government and society from cyber attacks, pp. 1–6. *5th IEEE International Conference on System of Systems Conference (SoSE): Sustainable Systems for the 21st Century*, Loughborough University (22–24 June).

Trim, P.R.J., and Lee, Y-I. 2011. Cyber social science and information assurance: A generic cyber security management model (GCSMM). Poster paper presentation. *The IAAC Symposium*, College of Physicians, London (7 September).

## Website

Information Governance Limited (now known as Infogov). http://www.infogov.co.uk/proteus_enterprise/index.php [assessed 11 May 2011].

# 11 *Threat Identification*

## 11.0 Introduction

The Cabinet Office (2011: 15–19) report entitled *The UK Cyber Security Strategy: Protecting and Promoting The UK in a Digital World* highlights the fact that criminals are undertaking fraud on an industrial scale and that identity theft and fraud online are serious problems and so too is the fact that the Internet has been used to exploit vulnerable people and children. Added to this is the fact that certain states and 'patriotic' hackers have engaged in various forms of espionage to their advantage, and as well as industrial and economic assets being at risk; such acts can also reduce a nation's military technological advantage and/or be used to attack a nation's critical infrastructure.

Terrorists have embraced cyberspace and undertake a range of activities including spreading propaganda, radicalizing people, raising funds and communicating and planning their operations. The problem is exacerbated by the fact that politically motivated activists launch attacks on websites. The objective appears to be to cause disruption, gain publicity, and inflict financial and reputational damage.

This chapter starts with UK Cyber Security Strategy and changing threats (Section 11.1), continues with cloud computing: opportunities and threats (Section 11.2) and follows with insights into counteracting cyber attacks (Section 11.3). The international context (Section 11.4) is given attention and a glimpse at organizational considerations is provided (Section 11.5). The chapter ends with a conclusion (Section 11.6).

## 11.1 UK Cyber Security Strategy and Changing Threats

By drawing on the UK Cyber Security Strategy (Cabinet Office, 2011), it is possible for senior managers to integrate the organization's cyber security strategy with those of partner organizations and to work closely with government representatives so that the nation has a robust cyber security strategy in place. The vision set out in the report, which aims to achieve a 'resilient and secure cyberspace' by 2015 (Cabinet Office, 2011: 8 and 21) will do much to get managers thinking about protecting the organization's intellectual property and commercially sensitive information. The following example indicates why safeguarding data and information is so important (Cabinet Office, 2011: 16): 'In the spring of 2011, Sony announced that criminals had successfully targeted the PlayStation network, compromising the personal details of up to 100 million customers and resulting in the network shutting down for several weeks. The costs to Sony are expected to total $171 million.'

As well as individuals and companies being at risk from attack, it has been made clear that government departments and agencies are also at risk. For example, Sir Iain Lobban (2013: 1), Director of GCHQ, has said, 'On average, 33,000 malicious emails a month are blocked at the gateway to the Government Secure Intranet – they contain sophisticated malware, often sent by highly capable cyber criminals or state-sponsored groups.'

There is no doubt that government, organizations and institutions, as well as individuals in society need to work more closely in order to make a country more robust and better able to counter the cyber threats that exist and the cyber threats of the future that are likely to emerge year on year. The UK government has, it is good to report, ratified the Budapest Convention on cyber crime and hopes that other countries will develop compatible laws. The UK government has invested in a number of initiatives to reduce the threats associated with cyberspace, and the proposed cyber security 'hub' should work well by promoting cooperation between private sector companies and the Government (Cabinet Office, 2011: 28):

- *exchanging actionable information on cyber threats and strengthening our response to incidents*
- *analysing new trends and identifying new and emerging threats and opportunities*
- *working to strengthen and link up our collective cyber security capabilities.*

Powell has highlighted the potential problem associated with terrorist attacks on communication networks (ENISA, 2008: 4) and this brings to the fore the fact that interdependencies exist between nations, organizations and infrastructures. Bearing this in mind, it is important to note that a nation's cyber security strategy needs to be placed in the context of an international cyber security strategy, hence the GISES Model (Trim, 2005a) is useful with respect to this. Information sharing between governments and organizations, and other relevant bodies and institutions, is necessary and to be applauded, as it will result in robust cyber security management systems and frameworks being put in place that are used to counteract a range of cyber attacks. However, caution is needed. For example, Judy Baker, Director of the Cyber Security Challenge UK, indicated that companies are finding it difficult to recruit specialist and skilled individuals (Baker, 2010) and this represents a major worry. Furthermore, Alan Paller, Director of the Sans Institute, has indicated that the US needs many thousands of individuals to counteract the work of those involved in cyber crime (Paller, 2010).

It is important to note that cyber attacks can be launched from any part of the world at any time, hence governments and international institutions need to cooperate more fully and raise awareness regarding these threats through public promotional campaigns. By putting in place more effective counter-attack measures, organizations will adopt and promote security, and this means that a change in organizational culture will result. As a consequence, pressure will be placed on universities to design and market relevant security management courses and programmes, and make executive and post-experience programmes of study available to a broad based audience.

## 11.2 Cloud Computing: Opportunities and Threats

Bearing the above in mind, it can be suggested that senior managers need to engage more fully in what is known as enterprise risk management (ERM). The enterprise risk management (ERM) approach has been criticized by some and misunderstood by others. Fox and Epstein's (2010: 3) work is of interest as it places risk within the organization's 'unique strategy, tolerance, culture and governance' and this may be considered a useful starting point, to understand and appreciate the issues and ramifications associated with risk. The work can be used by senior managers, as it outlines how they can apply an environmental and intelligence scanning system to identify risks and match the threat of risks with internal organizational vulnerabilities, and develop and implement an enterprise risk management cyber strategy (ERMCS) that ensures that prioritized risks are documented and evaluated, and contingency plans are drawn up relating to possible outcomes. By utilizing scenario planning and futuristic research methodologies, senior managers can develop security tools and systems, which can be deployed in partnership arrangements. It is important to note that organizational learning underpins organizational cultural change and in order to implement countermeasures effectively, continual monitoring is necessary and requires that a formal and systematic approach to environmental scanning (both internal to the organization and external to the organization are necessary). An effective monitoring system will have a number of advantages associated with it (ISO/FDIS, 2009: 20): the controls in place will be effective and efficient, both in design and operation; further information is obtained and this improves the risk assessment process; analysing and learning from events, changes, trends, successes and failures allows lessons to be learned; changes in the internal and the external context are detected – risk criteria, the actual risk, and revision of risk treatments and priorities; and the identification of emerging risks is automatic.

Experts and policy makers in the UK and the US have recognized that more needs to be done in order to encourage and develop the pool of cyber security professionals. For example, the report entitled *Cyber In-Security: Strengthening the Federal Cybersecurity Workforce* by Booz, Allen and Hamilton (2009: ii) indicated that the quality and the quantity of staff entering cyber security jobs, in both the private and public sectors, needs to be addressed because of the apparent shortfall (in both numbers and quality). Various issues and questions arise including:

- How robust is the recruitment process vis-à-vis the vetting of potential employees?
- How secure are computer systems vis-à-vis highly skilled and inquiring minds?
- How does the organizational value system embrace the aspirations of employees?
- If an employee is to engage in computer abuse, will the effects be limited only to the company or partner organizations? And how will this affect trust enhancement between partners?
- At what stage does the organization involve the police and/or make matters public?

The Sequence-of-Events Model was designed specifically so that managers could counteract cyber threats and devise a resilience oriented strategy that incorporated a sustainable counter-intelligence policy and strategy, and which placed the management of risk in a business–industry framework.

When addressing the issue of 'how to align security with the business', Briggs and Edwards (2006: 13) discovered that corporate security staff need to communicate widely and seek the views of non-security professionals in order that 'security is achieved through the everyday actions of employees right across the company'. Training and creating additional opportunities should reduce theft and absenteeism and acts of grievance (Briggs and Edwards, 2006: 44) and may prepare staff better to spot and deal with actual and/or potential attacks from organized crime syndicates and terrorists. Cornish et al. (2009: 3) indicated that 830,000 businesses in the UK during the period 2007–2008 experienced an online/computer related security incident and 84,700 personal identity fraud cases took place online. Extremist groups are known to use the Internet and so too are organized crime gangs engaging in money laundering. Trim et al. (2009: 347), in their work relating to organizational resilience, make it known that a collectivist approach to security should reduce the prospect of a disaster occurring. A collectivist approach to security requires that senior managers, experts and policy advisors adopt a united approach to solving cyber related attacks and that human factors as well as technological factors are brought into the equation. The main advantage of this approach is that it places cyber security in a broad context and takes into consideration various cultural, economic, social, political and technological factors (Trim and Lee, 2010, 2011).

## 11.3 Insights into Counteracting Cyber Attacks

Data was obtained from the IAAC Consumerisation of IT research workshop entitled 'Information Advisory Assurance Council (IAAC): Risk and Advanced Persistent Threat Agent Research Workshop', held in London on 6 December 2011. Prior to the workshop, Blyth (2011a) had circulated a positioning paper entitled 'The changing face of IA risk management'. In the paper, Blyth (2011a: 1) indicated that as regards the challenges associated with advanced persistent threat (APT) agents, it is useful to think in terms of defining two key terms:

- *Computer Network Attack (CNA): Includes actions taken via computer networks to disrupt, deny, degrade, or destroy the information within computers and computer networks and/ or the computers/networks themselves.*
- *Computer Network Exploitation (CNE): Includes enabling actions and intelligence collection via computer networks that exploit data gathered from target or enemy information systems or networks.*

Blyth (2011a: 1 and 2) also outlined a risk model and provided background information about sophisticated cyber attacks (Ghostnet, Operation Aurora and Stuxnet). Blyth (2011a: 2) explained that 'increased interconnectedness is providing opportunities for those that are intent on carrying out an attack to do so' and continued:

*In the past few years, three high profile computer network attacks have occurred and this illustrates how computer network attacks (CNA) have moved into the area of information acquisition and intelligence gathering via the application of zero-day exploits. This indicates that the nature and capabilities of threats and threat agents continues to evolve, and pose increasing challenges to senior management....To explore and understand the issues referred to above we need to put in place a series of definitions and concepts. The term advanced persistent threat (APT) is used to refer to an individual or group of individuals that are well motivated, well resourced and well trained in the art of computer network attack and computer network enumeration. Typical threat agents that fall into this group are: Foreign Intelligence Services (FIS) and Organized Criminal Syndicates. The term advanced evasion technique (AET) is used to refer to the CAN/CNE techniques that have been engineered to avoid detection and attribution. Analysis of the above allows us to explore the changing face of CAN/CNE. For example, recent attacks have focused on deploying advanced evasion techniques such as zero-day exploits to gain, and maintain, a persistent presence on the target system so as to exfiltrate information for political and economic ends. In particular attack outcomes include:*

- *The theft of an individual's online identity.*
- *The targeted theft and re-sale of intellectual property.*
- *The use of the Internet to engage in fraud and extortion.*
- *The use of the Internet for political influence.*

*These security incidents highlight the fact that cyber criminals and foreign state intelligence services are seeking to maintain a level of persistence on a victim's machine and are prepared to use sophisticated techniques to achieve that goal. These techniques include:*

- *targeted social engineering attacks that seek to manipulate existing social/trust relationships to facilitate exploitation of a targeted system; and*
- *the development and use of zero-day exploits and other advanced evasion techniques (AET) in order to manipulate existing social/trust relationships.*

For the Information Assurance Advisory Council research workshop held on 6 December 2011, Blyth (2011a) outlined the key challenges facing senior management and turned these challenges into questions to be addressed at the workshop:

1. *How can senior management detect an attack that they have never seen before, as they have no frame of reference for assessing the potential impact?*
2. *What information do we need to share to achieve the required level of understanding in order to implement effective countermeasures?*
3. *How can we develop architecture, develop, deploy and operate complex socio-technical systems such that any vulnerability contained in the system cannot be exploited?*
4. *How can we attribute a computer network attack to a specific attacker that is engineering it to avoid detection and attribution?*
5. *How do we measure and mitigate a level of risk when we do not know if we have been the victim of an attack?*
6. *How, if we have been attacked, can we quantify the damage/cost accurately if we have lost something as a result of the attack?*

Three papers were presented at the workshop: Tryfonas (2011) talked about 'Risk management in an uncertain world'; Ralph (2011) made reference to 'Situational awareness and advanced persistent threat agents'; and Blyth (2011b) talked about 'Risk, APT, AET and other dangerous things'.

Tryfonas (2011) raised a number of questions relating to the current context of risk management and posed two questions: (i) 'How could such interactions be modeled if things went wrong?'; and (ii) 'How can the impacts be adequately modeled?' Referring to open source intelligence, Tryfonas (2011) posed the question: 'What does a cyber weapon look like (Stuxnet)?' Ralph (2011) reinforced the point that those responsible for APTs are well organized and highly motivated. Ralph (2011) indicated that according to staff at Lockheed Martin, an APT cyber kill chain is composed of eight steps, which can occur over months:

1. reconnaissance
2. weaponization
3. delivery
4. exploitation
5. installation
6. command and control
7. actions
8. clean up.

Ralph (2011) posed the question: 'What is the method/delivery of attack?' Social engineering is used to get a target (victim) to install the tool and according to Ralph (2011), those preparing and implementing an APT are engaged in a constant effort to get their victim. The most successful attack is undertaken via email or by a placed data stick or web download. If the attack does not work the attacker tries a different approach. An attacker is persistent and looks for a new way or form to attack the selected victim. Bearing this in mind, Ralph (2011) is keen to point out that situational awareness is a key challenge for all concerned and those at risk should be vigilant (e.g. targets/victims are approached at conferences and/or via active probing via the network and/or via unexpected emails (spam)). Ralph (2011) posed the question: 'How can we link these different events together to identify an attack?' It is possible to use signal to noise ratios and signals to clutter. The key point to note is that those at risk have something that the attacker wants and one way to reduce risk is to have an effective training and awareness programme in place. The dilemma is, by expanding the envelope of business activity it may put the target at increased risk.

Blyth (2011b) suggested that there was evidence to suggest that Ghostnet, Aurora and Stuxnet were carried out by highly trained professionals and that they had tested the malicious software against the very best defences available before it was deployed in attack mode. Evidence suggests that the whole supply chain is vulnerable and managers need to take greater note of this. Furthermore, it is now necessary for managers in organizations to think of the security of their suppliers and what can be done in order to ensure that business operations cannot be penetrated. Obviously managers will need to pay more attention to outsourced operations and activities, the use of encryption, and malware that has been designed to extract data and leave without a trace; and be prepared to think of 'How can you detect an attack if you have no trace that it has occurred?'

After the papers had been presented at the workshop, the audience of 28 were provided with six questions to answer, which they did in a round-table discussion. Brief answers to the first three questions cited in the list above are provided below (Trim et al., 2012: 4–5).

## ANSWERS

1. How can senior management detect an attack that they have never seen before as they have no frame of reference for assessing the potential impact?
   Managers need to understand the behaviour of employees and take note of what they are sending out. The question surfaces: How much is the company prepared to spend on this? It seems likely that the organization's security model will be assessed and also, note will be taken of the level or degree of information sharing that goes on (internally and with external organizations). It is likely that individual managers

and/or the organization will be attacked and increased attention needs to be given to the controls that are in place. If the organization is attacked and a system does go down, is it possible for another system to take over? The key question becomes: 'Is the organization resilient?'

2. What information do we need to share to achieve the required level of understanding in order to implement effective countermeasures?

   Possibly the main question to be addressed is: 'What are the barriers to information sharing?' Managers need to pose the question: 'Who do we share information with?' Sharing means the blame culture mentality can be avoided and if a security breach does occur, it can be reported and a professional approach taken to rectifying the situation.

3. How can we develop architecture, develop, deploy and operate complex socio-technical systems such that any vulnerability contained in the system cannot be exploited?

   One has to accept the limitations and constraints that are in place and managers need to ensure that tools can be developed to analyse attacks accordingly. Possibly a range of methods as opposed to one method only should be used and more attention given to obtaining formal proof. It goes without saying that if a system fails then it should be fixed as soon as possible.

## 11.4 The International Context

Symantec (2010: 7) reported that Brazil has continued to experience increases in all categories of malicious code activity and one attack resulted in a massive power grid blackout, another resulted in a ransom request relating to the exposure of valuable data from a government source with various consequences. Another country experiencing malicious activity is India, indeed, malicious code, spam zombies and phishing hosts all increased from 2008 through 2009 (Symantec, 2010: 8). The Hydraq Trojan (referred to as Aurora) infected the computer systems of a number of large companies (Symantec, 2010: 8) and the attackers exploited information about companies and individuals found on social networking sites and an unknown vulnerability in computer technology in order to compromise computers. The degree of threat to companies is highlighted in the following quotation (Symantec, 2010: 8):

*Once the Trojan is installed, it lets attackers perform various actions on the compromised computer, including giving them full remote access. Typically, once they have established access within the enterprise, attackers will use the foothold that they have established to attempt to connect to other computers and servers and compromise them as well. They can do this by stealing credentials on the local computer or capturing data by installing a keystroke logger.*

*Usually, when this type of attack is performed against individuals or by less sophisticated attackers, the attack is used to gather all the information immediately available and move on to the next target. However, APT attacks are designed to remain undetected in order to gather information over prolonged periods.*

Evidence presented by Symantec (2010: 9) indicates that in 2009, hacking attacks accounted for 60 per cent of the identities exposed and that malicious code that was planted on the network gathered sensitive information and resulted in the theft of 130 million credit card numbers. The key point to note is that the attackers were able to carry out a data breach and thus remotely acquire data. It would appear that web based attacks have now replaced mass-mailing worm attacks, and social engineering methods such as spam messages are used to gather intelligence for the attacker, and once operationalized the user is lured to a website and unknowing to them, the browser and plug-in vulnerabilities are exploited (Symantec, 2010: 10). Once malicious code is installed in the user's computer they are at the mercy of those perpetuating the crime. Online banking activity is making it increasingly attractive for attackers to purchase crimeware kits such as Zeus and customize malicious code that has been designed to obtain data and information illegally (Symantec, 2010: 11). Crimeware kits are expected to remain sound business opportunities for criminals as there is a market for them.

Managers will need to pay attention to a number of points (Symantec, 2010: 19–34): malicious activity by country (especially the US, China, Brazil, Germany and India); web based attacks (compromised legitimate sites and especially crafted malicious sites that have been set up with the intention to target web users e.g. PDF activity aimed at distributing malicious PDF content); countries of origin for web based attacks (e.g. once a legitimate website has been compromised by an attacker, a user that visits the website can be attacked in one of two ways – a drive-by download that installs malicious code or the redirection of the user to a website that is hosting malicious code); data breaches that could lead to identity theft, by sector (educational institutions hold large amounts of sensitive data relating to staff and students and thus are a target, and so too are financial institutions and government departments); data breaches that could lead to identity theft, by cause (e.g. missing disks, insecure policy, and hacking activity); bot-infected computers (bots are installed computer programs that allow an attacker to control the computer via remote means and launch an attack such as denial of service, spam and phishing attacks, distribute spyware, adware and malicious code, and harvest information of a confidential nature); and threat activity – protection and mitigation (this requires that senior managers monitor network-connected computers in order to detect malicious activity and deploy firewalls and antivirus software).

In addition to the advice above relating to an effective threat activity programme, Symantec (2010: 33–34) recommends the removal of infected computers; companies need to deploy up-to-date anti-virus software and install necessary security patches; notify their ISPs of what they consider to be malicious activity; request that staff only open attachments from trusted or known sources; protect personal data via the Internet; implement a data loss protection solution; restrict access to sensitive information; comply with information storage and transmission standards; ensure that computers containing sensitive information are held in secure locations; ensure that sensitive information is accessed by authorized individuals only; and avoid having data on mobile devices that can be misplaced or stolen. Symantec (2010: 46–83) makes clear that managers/ administrators should also: monitor vulnerability mailing lists as well as security websites in order to keep up with new vulnerabilities affecting the organization's assets; monitor trends associated with malicious code and in particular analyse malicious code types (e.g. trojan, worm, virus, back door); monitor phishing, underground economy servers and spam trends); monitor the countries hosting phishing URLs (e.g. the US, South Korea,

Spain, Poland, Romania and Russia) and the most targeted sectors (e.g. financial, ISP, retail, insurance). Furthermore, managers/administrators will need to monitor the market for automated phishing toolkits; the countries of spam origin (the US, Brazil, India, South Korea, Poland, China, Turkey, Russia, and Vietnam); and how botnets are distributing spam, malicious code and phishing scams (Symantec, 2010: 71–83).

## 11.5 Organizational Considerations

The speed at which cyber criminals move can be deduced from the following quotation (McAfee, 2011: 17):

*Only two hours after the Japanese earthquake and tsunami struck we spotted the first potential scam donation site. During the few next hours we collected more than 500 malicious domains or URLs with the terms Japan, tsunami, or earthquake in their titles. Most were created in association with spam campaigns, false news sites to distribute malware, and especially fake charity actions. This behavior will never go away.*

Martin (2008) has highlighted the need for and relevance of developing information security standards that form the basis of security management and measurement activities. This may have the advantage of reducing misunderstandings in terminology and focusing attention on what is meant by holistic security. What is clear, is that companies in the private sector need to work with government in order to ensure that such initiatives are translated into workable plans and strategies.

It is also useful to reflect and remember that ENISA (2010: 15) understand risk to be: Risk = f(Asset, Vulnerability, Threat). However, managers need to develop an in-depth appreciation of risk and put in place a proactive threat identification process. This can be done by adopting the SATELLITE Model (Trim, 2004) and ensuring that the corporate security management component views security as a core activity (Trim, 2005b). At this point it is necessary to state that a number of internal stakeholders can be identified who are in addition to the managers and specialists already in place. The various stakeholders can be defined and grouped into four main categories (Chambers and Thompson, 2004: 8): discoverers, vendors, users and coordinators. It is useful to note that discoverers (individuals or organizations) find vulnerabilities and subgroups include a range of people – researchers, staff in security companies, users, government employees and coordinators (Chambers and Thompson, 2004: 16). Chambers and Thompson (2004: 17) indicate that vendors develop/maintain information system products/services that are judged to be vulnerable and subgroups include information security (Infosec) teams, product security teams, incident response teams, researchers, and a range of specialists including communications coordinators, legal officers and operators. Users are those that use a vendor's product which may be affected by a vulnerability and include governments and the owners and operators of critical infrastructure, and service providers (Chambers and Thompson, 2004: 18). The last group, coordinators, is composed of those that manage a single vendor's response/multiple vendors' response vis-à-vis a vulnerability (Chambers and Thompson, 2004: 18). Bearing this in mind, it seems appropriate that top management consider putting in place a group of people that can work within a stakeholder framework and who are charged with undertaking certain duties and liaising with appropriate external staff. For example: Infosec team (charged with maintaining or improving information system security); the product security team (address problems associated with a vendor's product); an incident response team (subgroup of the Infosec team); incident handler (an individual appointed to manage a response to a vulnerability); operators (those in charge of day-to-day activities associated with maintaining and improving information system resources); communication coordinators (organizational staff in charge of media issues); researchers (a range of individuals who undertake technical research to produce countermeasures); legal officers (individuals who identify, monitor and address legal issues in relation to vulnerabilities, e.g. product liability, contractual obligations and regulatory requirements); and law enforcement (individuals or groups that deal in legal and wider issues relating to national security) (Chambers and Thompson, 2004: 20–21).

## 11.6 Conclusion

When addressing the topic of cyber threats, it is unrealistic to think that the problems identified can be placed in a national security context only. The potential problem associated with attacks on communication networks has been made known and to deal with the problem effectively, international cooperation is needed. The decision to engage with a cloud computing services provider will require knowledge and a clear understanding of what is involved. What is clear is that those formulating an organization's cyber security strategy need to consider a wide range of issues that have a cultural, economic, social, political and technological base. However, it has to be accepted that not all governments have the same priority because some countries are more prone to attack than others and because of this, government representatives do not always consider that cyber security may be as high a priority as other government representatives claim.

## References

Baker, J. 2010. Talk at the Cyber Security Challenge UK, University College London (26 July).

Blyth, A. 2011a. The changing face of IA risk management. *Information Advisory Assurance Council (IAAC) Consumerisation of IT: Risk and Advanced Persistent Threat Agent Research Workshop*. Positioning Paper. London: BCS, The Chartered Institute for IT (6 December), 1–3.

Blyth, A. 2011b. Risk, APT, AET and other dangerous things. *Information Advisory Assurance Council (IAAC) Risk and Advanced Persistent Threat Agent Research Workshop*. Positioning Paper. London: BCS, The Chartered Institute for IT (6 December).

Booz, Allen and Hamilton. 2009. *Cyber In-Security: Strengthening the Federal Cybersecurity Workforce*. Washington, DC: Booz, Allen and Hamilton.

Briggs, R., and Edwards, C. 2006. *The Business of Resilience: Corporate Security for the 21ˢᵗ Century*. London: Demos.

Cabinet Office. 2011. *The UK Cyber Security Strategy: Protecting and Promoting the UK in a Digital World*. London: Cabinet Office (November).

Chambers, J.T., and Thompson, J.W. 2004. *Vulnerability Disclosure Framework: Final Report and Recommendations by the Council*. National Infrastructure Advisory Council (NIAC).

Cornish, P., Hughes, R., and Livingstone, D. 2009. *Cyberspace and the National Security of the United Kingdom: Threats and Responses*. Chatham House Report. London: Royal Institute of International Affairs.

ENISA. 2008. *Report on 4th ENISA CERT Workshop*. Athens: European Network and Information Security Agency (ENISA) (June).

ENISA. 2010. *Mapping Security Services to Authentication Levels: Reflection on STORK QAA Levels*. Heraklion, Greece: European Network and Information Security Agency.

Fox, C.A., and Epstein, M.S. 2010. *Why is Enterprise Risk Management Important for Preparedness?* White Paper. New York: Risk Insurance Management Society, Inc.

ISO/FDIS 2009. *International Standard: Risk Management – Principles and Guidelines*. Reference Number ISO/FDIS 31000: 2009 (E). Geneva: ISO.

Lobban, I. 2013. *Countering the Cyber Threat to Business*. London: Institute of Directors.

Martin, R.A. 2008. Making security measurable and manageable. Software Assurance Measurement Working Group. Department of Homeland Security/The MITRE Corporation. http:// buildsecurityin.us-cert.gov/swa/ecosystem.html [accessed 1 December 2011].

McAfee. 2011. *McAfee Threats Report: First Quarter 2011*. Santa Clara, California: McAfee Labs.

Paller, A. 2010. Talk at the Cyber Security Challenge UK, University College London (26 July).

Ralph, S. (2011). Situational awareness and advanced persistent threat agents. *Information Advisory Assurance Council (IAAC) Consumerisation of IT: Risk and Advanced Persistent Threat Agent Research Workshop*. Positioning Paper. London: BCS, The Chartered Institute for IT (6 December).

Symantec. 2010. *Symantec Global Internet Security Threat Report: Trends for 2009. Volume XV*. Mountain View, California: Symantec Corporation (April).

Trim, P.R.J. 2004. The strategic corporate intelligence and transformational marketing model. *Marketing Intelligence and Planning*, 22 (2), 240–256.

Trim, P.R.J. 2005a. The GISES model for counteracting organized crime and international terrorism. *International Journal of Intelligence and CounterIntelligence*, 18 (3), 451–472.

Trim, P.R.J. 2005b. Managing computer security issues: Preventing and limiting future threats and disasters. *Disaster Prevention and Management*, 14 (4), 493–505.

Trim., P.R.J., Jones, N., and Brear, K. 2009. Building organisational resilience through a designed-in security management approach. *Journal of Business Continuity & Emergency Planning*, 3 (4), 345–355.

Trim, P.R.J., and Lee, Y-I. 2010. A security framework for protecting business, government and society from cyber attacks. *5th IEEE International Conference on System of Systems (SoSE): Sustainable Systems for the 21st Century*, Loughborough University (22–24 June), 1–6.

Trim, P.R.J., and Lee, Y-I. 2011. Cyber social science and information assurance: A generic cyber security management model (GCSMM). Poster paper presentation. *The IAAC Symposium: Information Assurance: Meeting Challenges of Changing Times*, College of Physicians, London (7 September).

Trim, P.R.J., Blyth, A., Tryfonas, T., Ralph, S., and Austin, J. 2012. Risk and advanced persistent threat agent: Context and counteracting strategy. *IAAC Consumerisation of IT Workshop Research Report*. London: Information Assurance Advisory Council, 1–8.

Tryfonas, T. 2011. Risk management in an uncertain world. *Information Advisory Assurance Council (IAAC) Risk and Advanced Persistent Threat Agent Research Workshop*. Positioning Paper. London: BCS, The Chartered Institute for IT (6 December).

# 12 *Competitor and Marketing Analysis*

## 12.0 Introduction

This chapter draws on the content of several other chapters and views competitor and marketing analysis from the perspective, not of the market and accompanying analysis of the market, but an appreciation of marketing conditions and the market opportunity. A strategic marketing approach brings into context the strategic market management perspective advocated by Aaker (1992).

First attention is given to Proteus's capabilities (Section 12.1) and this is followed by insights into the consumerization of IT (both internal and external considerations are highlighted) (Section 12.2). Consideration of current cyber security issues and challenges (Section 12.3) is followed by preventing cyber attacks (Section 12.4). The mapping of key variables and characteristics (Section 12.5) is followed by the South Korean security market (Section 12.6). A conclusion (Section 12.7) is provided.

## 12.1 Proteus's Capabilities

A teleconference and web demonstration to highlight the capabilities of Proteus was provided by a senior manager on 22 June 2012 from 7pm to 8pm, and the results are outlined below. This material can be considered to be an internal component.

### RISK MANAGEMENT

Risk is viewed from the perspective of what is 'fit for purpose', in other words the approach to risk is limited to risk assessment and management and does not extend to risk analysis. Hence Proteus does not include a risk analysis tool but one could, if needed, be built in. What Proteus does do, is link the risk task when the control requires it to the risk engine, which is then linked to the business impact tool. There is a distinction between risk analysis and management. The CIA (confidentiality, integrity and availability) risk interpretation from standards focuses attention on levels of risk. So it operates in semi-real time and a risk analysis tool can be built in to provide a better interpretation of risk by taking into account the interdependencies and arriving at a better understanding as to how multiple impacts will affect the organization's vulnerability level and how managers within the organizational structure can relate better to the countermeasures in place, which then act in unison or in a pre-planned manner.

## BUSINESS IMPACT ASSESSMENT

With respect to provisioning (BC00631), cross-reference controls can be linked, meaning that the potential disruptions can be identified and this has implications for the process itself. Various disruptions and their impacts can be defined in time based terms: 1 hour, 4 hours, 8 hours, 1 day, 2 days etc. Disruptions are time specific (e.g. tolerance) and can be classified in terms of financial disruption. At stage 4 of the process, it is possible to build in resources and undertake a business assessment with the assets. Having done a risk assessment it is possible to establish a risk priority number from the risk assessment (hours, 2 days used in the process). And link to individual people, i.e. managers. At stage 5 of the process, an overall assessment can be made and this means that criticality can be established, recommended values produced and responsibility assigned to individual managers. Managers can look at the risk assessment and establish the possible impact on the business. Individual managers can accept the diagnosis and Proteus can be used to assign tasks, which is useful as it leaves an audit trail.

## RISK ASSESSMENT

Risk assessment is in the form of a four stage process. Stage 1 relates to risk assessment details and stage 2, CIA (confidentiality, integrity and availability), processes the assets it is supporting and relies on the manager's judgement. Stage 3 is identifying threats, and various threats identified may be cracking keys and cracking passwords, and stage 4 is the available countermeasures to reduce risk on the asset. Risk is denoted on a scale of 1 to 5. The table used outlines the following in order: the asset, countermeasures, likelihood, vulnerability, RPN, and Justification. The value assessment is, for example, 1140, which is multiplied by the RPN (which is 16), which produces a total risk score of 18,240. This is communicated to an individual manger and if he accepts it, he signs it off, and a designated manager/individual receives an email, which outlines the risk assessment in report form, and if the designated manager accepts the risk he signs it off and submits the response accordingly. He then has a given period in which to put matters right and is held accountable for doing so.

## BUSINESS CONTINUITY

Business continuity needs to be thought of in terms of the process of sustaining more provisioning. A question can be posed: Which services are critical to this process (Internet, wireless, network, fixed line telephony, email)? Stage 3 relates to work around procedures and stage 4 relates to critical data. Stage 9 is contacts and stage 10 is responsibility and acceptability. The process is then signed off.

## POLICY MANAGEMENT

There is a link to the document emailed to the manager, and the email asks that the manager goes to the document and answer questions on it; and the compliance manager sees that it has been done.

## GRAPHICAL USER INTERFACE

This allows for physical reporting.

## COMPLIANCE

Standards, questions posed and assigned to managers(s). It can be noted that there are different standards for different industries, accepted in Europe, and utilized by Proteus.

## CONTROL

Questions from consultants are built in, hence the planning process is built in. This is advantageous as the auditor can see that it has been done.

## GOVERNANCE

Allows for a company's policy to be checked against a range of standards.

## AUDIT POINTS

An audit point, department or site, and various groups defined according to them being a user, an asset or a control. Proteus can be used as part of the auditing process as it has a list of pre-set questions (or different questions based on the standard relating to the industry).

## SECURE

Only the appropriate managers identified and designated receive the emails so it is a list of privileged names.

## UNIQUENESS

Proteus is flexible and incorporates a different set of risk values that can be used by different business units operating in different business environments to assign a risk value to a particular asset. Some risk values associated with different assets can be compared and this provides senior management with some indication of the organization's overall vulnerability. Proteus can be adapted to different business environments (the public and private sectors and different countries).

Proteus is used by highly skilled and industry specific people who are knowledgeable about the business environment in which the organization operates. Proteus is an operating tool that assists the development of the planning process and allows relevant and fact based decisions to be made and implemented in real time. By linking business impact with the risk associated with the asset, managers can prioritize the risk and the risk can be managed in real time.

Proteus can be used by those engaged in enterprise risk management as it allows individual managers, some of whom only see or are concerned with a particular aspect of the business operation, to assign a specific risk assessment/task to an asset and then report to the risk manager (who is also receiving similar reports from different managers) who then prioritizes the risk associated with the individual assets.

The next step of action requires that the risk manager evaluates the situation and authorizes action, for example, indicates to each corresponding manager what they need to do and by when.

## 12.2 Consumerization of IT

The Information Assurance Advisory Council (IAAC, 2012) Consumerisation of IT workshop held in London on 19 June 2012, provided some useful insights into a range of internal and external factors that management need to take into consideration vis-à-vis market opportunity. Reference to the main points appears below.

### CONSUMERIZATION OF IT MAIN POINTS

1. Consumerization of IT and BYOD is increasing the risk associated with vulnerability and tracking is key (Wilson, 2012).
2. As regards cameras and video recording facilities built into the device it is possible to transfer data between points therefore the human factor needs more attention (industrial espionage) (Wilson, 2012).
3. If staff use BYOD to work they can download documents and are at risk from having hackers break into their machine or may be inadequately safeguarding the data/information and it could be accessed by others via the cloud for example (Wilson, 2012).
4. Potential loss from a smartphone device due to Android platform vulnerability and interconnectedness of platforms (system network) (Wilson, 2012).
5. Does the manufacturer/vendor comply with recognized standards so that the device is considered safe to use (Wilson, 2012).
6. Customer relationship management is no longer viewed as a corporate issue but is related to social media and the person that manages the service for the social media is responsible for CRM (e.g. incorporates outsourcing) (Wilson, 2012).
7. Who is the risk owner? The company or an individual e.g. in terms of managing the asset safely (Wilson, 2012).
8. Mobile application registered by the organization (Wilson, 2012).
9. The tools for application need to be viewed in the context of the task undertaken, and attention needs to be given to the platform and the technical capabilities covered in the corresponding standard(s) (Wilson, 2012).
10. The corporate/user interface needs to be given attention as this may be a potential vulnerability, hence an emergency response team needs to be in place to deal with all types of incidents (ranging from technical expertise to media expertise) (Wilson, 2012).
11. Security issues are driving information flow and technical capability which need to be addressed in terms of pressure to be a more open company in terms of data made available to the public (Wilson, 2012).
12. Raised level of threat associated with platform design, outsourcing and the change in human behaviour when the user is online (Collins, 2012).

13. The role and nature of information assurance has to be placed in the context of trustworthy behaviour and the non-release of sensitive data and information to social networks.

14. The legal framework needs to be improved and/or reflect the changes in the environment as the tools and techniques used currently are different from those developed in the 1940s (Collins, 2012).

15. The operating environment is changing and the values and belief systems determine what data and information is available to the public (Collins, 2012).

## 12.3 Consideration of Current Cyber Security Issues and Challenges

The main conclusions in the form of current cyber security issues and challenges emanating from the SMi Cyber Defence Conference that was held in London from 18 to 19 June 2012, are, together with the source, cited below.

1. Organizations need to consider the use of integrated, multi-media channels and make use of multi-media tools if an attack is launched. If an attack has got through, management need to (Mehringer, 2012): (i) investigate and confirm the incident; (ii) prepare a communication response; and (iii) notify the media, subscribers and the public.

2. Problems associated with software vulnerability (Mehringer, 2012). Whose responsibility is it to put matters right? Manufacturer, vendor and/or user. What role should law enforcement play? Need for cooperation between all parties. Need to improve the quality of software through private-public partnerships (Bryant, 2012).

3. A more integrated approach needs to be taken vis-à-vis how different industrial sectors deal with and relate to risk, and in particular how companies calculate the risk associated with interdependencies (Panzieri, 2012). Tracking and tracing such attacks is important and should allow management to better understand the vulnerabilities evident (Panzieri, 2012). Risk management can be enhanced through information sharing and collaborative arrangements, and should be aimed at identifying probable impacts (Panzieri, 2012). The role of the emergency decision team needs to be thought through (Panzieri, 2012).

4. It has been suggested that cyber attacks are asymmetric, anonymous and anarchic; and they are versatile, they change shape, the identity of those involved is hidden, and they are extremely rapid (Roehrig, 2012). If a cyber attack is unsuccessful renewed attempts will be made until a way in has been found via a different attack vector (Roehrig, 2012). The problem is growing and so is the complexity, therefore, information and intelligence sharing relating to forensics needs to occur and for this to happen trust must be evident (Roehrig, 2012). In order to defend against cyber attacks, there must be cooperation between the military and civilian sectors, based on mutual interest and this needs to extend beyond the national level to the international level (Roehrig, 2012). Need to build a common culture of cyber defence based on education and training that incorporates networking and interoperability (Roehrig, 2012).

5. A cyber weapon is known to not have a single purpose, have multiple payloads, are secretive projects, with layers of approval, with trusted teams in place, and timeline reduced with operational objectives and efficiency (Lee, R., 2012).

6. Society needs to review how effective the country's laws and punishments are with respect to deterring cyber attacks (Aston, 2012). As well as actual cyber attacks software exists to create the impression an attack is underway when in reality it is a diversion and an attack is being carried out elsewhere (Sandhu, 2012).

7. Organizations need to engage in risk management assessment and prioritize their investments in cyber defence so that they have trusted security operations in place (Pevtschin, 2012). An impact analysis needs to include economic impacts and organizational and operational impacts, thus coordination of pre-emption and reaction cannot and should not be driven by industry alone (Pevtschin, 2012).

8. Good systems can be implemented badly hence it is imperative that people follow the procedures and continual checking is needed, hence organizational learning needs to be considered more than it is at present (Barrington Brown, 2012). Managers need to be aware of social engineering techniques for the attacker to deploy malware to carry out acts of industrial espionage and in particular attention needs to be given to how to prevent staff from giving out sensitive data that can be used for sophisticated social engineering programmes (Thon, 2012).

9. When considering the range of threats in existence (conflict, terrorism, sabotage, espionage, criminality, activism, vandalism) it is important to think of how such incidents differ in intensity and what the residual risk is (Vernez, 2012). When weighing up the possible impacts of international threats it is important to think in terms of the investment needed in countermeasures, and the balance between technology and the role of management in terms of low and high intensity (Vernez, 2012). All members of the population are at risk and cyber represents a high level of variability of possible attack, hence an awareness programme needs to take into account adequate and continual monitoring (Vernez, 2012).

## 12.4 Preventing Cyber Attacks

Trim and Lee (2011) gave a talk entitled 'A pro-active approach to managing cyber security threats' at the CAMIS Integrated Governance, Risk and Compliance Conference and Knowledge Sharing Event, incorporating the iGRC Consortium demonstration and network sensor devices at Birkbeck, University of London on 15 December 2011. A questionnaire composed of six questions entitled 'Preventing Cyber Attacks' was distributed to 25 of the delegates attending the conference and 12 completed questionnaires were returned at the end of the day, representing a response rate of 48 per cent. Forty people attended the conference, however, some did not attend for the full duration and some declined to complete the questionnaire. The responses, in summary form, to each individual question are contained in Appendix 6: Preventing Cyber Attacks survey results. A summary of the results is included in Table 12.1.

**Table 12.1    Preventing Cyber Attacks**

*Action to protect against cyber attack(s).*

Foresight risk policy (operational and strategic) in place.
BYOD policy in place.
In-house security awareness programme (education and training).
Effective contingency responses devised.

*Cyber security issues to be addressed.*

Integrated information system to protect personal, private and company data and information breaches.
Social engineering, advanced persistent threats, state espionage, compliance and regulatory action.
Consumerization and new market offerings.

*Effectiveness of existing risk management models.*

Need to better understand the organization's risk appetite and the risk consequences from both a quantitative and qualitative perspective.
Need to understand the human factor aspects.
More effective coordination between different organizations e.g. governments and business.

*Cyber security management framework to counter cyber attacks.*

Industry standards and increased cooperation.
Efficient deployment of controls and countermeasures.
Organizational strategy underpinned by the concept of resilience.

*An effective organizational knowledge base that embraces risk, compliance and governance.*

A monitoring system needs to be put in place.
Better strategic (external) intelligence.
Sharing knowledge with competitors and government agencies.

*Government, industry and academia and an adequate pool of skills to counter cyber attacks.*

A set of broad based education and training programmes.
Situational awareness to be incorporated in a range of courses and programmes (develop undergraduate and postgraduate security and resilience programmes of study).
Executive courses and programmes of study for senior and junior managers.
Common strategic intelligence forum covering all aspects.

# 12.5 Mapping of Key Variables and Characteristics

The main unmet customer needs identified through the analysis and interpretation of the research findings include some specific unmet needs and some more generally defined and wide-ranging unmet needs. The 28 unmet needs have been identified and placed in a list in Appendix 7. The 28 unmet customer needs identified were synthesized and are shown in Figure 12.1.

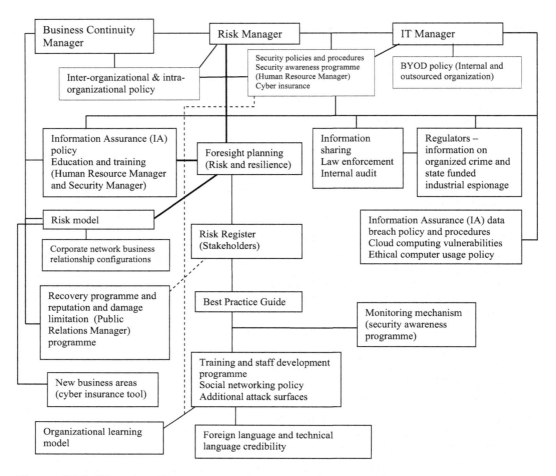

**Figure 12.1 Mapping Management Inputs Against Functions**

## 12.6 South Korean Security Market

Table 12.2 below represents a SWOT analysis of the Republic of Korea homeland security market. The British government is keen for UK companies to penetrate this market and evidence suggests that the relations between the two countries are strong and growing in importance.

In order to do business in South Korea, it is essential that company representatives (Lee, K., 2012): (a) adopt a customer approach (introduction and demonstration meeting, keep updating end users); (b) adopt a realistic pricing strategy (reasonable price includes agent fee, research competitors' prices and identify the needs of end user's budget range); (c) focus on quality (high performance, offer diverse models to meet buyer's needs); and (d) provide appropriate after-sales service (competitive warranty, secure after-sales service).

**Table 12.2   South Korean Security Market**

### SWOT Analysis for ROK Homeland Security Market

| Strengths | Weaknesses |
|---|---|
| Advanced ICT/electronics industries<br>Excellent mobile network<br>Fast developing security industry<br>Purchasing power for cutting edge security equipment/device/solution | Language barrier<br>Bureaucracy<br>Lack of understanding in overseas security products |
| **Opportunities** | **Threats** |
| Emerging government budget for Homeland Security<br>Increasing demand for high-tech software solution<br>Growing demand for security equipment/devices of counter-terrorism<br>Upcoming high-value projects such as new airport terminal and Winter Olympics | Well-established US competitors<br>Growing Korean competitors<br>Excessive margins of local agents<br>Low price competitiveness of UK products<br>Delay in after-sales service |

*Source*: British Embassy Seoul (2012: 7). Reproduced with permission.

It is worth noting that more than 95 per cent of the homes in South Korea have permanent access to the Internet and there have been a number of cyber attacks on the country, one of which affected 35 million accounts on a social network (British Embassy Seoul, 2012: 46). There was also an attack on a government-backed bank (British Embassy Seoul, 2012: 46).

To enter the Korean market it is essential that an overseas company deals with an eligible Korean partner agent and in order to establish a good personal relationship, western managers need to respond quickly and communicate regularly with Korean managers) (British Embassy Seoul, 2012: 56 and 62).

## 12.7 Conclusion

By drawing on primary data and secondary data sources, it is possible to produce a competitor and marketing analysis within which product development can take place. The strategic marketing approach is useful for comparing internal organizational capabilities with external opportunities, in the sense that market dynamics provide first mover opportunities. Marketers that are able to identify and formulate policy to take advantage of unmet needs will place their company at an advantage, and when mature markets are evident, new and evolving overseas markets become attractive. South Korea represents a market opportunity and in order to survive in such a market, it is essential that British companies embrace the way of doing business there and are prepared to continually improve their products and services through time.

# References

Aaker, D.A. 1992. *Strategic Market Management*. Chichester: John Wiley & Sons Limited.

Aston, S. 2012. Cyber security threats and Microsoft strategy. *SMi Cyber Deference Conference*, Copthore Hotel, London (18 June).

Barrington Brown, C. 2012. UK cyber ops and resource management. *SMi Cyber Deference Conference*, Copthore Hotel, London (19 June).

British Embassy Seoul. 2012. *Republic of Korea Homeland Security Market*. Seoul: DSO, Defence and Security Section, British Embassy (April).

Bryant, I. 2012. Improving cyberspace trustability through software. *SMi Cyber Deference Conference*, Copthore Hotel, London (18 June).

Collins, B. 2012. Environmental impacts on IA. *IAAC Research Workshop. Consumerism: Same Old IA Issues ... or Not?* BCS, The Chartered Institute for IT, London (19 June).

IAAC. 2012. *Consumerism: Same Old IA Issues ... or Not?* London: BCS, The Chartered Institute for IT (19 June).

Lee, K. 2012. *Republic of Korea Homeland Security Market*. Fareham: Northorp Grumman (2 May).

Lee, R. 2012. The future of nation-state cyber weapons. *SMi Cyber Deference Conference*, Copthore Hotel, London (18 June).

Mehringer, S. 2012. Cyber attacks: NATO takes a direct hit. *SMi Cyber Deference Conference*, Copthore Hotel, London (18 June).

Panzieri, S. 2012. The Italian national cyber security approach. *SMi Cyber Deference Conference*, Copthore Hotel, London (18 June).

Pevtschin, V. 2012. The EOS cyber security working group white paper update. *SMi Cyber Deference Conference*, Copthore Hotel, London (18 June).

Roehrig, W. 2012. Cyber defence: The role of EDA. *SMi Cyber Deference Conference*, Copthore Hotel, London (18 June).

Sandhu, M. 2012. Protecting the World's IP: Putting an end to targeted attacks. *SMi Cyber Deference Conference*, Copthore Hotel, London (18 June).

Thon, R. 2012. Social media and the Norwegian National Security Authority (NOR NSM). *SMi Cyber Deference Conference*, Copthore Hotel, London (19 June).

Trim, P.R.J., and Lee, Y-I. (2011). A pro-active approach to managing cyber security threats. *The CAMIS Integrated Governance, Risk and Compliance Conference and Knowledge Sharing Event, Incorporating the iGRC Consortium Demonstration and Network Sensor Devices*, Birkbeck, University of London (15 December).

Vernez, G. 2012. Cyber security awareness campaigns. *SMi Cyber Deference Conference*, Copthore Hotel, London (19 June).

Wilson, P. 2012. Embedded into the company's structure? Or an add on? *IAAC Research Workshop. Consumerism: Same Old IA Issues ... or Not?* BCS, The Chartered Institute for IT, London.

# Appendix 6
# Preventing Cyber Attacks
# Survey Results

Bearing in mind the fact that cyber attacks on organizations are becoming more sophisticated, please provide answers to the following six questions.

## Question 1: What can managers do in order to prevent those responsible for launching a cyber attack(s) from achieving their goals?

SUMMARY OF RESPONSES

1. Ensure that staff do not use other people's/their colleague(s) computer.
   Ensure that staff do not use the a company computer(s) for their own personal use (e.g. online shopping).
   *Company must communicate risk internally to staff.*

2. Formulate and implement an in-house and partner company security awareness programme.
   *Liaise with law enforcement personnel and share information.*
   *Implement an effective public relations campaign with government.*

3. Do the basics – good housekeeping.

4. Review current investment in IT.
   *Protective means and reference to best practice – change programme.*

5. Recognize the difference between an attack and a failure made.
   *Plan and practise contingency responses.*
   *Take a proactive approach to capability generation.*

6. Identify potential cyber vulnerabilities.
   *Perform risk assessment to determine critical risk.*
   *Apply controls to protect against these risks.*

7. Take the threat seriously.
   *Be prepared: Good governance, effective risk management and train people.*

8. Protection.
   *Keep staff informed.*
   *Audit.*

9. iGRC and CAMIS – new stuff e.g. tools and techniques.
   *Have education and awareness for themselves and individually.*
   *Goals by understanding the environment they operate in.*

10. Undertake a foresight programme to 'predict' current and future threats.
    *Make processes to assure systems, networks and data.*
    *Educate and train users against threats.*

11. Be aware of the issues.
    *Allocate sufficient resources to manage them.*

12. Training and detection.
    *Defence in depth.*

## Question 2: What cyber security issues will need to be addressed in the next 10 years?

### SUMMARY OF RESPONSES

1. Company will need to provide a better understanding of why integrated information is important and explain the role that information systems play.
   *Management need to provide education and training in security awareness.*
   *Protect personal, private and company data and information.*

2. Advanced persistent threats.
   *Increased state espionage programmes.*
   *Global compliance and regulatory action.*

3. Raise the profile to board level.

4. Is it a weapon of intent foe or friend?
   *What are the aims of those doing it and how can this be thwarted?*
   *How can government transform industry to protect the UK economy?*

5. Combat the insider threat.
   *Define an internationally agreed legal framework.*
   *Get inside the adversary's decision cycle.*

6. Identify theft/payment fraud.
   *Corporate bullying – e.g. Denial of Service.*
   *Description to 'social' services as a different form of working (e.g. power, guidance, systems, defence systems, communications).*

7. Attack to and from mobile devices (both personal, e.g. smartphones, and networked devices, e.g. CCTV Systems, burglar alarms etc.).
   *Advanced/persistent (i.e. long-term) social engineering.*

8. Cloud/IDM/mobile.
   *Segregation.*
   *Inclusion.*

9. Consumerization.
   *Differing perspectives of consumers and where the boundaries lie.*
   *Have a full understanding of the information world.*

10. Risk caused by introducing new/evolving technology with existing legacy systems and the unknown interactions.
    *As assessment of 'impact' potential.*

11. Complexity.
    *Location data.*
    *Attacks on process control systems (SCADA etc.).*

12. Insecurity and end devices.
    *Trust.*

# Question 3: How useful are existing risk management models with respect to improving an organization's security awareness?

## SUMMARY OF RESPONSES

1. More attention is needed to understand risk model.
   *People in charge need to better understand risk and its consequences.*

2. The current risk management models are partially useful, however, more attention is needed to risk assessment and quantitative and qualitative approaches to risk.

3. Current models are useful but not if they are used in isolation – they need to be integrated within operations.

4. Reactive and slow.
   *No real time dynamic to move from corrective to preventive.*

5. Not very – threats are not sufficiently understood throughout organizations.
   *Information value not understood.*
   *Risk appetite inconsistent (because knowledge is not consistent).*

6. Poor: identify threats and controls.
   *Poor: assuming that controls are in place.*
   *Poor: co-ordination between different organizations e.g. governments, business etc., should work together and also work with other countries.*

7. Existing models are too far removed from the message that needs to go out to people.

8. Very useful but maybe a little stiff.
   *Not easily integrated with personnel.*

9. Static and too slow.
   *Tools do not reflect the real world.*
   *Provide a baseline but not dealing with a rapidly changing and uncertain environment.*

10. Not useful at keeping pace with new technology.
    *Not human focused.*
    *Need to give value to the risk identified.*
    *Models are based on areas of commercial risk which are not always applicable to information or cyber.*

11. They vary and there are too many of them.

12. Not mapped to business.

## Question 4: What factors do managers need to take into consideration when devising a cyber security management framework to counter cyber attacks?

### SUMMARY OF RESPONSES

1. Managers need to know who their staff are.
   *Provide better security awareness training based on an individual's function/level of operation.*
   *Identify main and key members of staff and control access to data and information.*

2. Industry standards and increased cooperation.
   *Costs involved.*
   *Prioritizing risks.*
   *Impact analysis and foresight planning.*

3. People, process, technology and business strategy.

4. Referencing to best practice.
   *Efficient deployment of controls.*
   *Effective deployment of countermeasures.*

*Up-to-date awareness of threats.*
*Management framework for active GRC enabled by web based technology.*

5. Value of information assets.
   *Risk analysis process.*
   *Skills development and leadership.*

6. Vulnerabilities.
   *Consequences.*
   *Countermeasures.*

7. We have developed one.

8. Organizational strategy.
   *People.*
   *Detection.*

9. People and how they interface with their required information.
   *Not too bureaucratic.*
   *Not too costly.*

10. Real time/dynamic system.
    *Open architecture to be modular or agnostic.*
    *Resilient to attack/interferences.*

11. Too many to list.

12. Dynamic nature.
    *Evolution of threats.*

# Question 5: How can managers develop an effective organizational knowledge base that embraces risk, compliance and governance?

## SUMMARY OF RESPONSES

1. A monitoring system needs to be put in place.
   *The CEO needs to take responsibility for overseeing and monitoring the operation.*
   *Better strategic intelligence and foresight is needed.*
   *Up-to-date intelligence is needed as regards what is happening in the external environment (e.g. competitors and other developments).*

2. Through training and staff awareness programmes.
   *Sponsoring marketing and promotional campaigns.*
   *Sharing knowledge with competitors and government agencies.*

3. Institutionalize GRC disciplines across all corporate business functions.

4. Regular knowledge, process and technology reviews to generate updates.
   *Performance gap analysis company versus outside world.*
   *Red Team reviews run by progressives.*

5. Introduce cyclical learning process (OODA).
   *Share understanding of risk appetite.*
   *Formalize observed learning.*

6. Leverage knowledge of security community within their organization.
   *Collaborate with other organizations.*
   *Overall: take the problem seriously.*

7. Good governance.

8. Involve staff – benchmarking.

9. Ensure this is done throughout the organization.
   *Risk becomes a common language.*
   *Done in a consistent way and approach across all relevant areas/functions to their organization.*

10. Educate and train employees (Taken back and tried at home).
    *Have knowledge management system that captures both tacit and intangible information.*
    *Ownership of the risk needs to be identified.*
    *Optimise the processes (passive) and ensure healthy environment.*

11. Do not think generalized managers should do this!

12. Train users on what to read in knowledge base and why it adds value.

# Question 6: How can government, industry and academia work more closely together to ensure that an adequate pool of skills exist to counter the various forms of cyber attacks?

## SUMMARY OF RESPONSES

1. A set of broad based education and training programmers are needed.
   *Situational awareness needs to be incorporated in a range of courses and programmes.*
   *Strategic intelligence needs to be viewed from the perspective of information sharing and on a selective basis included in education programmes.*

2. Jointly develop undergraduate and postgraduate security and resilience programmes of study.
   *Executive courses and programmes of study for senior and junior managers.*

3. Raise the visibility of corporate security career progression path.

4. Given funding stream.
   *Doctrinal Directorate.*
   *Management with context and value adding action plans.*
   *The wherewithal to convert cost and effort to realisable revenue.*

5. Incentivise by assuming the 'What's in it for me' question.
   *Government to invest in cyber education at all levels – especially secondary and primary.*
   *Government-led forum with influence on policy.*

6. They are not scared enough yet!
   *They need to recognize that it is a shared risk and responsibility.*
   *Business cannot just rely on government to address the problem alone.*

7. Build good attack intelligence and share this with the people who need to know, with the level of depth necessary.

8. Collaborative projects – including students.
   *More specialized education in schools.*
   *International collaboration.*

9. Common strategic intelligence forum in all aspects.
   *Hybrid and complexity thinker i.e. polymaths.*
   *Devise an information society pool of knowledge hub.*

10. UK to establish 'research capacity' model rather than a 'production' model for R&D in field of cyber space.
    *Industry undertake role of CSOC of identifying threats and reporting these to various stakeholders.*

11. Most training is generalist courses, e.g. cyber elements and marketing courses.

12. Short-term research projects e.g. 3 year PhD/KTP too long.

# Appendix 7
## List of Unmet Customer Needs

1. Risk and resilience are to be linked and thought of in the context of foresight planning. The risk manager should add notes into the feedback update box in the software tool to detail current and future thinking/policy decisions.
2. Areas associated with information breaches are to be identified and information assurance (IA) policy is to be aligned with and placed in the context of cyber security. The risk manager should add notes into the feedback update box in the software tool to detail current and future thinking/policy decisions.
3. As regards the process of information sharing, organizational and law enforcement agency/personnel and their needs are to be built into the software tool capability so as to improve the reporting of incidents (in real time) and allow law enforcement organizations to have immediate access to the type of threat(s) emerging.
4. The reporting outlined in point 3 needs to be highlighted in the organization's set of risk registers and such information needs to be reported (through the risk manager) by the company to the customers, shareholders and other stakeholders.
5. With respect to point 4, once the information has been coordinated, a best practice guide(s) can be produced and/or updated and built into the software tool capability. (Link with training and staff development programmes).
6. Civil law issues and e-disclosure, for example, need to be embedded in the concept of organizational learning adopted by the organization, and built into the software tool capability.
7. Security policies and procedures need to be invoked in order to eradicate the possibility of data/information being leaked from a storage site and from equipment that is given up for recycling. The risk manager and/or IT manager should add notes into the feedback update box in the software tool to detail current and future thinking/policy decisions.
8. The risk model/calculation process needs to quantify the risk associated with a data/ information leak and be timed to be hourly informative as opposed to days or weeks (and built into the software tool capability for attention by the risk manager).
9. The risk model/calculation process needs to quantify the risk associated with a data/information leak in the context of a recovery programme and a reputational damage programme.
10. The corporate network configurations of all business relationships, internal and external to the organization, need to be mapped so that the risk nodes (areas of vulnerability) can be identified and the risk associated with the node quantified.
11. Managers need both a foreign language compatibility and a technical language compatibility in order to classify matters (categories and mechanisms) so that communication is fluid (possibly via the risk manager).

12. As regards employees' behaviour, the behaviour of employees needs to be monitored during work hours, but reinforced through other internal or self-monitoring and security awareness programmes and mechanisms.

13. If a computer device is lost or stolen, it should be automatically wiped and this needs to be logged. Employees who use their own device at work (BYOD) or take home a company owned device need to sign a contract permitting the device to be wiped of all files. This can be mapped, monitored and checked by the software tool (e.g. under the attention of the IT manager).

14. If a computer device is loaned to an outsource organization or used by an outsource employee, the device should be automatically wiped at a set point in time and the outsource company must sign a contract permitting the device to be wiped of all files. This can be mapped, monitored and checked, and built into the software tool capability (e.g. for the attention of the IT manager).

15. If a breach has occurred, the company will delete all the files on the computer and check/demand that any partner organization does the same. This can be mapped, monitored and checked, and built into the software tool capability (e.g. for the attention of the IT manager).

16. All agreements (between the organization and the employees) relating to files being erased must be extended to relevant devices: computers, iPods and Notebooks for example. Inter-organizational and intra-organizational policy.

17. As regards the data breach cases/case examples that are reported to the regulators, a list can be made of those that relate to organized crime and/or state funded industrial espionage. Guidelines can be produced to highlight proven cases and a feedback or risk manager update box added in the software tool to detail current and future thinking/policy decisions.

18. Social networking web sites need to be graded for risk and other sources of possible and actual penetration by an illegal agent recorded and the risk manager should add notes into the feedback update box in the software tool to detail current and future thinking/policy decisions.

19. Additional attack surfaces (smartphones and personal mobile devices for example) need to be itemized and the risk assigned and a feedback update box in the software tool included to detail current and future thinking/policy decisions (e.g. risk manager involvement).

20. A cloud dimension and check list (e.g. risk, vulnerability) needs to be included so that actual and potential risks can be included/itemized and the level of risk of each identified and assigned.

21. Ethical considerations and decisions relating to computer usage and user behaviour need to be included and risk assessments offered.

22. Cyber insurance needs to be given consideration and in particular the risk assessment needs to include: the risk(s) associated with certain networks, data stored on networks, the physical damage that may result from an attack and the financial and emotional harm caused; costs (forensic costs in particular), risk mitigation costs, physical costs; losses of intellectual property rights; physical injury claims; emotional distress/damage; personal injury and damage; privacy liability; security liability and contractual liability; extortion, fraud and the bad behaviour

of employees; reputational damage; liability associated with the media; content on websites; the insider threat; the work of hacktivists; state sponsored (industrial espionage) attacks; EU directives; the SEC Guide; non-physical risks; liability for data/privacy; first party damage; loss or damage to digital assets; non-physical business interruption and management need to know the value of the company's assets, the value of its R&D and trade secrets; issues relating to potential faulty software; the real time performance associated with management controls that are in place; have an appreciation of product recall insurance that covers a faulty product and product liability. Attention needs to be given to a cloud provider and associated insurance risk cover; the conditions imposed on or by cloud users and cloud providers need to be specified/ranked and rated on a scale from 1 (low risk) to 4 (high risk).

23. A possibility exists for a market for Proteus in the sense that those companies that purchase Proteus would, through business continuity planning, be less at risk than those that did not, so its possible they could be offered a lower insurance rate as they should be judged to be less at risk than companies not using Proteus. Furthermore, how could Proteus be extended to include an insurance element? Link with risk mitigation and risk level.

24. A distinction needs to be made between cyber and information assurance (IA) education and training and closer cooperation is encouraged between industry, government departments and agencies, and academia, to provide tools and courses and programmes as well as research to ensure the nation has the necessary skill base in place. This suggests a link is formed with e-skills UK, The Sector Skills Council for Business and Information Technology.

25. With respect to point 24, a feedback update box in the software tool can be incorporated to detail what courses and programmes are available to employees, the employees of partner organizations and customers, and where they are run and who provides them (internal and external providers) and who monitors staff development (the risk manager, human resources manager, IT manager and security manager in unison for example).

26. In-house security awareness programmes need to be devised as additional services to inform staff about the threats so that they do not engage in risky practices and put the organization in jeopardy. A logical and well crafted security awareness programme should help the company to mitigate risks and educate employees to spot inappropriate behaviour among company staff and it should link with risk, compliance and governance policy and strategy.

27. Security awareness programmes need to be linked with organizational learning, and this needs to be mapped by staff in the human resource management department/function.

28. As regards, reputational damage, top management need to ensure that staff are more transparent about the type of vulnerability they are aware of and need to document such risks in a risk register, which must be comprehensive and up-to-date. Immediate responsibility: risk manager.

**CHAPTER 13** Governance and Compliance Decision Making Process

## 13.0 Introduction

The enterprise governance approach advocated by Fahy et al. (2005: 3) can be considered both holistic and practical. Placing corporate governance in context is necessary because 'Enterprise Governance is based on the principle that good governance alone cannot make an organisation successful' (Fahy et al., 2005: 2). Indeed, we are currently living in an age that is witnessing a rapid development in organizational connectivity, which is forcing managers to develop and amend current business models into something that may be considered sustainable. This era of transformation that we are going through should be embraced from several perspectives, as it will result in transformational change as a result of security being placed at the top of senior management's agenda.

It has been suggested that the Generic Cyber Security Management Model (GCSMM) (Trim and Lee, 2010: 5) represents a useful extension for achieving a:

*greater linkage between commerce and industry, government and academia, it is hoped that a more pro-active approach to cyber security will be established. This being the case, it can be argued that a hands-on approach to making an organization resilient will be needed, in the sense that resilient management systems and processes will provide greater protection against multi-dimensional attacks.*

In this chapter, linking organizational resilience with corporate governance (Section 13.1) has been addressed and is followed by the organizational decision making approach (Section 13.2). New business models (Section 13.3) are given attention and so are future impacts (Section 13.4). The topic of information security governance (Section 13.5) is addressed and lessons learned (Section 13.6) are included. The chapter ends with a conclusion (Section 13.7).

## 13.1 Linking Organizational Resilience with Corporate Governance

By linking organizational resilience with corporate governance it is possible to better understand how performance, conformance and corporate responsibility (Fahy et al., 2005: 3) are integrated with the people, processes and systems approach. Figure 10.1

(Trim and Lee, 2011), represents an extension of earlier work undertaken by Trim and Lee, (2010: 5), and places the development of an organization's cyber security strategy within the context of three interlinked circles representing (i) the external environment; (ii) risk assessment which is embedded within the organization's strategic value system; and (iii) the integration of security within the organization's functions and an emerging security culture within the organization.

The GCSMM (Trim and Lee, 2010: 5, 2011) allows senior management to improve and refine the linkage between a company's cyber security strategy and the company's ability to attract and maintain cyber security specialists. By integrating security with intelligence, and other functional areas, it is possible to embrace more effectively the GISES (Global Intelligence and Security Environmental Sustainability) Model (Trim, 2005) and to link the GISES Model with the SATELLITE (Strategic Corporate Intelligence and Transformational Marketing) Model (Trim, 2004). The intelligence oriented and multi-disciplinary security approach embedded in these models should enable the risk manager and his/her colleagues (assistant risk managers) to link corporate security with strategic corporate intelligence, and to provide the necessary stimulation for the development of a security culture within the partnership arrangement. What we need to do at this juncture is recognize that 'by integrating security more firmly into the organization's structure, it should be possible to reduce the organization's level of risk and facilitate information sharing. Information sharing should enhance co-operation between partner organizations and add to the defensive capability vis-à-vis establishing effective counter-cyber attack measures' (Trim and Lee, 2010: 4). However, in order to achieve our changing set of security objectives, it is necessary to revaluate the organization's security priorities and to place cyber security in a firmer light. This means reviewing our understanding of organizational resilience and placing resilience in a partnership or community context. This does have ramifications for the type of risk communication strategy and this needs to be noted by top management.

By revisiting the fact that top management need to deliver value to shareholders, it is possible to think of the enterprise governance model, which incorporates three dimensions: *performance, conformance* and *corporate responsibility* (Fahy et al., 2005: 2–10), from the stance of providing a platform from which organizational resilience can be developed. Fahy et al. (2005: 3–5) refer to performance in terms of how well an organization does with respect to systems, people and processes, in creating value for shareholders. With respect to conformance; of key interest here is corporate accountability and how well management do in terms of regulatory codes, corporate legislation and accounting standards (Fahy et al., 2005: 5–7). According to Fahy et al. (2005: 5), corporate governance addresses five main areas: risk management and internal controls; corporate culture; stewardship and accountability; board operations and composition; and monitoring and evaluation of activities. Corporate responsibility has been successfully built into various business models and is most likely to continue to be so in the foreseeable future because corporate responsibility is known to address six main areas (Fahy et al., 2005: 7–8): managing/reducing environmental, societal and cultural impact; protecting intangible assets such as reputation; promoting best practice vis-à-vis corporate ethics and governance; engaging in risk management; establishing traceability in supply chain management and procurement; and enhancing employee motivation and productivity.

Fahy et al. (2005: 163) state that 'in its simplest form, corporate governance is the systems and processes put in place to direct and control an organisation in order to increase performance and achieve sustainable shareholder value'. But this can only be achieved provided that management have undertaken an adequate threats analysis and are prepared to invest resources in securing any organizational weaknesses within the organization that have emerged.

## 13.2 Organizational Decision Making Approach

Fahy et al. (2005) have indicated that corporate governance needs to take into account the effectiveness of management structures, the role that directors play, and the accuracy of corporate reporting. It can be assumed that the past crises in the banking and financial sector and the current debate regarding the role of banks and the payment of huge bonuses to fund/investment managers will spur shareholders to seek transparency vis-à-vis business operations. As a consequence, individual managers are likely to be held more accountable for their actions. It is with this in mind that management need to think of the organization being compliant.

## 13.3 New Business Models

It is acknowledged that in an interconnected world, international cooperation involving sharing information relating to cyber issues is crucial as: 'Without such cooperation, our collective ability to detect, deter, and minimize the effects of cyber-based attacks would be greatly diminished' (The White House, 2003: 8). This suggests that when looking at the issue of cyber security from a stakeholder perspective, we need to think in terms of developing a business model that has a robust security dimension to it.

New business models are emerging and what has to be remembered is that management is looking for new ways to preserve their organization's market position and as a consequence delayering may be occurring, outsourcing may be evident and subcontracting important services may be preferred. As management are concerned with profit maximization and value creation, it has to be borne in mind that value capture, which is the means by which a business is rewarded for the value it creates and which is dependent upon competitive differentiation (Fitzroy and Hulbert, 2005: 46) is fundamental to an organization achieving sustainability. It is because of this that management need to think more deeply about compliance and the fact that 'Compliance is now a measurement of responsibility to the stakeholder, the environment and the community' (Fahy et al., 2005: 231). So, yes, a new business model will emerge and with it, a new form of leadership.

What management need to understand is that as an organization becomes more connected, it will become more 'net-centric'. The Defense Science Board (2009: ix) has provided an insight into what becoming 'net-centric' involves:

*This entails networking many different sources of sensor and informational data with multiple processing nodes and geographically distributed users to achieve unprecedented levels of situational awareness, data distribution, and operational coordination. Net-centric operations bring both an increase in capability as well as increased dependence on the viability of the network. Thus, new vulnerabilities are created.*

CPNI have done much to improve governance, for example, the HoMER (Holistic Management of Employee Risk) approach offers guidance and advice to senior management regarding how the risk associated with employees can be reduced. For example (CPNI, 2012a):

*HoMER is an interactive guidance document designed to help organisations manage these risks. The guidance provides examples of good practice principles, policies and procedures, backed up by case studies. The guidance will help organisations build effective countermeasures, and respond to and recover from incidents when they occur.*

*HoMER is aimed at board members and other owners of people risk and shows users the steps that can be taken to change their organisation's approach to personnel security. Through creating a positive culture supported by strong corporate governance and a fair, compliant and transparent legal framework, an organisation can successfully prevent, protect and manage employee risk.*

CPNI (2012b) advises:

*Risk of damage from the actions of employees or contractors working on your behalf. Most incidents stem from errors or omissions but there is also a threat of malicious activity including, in extreme cases, actions by criminals, terrorists or foreign powers....HoMER provides guidance or organizational governance, security culture, and controls to help you mitigate people risk. The key elements of HoMER are:*
- *Take a risk-based approach*
- *Manage people risk holistically*
- *Develop the security culture needed by the business*
- *Appoint a senior single owner of people risk*
- *Act in an ethical, legal and transparent manner.*

CPNI (2012b) have also listed the questions that non-executive directors need to ask the chief executive officer of an organization:

- *Who is accountable for all elements of people risk in your organization?*
- *When did your organization last undertake a people risk assessment?*
- *Does your organization have integrated measures in place to identify and manage people risk?*
- *How confident are you that your organization would be protected against the likelihood of a major incident due to an accidental or deliberate action on the part of its people?*
- *Does your organization understand the impact that an incident would have on it and on the board's reputation?*

It is clear from the guidance provided by CPNI (2012b) that technical security, physical security and personnel security are key, and that information assurance is a critical factor as well. This does to some degree focus attention on the role of government and how staff within organizations are able and willing to engage with government representatives to change and/or amend the law relating to the prevention of fraud. Technological developments occurring in the area of cloud computing are also of interest because of the interest being shown in cloud computing and the fact that new concepts will emerge that need to be better understood than is the case at present. West (2010: 2) has suggested: 'Countries need to harmonize their laws on cloud computing so as to reduce current inconsistencies in regard to privacy, data storage, security processes, and personnel training.' For example, West (2010: 3) has noted that there are times when 'courts often support greater privacy rights with local rather than remote file storage.... Potential security problems need to be addressed, but sometimes this involves increasing the level of real or imagined privacy threats'. As West (2010: 3) says, 'the lack of uniformity in standards across nations' is also a worry and means that there are issues relating to privacy, security, storage and accessibility that need addressing. This takes us back to the HoMER concept and the valuable work that CPNI are doing and which needs to be embraced by managers, as it reinforces the concept of resilience.

The work of Howard et al. (2011) is of interest because it outlines the direct action taken by governments around the world to disconnect the digital networks in their country. Howard et al. (2011: 1) found that since 1995, 99 countries have been involved in 606 unique incidents that actually disconnected Internet exchange points or if they did not go that far instead they blocked significant amounts of traffic entering the country's networks. The reasons for such action varied from political actions to social actions to safeguard the public. Howard et al. (2011: 7) state:

> The lasting impact of a temporary disconnection in Internet service may actually be a strengthening of weak ties between global and local civil society networks. When civil society disappears from the grid, it is noticed. What lasts are the ties between a nation's civic groups, and between international non-governmental organizations and like-minded, in-country organizations. Certainly not all of these virtual communities are about elections, but their existence is a political phenomenon particularly in countries where state and social elites have worked hard to police offline communities. Thus, even the bulletin boards and chat rooms dedicated to shopping for brand name watches are sites that practice free speech and where the defense of free speech can become a topic of conversation. The Internet allows opposition movements that are based outside of a country to reach in and become part of the system of political communication within even the strictest authoritarian regimes. Today, banning political parties could simply mean that formal political opposition is now organized online, from outside the country. It could also mean that civil society leaders turn to other organizational forms permitted by the network technologies. When states disconnect particular social media services, student and civil society leaders develop creative workarounds and relearn traditional (offline) mobilization tactics. This almost always means that target sites, such as YouTube, Facebook, and Twitter, are accessible through other means.

## 13.4 Future Impacts

As regards the issue of impact, the Ministry of Defence (MoD, 2010: 6) has provided guidance in the sense it defines a *strategic shock* as 'a high impact event that results in a discontinuity or an abrupt alteration in the strategic context. The strategic shock can either be expected or unexpected; the important point is that it dislocates the strategic context from the trends that have preceded it'. The points below have been taken from the MoD (2010) study and are in the original form. They are relevant because they place the various subtopics in context.

The MoD (2010: 10) has indicated that globalization 'is *likely* to raise the level of interdependence between states and individuals within the globalised economy'; 'Resources, trade, capital and intellectual property are *likely* to flow through this core, and rely on complex networks of physical and virtual infrastructure that are *likely* to be vulnerable to physical disruption or cyber attack by multiple actors....Consequently, increasing dependency on this infrastructure, and the global supply chains that underpin globalisation, *will* leave the global economy vulnerable to disruption. Ensuring the security of this globally distributed infrastructure is *likely* to be of multilateral interest' (MoD, 2010: 11); 'Conflict is *likely* to involve a range of transnational, state, group and individual participants who *will* operate at global and local levels' (MoD, 2010: 13).

'Innovative communication techniques *will* create a network-enabled audience. Adaptive adversaries *will* seek to utilise the media and the opponent's political system to their advantage' (MoD, 2010: 13–14); 'The differences between state, state-sponsored and non-state adversaries *will* blur. The range of threats will diversify, as technology and innovation opens up novel avenues of attack and adaptive adversaries exploit opportunities' (MoD, 2010: 15); 'Cyberspace *will* be widely exploited by all types of actors, but the effects of their actions are likely to vary. Attribution, intent and legitimacy of cyber-attacks *will* all be disputed' (MoD, 2010: 17); 'Strategic shocks *will* occur, although their character and detail remain unpredictable. Complex interconnected and interdependent systems *will* be subject to systematic risk and the potential of cascading failures. Organisations that are built around agility and versatility are the most *likely* to be successful at adapting to events' (MoD, 2010: 17).

'Success in future conflict, especially against adaptive and agile adversaries, *will* require a shift away from kinetic to influence activity, underpinned by a greater understanding of the enemy. This understanding *will* require more emphasis on intelligence gathering, cultural awareness, individual and collective training, and focused comprehensive approaches' (MoD, 2010: 17); 'Technology *will* facilitate the organisation of protests and high impact terrorist attacks that occur rapidly, and without fore-warning, and seek to achieve symbolic effects that create the greatest media impact' (MoD, 2010: 30).

'As the globalised economy becomes increasingly dependent on knowledge-based industries, creativity and innovation, the importance of advanced education *will* increase. However, global access to education *will* remain variable, although ICT based initiatives are likely to improve basic skills in numeracy and literacy....The increasing role that ICT will play in future society is *likely* to lead to the vast majority of individuals developing the skills required to use and operate such technology' (MoD, 2010: 31); 'The majority of individuals are *likely* to have access to network connections leading to large-scale changes in identity through the use of multiple online profiles. Remote working is *likely* to become the norm with controlled network spaces representing the new work environments' (MoD, 2010: 34); 'Developments in social networking technology *will* continue to facilitate the rise of "citizen journalism" and make it increasingly difficult for even the most autocratic states to control access to information, especially as globalised connectivity allows local news stories to be broadcast instantaneously across the globe' (MoD, 2010: 34).

'Security of global supply chains, and access to the "global commons" and global markets *will* be a priority for virtually all states. Effective governance, regulation, operation and control of the networks that underpin economic activity will be an ever-present concern' (MoD, 2010: 40); 'Technology has already broadened the scope of conflict from the land, maritime and air environments to encompass cyberspace and space. It offers new possibilities for conflict and is exploited through innovations in organisation, strategy and tactics. Out to 2040, rapid technological innovation *will* have a significant impact on the evolving character of conflict' (MoD, 2010: 78).

'The development of networked systems *will* continue. Access to information *will* spur knowledge and understanding, and act as a critical enabler in future conflict. Irregular actors *will* continue to use widely available technology such as the Internet to both conceal and promote their activities' (MoD, 2010: 79); 'Economic, financial, legal and diplomatic conflict are all *likely*, challenging legal norms, and requiring coordinated and integrated responses in order to protect from and respond to attacks. Orbital space and cyberspace *will* be part of the battlespace in the same manner as the air, land and maritime environments'(MoD, 2010: 84).

'Even in the developed world, some non-state actors are *likely* to deploy capabilities beyond the ability of law enforcement agencies to counter in isolation, requiring the use of military, paramilitary or other security forces, such as cyber security groups. However, not all actors *will* embrace this form of multi-modal conflict, with some restrained by ethical, cultural or legal constraints from operating across the full spectrum. In particular, some states *will* lack the confidence in their own cohesion to develop the force structures necessary to conduct irregular conflict' (MoD, 2010: 85); 'Out to 2040, global interdependence and reliance on complex systems is *likely* to continue to increase. This provides many benefits, but *may* make future strategic shocks and the systematic failures more frequent and pervasive than the past' (MoD, 2010: 91).

'The pervasiveness of ICT *will* enable more people to access and exploit sophisticated networks of information systems' (MoD, 2010: 100); 'Globalisation *will* provide diverse opportunities for organised criminal groups, which are *likely* to increasingly exploit adaptable and flexible networks that allow them to be based in ungoverned spaces' (MoD, 2010: 103); 'Organised criminals and illicit groups are *likely* to increasingly take advantage of legitimate company structures to conduct or hide their criminal activity, leading to higher levels of global corruption and illicit trade, often involving the use of cyberspace' (MoD, 2010: 103); 'Criminal networks *will* exploit new technologies to circumvent law enforcement activities and to gain further financial advantage' (MoD, 2010: 103).

'There *will* be changes in network technology driven by: the need to improve end-to-end security; the requirement to support large numbers of Internet-enabled devices; and the ability to directly convert from optical to wireless connectivity. The evolution of ICT devices *will* be driven by their increasingly wide range of applications and rising demand by society. Increased Internet penetration across the globe, particularly in heavily populated areas, *will* influence Internet content and ownership' (MoD, 2010: 138); 'Information *will* increasingly be transient in nature, generated and tailored to meet need, provide the context to queries, and interact with cyberspace by these and more advanced mediums. As a consequence it *will* become progressively more difficult to identify sources and validate the information that has been provided. Access to personal data, and its subsequent exploitation, *will* have to be safeguarded with commitments to protect user privacy and control' (MoD, 2010: 140).

'Offensive cyberspace capabilities *will* be used to penetrate and attack electronic-rich systems, networks and infrastructure' (MoD, 2010: 150); '…the impact of cyber-attacks is *likely* to range from incremental to catastrophic' (MoD, 2010: 150); 'The incidents of cyber-espionage, cyber-terrorism and cyber-criminality *will* increase, especially across distributed virtual communities, raising ethical dilemmas. Protection of cyber assets *will* extend into active defence of civilian logistics and other supporting contractor organisations' (MoD, 2010: 150).

'Defending and ensuring continuity of such interdependent systems *will* require trusted government and industrial partnerships, and the adoption of new approaches to ethical and technological cyber-management. Information infrastructure personnel *will* require a significantly different approach from physical infrastructure protection teams' (MoD, 2010: 150); 'At the international level, the few existing laws concerning control of cyberspace *will* be reviewed, but national interests concerning the military use of cyberspace *will* delay progress towards agreement. The security and intelligence consequences *will* continue to be debated within the legal frameworks' (MoD, 2010: 150).

The findings of *Global Risks*, a report produced by the World Economic Forum (2012: 24–25), and which drew on the expertise of 469 experts and industry leaders, suggests if there was a cyber disruption that caused cascading failures of critical infrastructures and networks then a critical systems failure could occur that undermined global governance. It is for this reason that a case can be made for developing the GISES Model (Global Intelligence and Security Environmental Sustainability) (Trim, 2005) and placing it in a cyber environment context.

## 13.5 Information Security Governance

Conner and Coviello (2003) made clear the fact that cyber security was to be addressed by people at the apex of the organization and that corporate governance was the key to making information security secure. Conner and Coviello (2003: 2) recognized that organizations were diverse and so were their needs, and as a consequence they were required to think in terms of developing an approach to information security governance that management considered would be appropriate for the organization. A number of principles were put forward that would assist management to develop a programme that would take into account the organization's needs (Conner and Coviello, 2003: 2 and 9):

- *CEOs should have an annual information security evaluation conducted, review the evaluation results with staff, and report on performance to the board of directors.*
- *Organizations should conduct periodic risk assessments of information assets as part of a risk management programme.*
- *Organizations should implement policies and procedures based on risk assessments to secure information assets.*
- *Organizations should establish a security management structure to assign explicit individual roles, responsibilities, authority and accountability.*
- *Organizations should develop plans and initiate actions to provide adequate information security for networks, facilities, systems and information.*
- *Organizations should treat information security as an integral part of the system life cycle.*

- *Organizations should provide information security awareness, training and education to personnel.*
- *Organizations should conduct periodic testing and evaluation of the effectiveness of information security policies and procedures.*
- *Organizations should create and execute a plan for remedial action to address any information security deficiencies.*
- *Organizations should develop and implement incident response procedures.*
- *Organizations should establish plans, procedures and tests to provide continuity of operations.*
- *Organizations should use security best practices guidance, such as ISO 17799, to measure information security performance.*

It can be noted that management are being asked to place information security governance at the top of the agenda and to place information security in the context of governance. What emerges from the debate on cyber crime is 'that there is no easy technological answer to cyber crime...hardware solutions are likely to unduly restrict computer users in their activities while software solutions require constant updating and a more advanced understanding of the technology to be truly effective' (House of Commons, 2012: 19). Taking the above into account, it is possible to map out the responsibilities and functional roles associated with information security governance (Conner and Coviello, 2003: 20). An information security governance framework is outlined in Table 13.1. The reader will note from the table that the overarching aims and objectives are defined in an Information Security Governance Charter and the organizational value system is security oriented.

**Table 13.1  Information Security Governance Framework**

| | |
|---|---|
| Overarching aims and objectives. | Defined and outlined in terms of an Information Security Governance Charter. |
| Organizational roles and responsibilities. | Defined in terms of the board; individual senior managers; individual functions; and specialist external knowledge providers. |
| Educational and training provision. | Recruitment; staff development (various levels); placements/internships; and university courses and training courses. |
| Intra-organizational relationships. | Internal cyber security policies and processes. Plans Mechanisms Audits |
| Inter-organizational relationships. | Externally oriented cyber security policies and processes. Suppliers Customers Partnerships (e.g. joint venture arrangements) |
| Organizational value system and best practice. | Security oriented. A commitment to information assurance A commitment to cyber security |

Organizational learning can be considered fundamental to a corporate governance mentality being adopted by employees in an organization because it should ensure that an appropriate management structure, processes and systems are put in place to turn ideas into actions which are then turned into plans and implemented as policies and strategies. Bearing these points in mind, it is possible to take on board the points put forward by CPNI/SANS (2012):

1. **Inventory of Authorized and Unauthorized Devices**
   **Reduce the ability of attackers to find and exploit unauthorized and unprotected systems**: active monitoring and configuration management is in existence and is aimed at maintaining an up-to-date inventory of devices vis-à-vis the company's network (e.g. servers, workstations, laptops and remote devices).

2. **Inventory of Authorized and Unauthorized Software**
   **Identify vulnerable or malicious software to mitigate or root out attacks**: a list of authorized software per system and tools to track software that has been installed (e.g. type, version and patches) needs to be in existence. In addition, monitoring with regards to unauthorized/unnecessary software needs to take place.

3. **Secure Configurations for Hardware and Software on Laptops, Workstations and Servers**
   **Prevent attackers from exploiting services and settings that allow easy access through networks and browsers**: a secure image for all new systems used by the company is established and the standard images are secured on servers that are regularly validated and updated. A configuration management system needs to be in place to track images.

4. **Continuous Vulnerability Assessment and Remediation**
   **Proactively identify and repair software vulnerabilities reported by security researchers or vendors**: automated vulnerability scanning tools are run on a regular basis against all systems so that vulnerabilities can be identified and problems fixed within a 48 hour period.

5. **Malware Defences**
   **Block malicious code from tampering with system settings or contents, capturing sensitive data or spreading**: automated anti-virus and anti-spyware software is used to monitor and protect workstations, servers and mobile devices on a continual basis. In addition, anti-malware tools on all the company's machines are updated automatically on a daily basis. In addition: 'Prevent network devices from using auto-run programs to access removable media.'

6. **Application Software Security**
   **Neutralise vulnerabilities in web based and other application software**: internally developed and third party application software is tested for various security flaws (e.g. coding errors and malware). Web application firewalls are deployed so that all the traffic is inspected and also, checking is carried out to ensure that errors in user inputs (e.g. by size and data type) are found.

7. **Wireless Device Control**
   **Protect the security perimeter against unauthorized wireless access**: wireless devices can only be connected to the network if they match an authorized configuration and security profile. Additionally, they need to have a documented owner assigned and a defined business need. All the wireless access points need to

be manageable *vis-à-vis* enterprise management tools. The scanning tools deployed needs to detect wireless access points.

8. **Data Recovery Capability**
   **Minimise the damage from an attack**: a trustworthy plan of action needs to be drawn up so that all traces of an attack are removed and all the company's information is automatically backed up. This is so that each system (e.g. the operating system, application software and data for example) can be fully restored. Advice provided is to back up all systems on a weekly basis; if it is a sensitive system, it should be backed up more often and the restoration process should be tested on a regular basis.

9. **Security Skills Assessment and Appropriate Training to Fill Gaps**
   **Find knowledge gaps, and fill them with exercises and training**: a security skills assessment programme needs to be developed and training needs to be mapped against skill requirements for each job. The results can be used to allocate resources to improve security practices.

10. **Secure Configurations for Network Devices such as Firewalls, Routers and Switches**
    **Preclude electronic holes from forming at connection points with the Internet, other organizations, and internal network segments**: as regards each network device, it is important to compare firewall, router and switch configurations against existing standards. Any deviation from the standard configuration must be documented and approved. It is also suggested that 'any temporary deviations are undone when the business need abates'.

11. **Limitations and Control of Network Ports, Protocols and Services**
    **Allow remote access only to legitimate users and services**: host based firewalls and port-filtering are to be put in place and as regards scanning tools, these are required to block traffic that is not allowed. Web servers, mail servers, file and print services, and also domain name systems (DNS) servers all need to be configured properly in order that remote access is limited. Other advice provided is: disable automatic installation of what is known as unnecessary software components and move servers inside the firewall. As regards the latter, it needs to be remembered that remote access might be needed for business purposes.

12. **Controlled Use of Administrative Privileges**
    **Protect and validate administrative accounts on desktops, laptops and servers to prevent two common types of attack**: '(1) enticing users to open a malicious e-mail, attachment, or file, or to visit a malicious website; and (2) cracking an administrative password and thereby gaining access to a target machine. Use robust passwords that follow Federal Desktop Core Configuration (FDCC) standards.'

13. **Boundary Defence**
    Control the flow of traffic through network borders, and police content by looking for attacks and evidence of compromised machines: in order that this is achieved, a multi-layered boundary defence needs to be established 'by relying on firewalls, proxies demilitarised zone (DMZ) perimeter networks, and other network-based tools. Filter inbound and outbound traffic, including through business partner networks ("extranets")'.

14. **Maintenance, Monitoring and Analysis of Security Audit Logs**
    **Use detailed logs to identify and uncover the details of an attack, including the location, malicious software deployed, and activity on victim machines**: for example, standardized logs can be generated for each hardware device and the software that is installed on it (e.g. 'date, time stamp, source addresses, destination addresses, and other information about each packet and/or transaction)'. It is recommended that logs are stored on dedicated servers, and biweekly reports are run in order to identify and document anomalies.

15. **Controlled Access Based on the Need to Know**
    **Prevent attackers from gaining access to highly sensitive data**: in order to achieve this, it is essential that critical data is separated from information that is easily available to various internal network users and that a multi-level data classification scheme is in use. It is essential that 'only authenticated users have access to nonpublic data and files'.

16. **Account Monitoring and Control**
    **Keep attackers from impersonating legitimate users**: having reviewed all the system accounts, those that are not identified with a business process and owner can be disabled. In addition, system access can be revoked in the case of terminated employees/contactors and dormant accounts can be disabled. It is also necessary to encrypt and isolate files linked with such accounts and to assign robust passwords that are known to conform to FDCC standards.

17. **Data Loss Prevention**
    **Stop unauthorized transfer of sensitive data through network attacks and physical theft**: the movement of data across network boundaries needs to be monitored and scrutinized by both electronic and physical means. This should minimize exposure to attackers and a centralized management framework can be put in place to monitor people, processes and systems as required.

18. **Incident Response Capability**
    **Protect the organization's reputation, as well as its information**: an incident response plan needs to be developed that will allow an attack to be discovered quickly, and then action taken to limit the damage. This means 'eradicating the attacker's presence, and restoring the integrity of the network and systems'.

19. **Secure Network Engineering**
    **Keep poor network design from enabling attackers**: a robust, secure network engineering process must be used 'to prevent security controls from being circumvented. Deploy a network architecture with at least three tiers: DMZ, middleware, private network. Allow rapid deployment of new access controls to quickly deflect attacks'.

20. **Penetration Tests and Red Team Exercises**
    **Use simulated attacks to improve organizational readiness**: this means conducting on a regular basis both internal and external penetration tests that can mirror an attack and thus vulnerabilities can be identified and just as importantly, the potential damage can be estimated. Red Team exercises can be used periodically to test defences and also response capabilities.

## 13.6 Lessons Learned

Much attention at present is being given to the insider threat and the work by Randazzo et al. (2004: 1–2) entitled *Insider Threat Study: Illicit Cyber Activity in the Banking and Finance Sector*, which can be considered informative in the sense that it makes reference to a variety of insider acts including employees altering credit reports, changing data in trading systems and the implementation of a 'logic bomb' that deleted a large number of files. The key point to note is that these acts were committed by employees who were authorized to carry out tasks using information systems.

Randazzo et al. (2004: 4) state: 'The overall goal of the collaborative effort is to develop information and tools that can help private industry, government, and law enforcement identify cyber security issues that can impact physical or operational security and to assess potential threats to, and vulnerabilities in, data and critical systems.' When studying what an insider may have done and the damage caused, it is useful to think in terms of (Randazzo et al., 2004: 4):

1. *components of the incident;*
2. *detection of the incident and identification of the insider;*
3. *pre-incident planning and communication;*
4. *nature of harm to the organization;*
5. *law enforcement and organizational response;*
6. *characteristics of the insider and the organization;*
7. *insider background and history; and*
8. *insider technical expertise and interests.*

Research revealed that as regards 81 per cent of the incidents, the insiders knew what they were going to do as they had planned it in advance of committing the act (Randazzo et al., 2004: 10). It is also worth noting that a high percentage of detection was by individuals not involved in security (61 per cent) and just over one-third of the incidents were reported by customers (Randazzo et al., 2004: 16). It also emerged that many of the insider attacks originated at the office during normal working hours and the implication here is that staff need to be made aware of what might be regarded as suspicious behaviour of co-workers (Randazzo et al., 2004: 20).

Bearing the above in mind, a case can be made for incorporating the organizational strategic governance framework (Figure 3.2) with insights drawn from above, and a Governance and Compliance Decision Making Process can be produced (Figure 13.1).

## 13.7 Conclusion

As early as 2004 there were calls to provide better protection for Internet users and to make the Internet more resilient. For example, Conrades (2004: 9) called for more education and awareness regarding the Internet and its use, but most importantly, asked that more attention be given to education in order that a common level of security understanding was achieved among software developers and in particular, that security education was available and made more accessible. This can be regarded as timely and valid, and something senior management need to take note of.

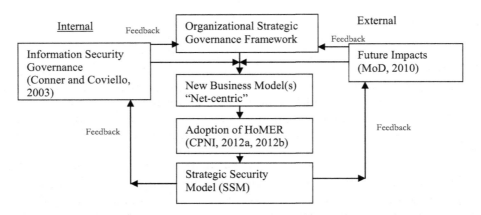

**Figure 13.1 The Governance and Compliance Decision Making Process**

# References

Conner, F.W., and Coviello, A.W. 2003. *Information Security Governance: A Call to action.* Washington, DC: National Cyber Security Summit Task Force (December).

Conrades, G.H. 2004. *Hardening the Internet: Final Report and Recommendations by the Council.* Washington, DC: National Infrastructure Advisory Council.

CPNI. 2012a. *Holistic Management of Employee Risk (HoMER).* CPNI website: http://www.cpni.gov.uk/ highlights/homer-news/ [accessed 1 October 2012].

CPNI. (2012b). *Holistic Management of Employee Risk (HoMER): New guidance to help organisations to reduce the risk from their employees.* London: Centre for the Protection of the Protection of National Infrastructure.

CPNI/SANS (2012). *20 Critical Security Controls for Effective Cyber Defence.* (Referred to as version 3.1). London: Centre for the Protection of the Protection of National Infrastructure and SANS: www. cpni.gov.uk/advice/cyber/critical-controls/ and www.sans.org/critical-security-controls/

Fahy, M., Roche, J., and Weiner, A. 2005. *Beyond Governance: Creating Corporate Value Through Performance, Conformance and Responsibility.* Chichester: John Wiley & Sons Limited.

Fitzroy, P., and Hulbert, J. 2005. *Strategic Management: Creating Value in Turbulent Times.* Chichester: John Wiley & Sons Limited.

House of Commons. 2012. *Malware and Cyber Crime: Twelfth Report of Session 2010–12.* London: The Stationery Office Limited (2 February).

Howard, P.N., Agarwal, S.D., and Hussain, M.M. 2011. The dictators' digital dilemma: When do states disconnect their digital networks? *Issues in Technology Innovation Number 13.* Washington, DC: The Center for Technology Innovation at Brookings, The Brookings Institution (October).

MoD. 2010. *Global Strategic Trends – Out to 2040.* London: Ministry of Defence.

Randazzo, M.R., Keeney, M., Kowalski, E., Cappelli, D., and Moore, A. 2004. *Insider Threat Study: Illicit Cyber Activity in the Banking and Finance Sector.* US Secret Service National Threat Assessment Center and CERT Coordination Center. Pittsburgh, PA: Software Engineering Institute, Carnegie Mellon University (August).

The Defense Science Board. 2009. *Capability Surprise: Volume 1: Main Report.* Washington, DC: The Defense Science Board.

The White House. 2003. *The National Strategy to Secure Cyberspace.* Washington, DC: The White House.

Trim, P.R.J. 2004. The strategic corporate intelligence and transformational marketing (SATELLITE) model. *Marketing Intelligence and Planning,* 22 (2), 240–256.

Trim, P.R.J. 2005. The GISES model for counteracting organized crime and international terrorism. *International Journal of Intelligence and CounterIntelligence,* 18 (3), 451–472.

Trim, P.R.J., and Lee, Y-I. 2010. A security framework for protecting business, government and society from cyber attacks, pp. 1–6. *5th IEEE International Conference on System of Systems Conference (SoSE): Sustainable Systems for the 21st Century,* Loughborough University (22–24 June).

Trim, P.R.J., and Lee, Y-I. 2011. Cyber social science and information assurance: A generic cyber security management model (GCSMM). Poster paper presentation. *The IAAC Symposium,* College of Physicians, London (7 September).

West, D.M. 2010. Steps to improve cloud computing in the public sector. *Issues in Technology Innovation, Number 1.* Washington, DC,: The Center for Technology Innovation at Brookings, The Brookings Institution (July).

World Economic Forum. 2012. *Global Risks 2012.* Geneva: World Economic Forum.

# 14 Integrated Security Mechanism

## 14.0 Introduction

Risk managers and security managers are fully aware that data and information needs to be fully protected, however, those that produce data and information do not necessarily own it, and this is an important point to note. The ownership of data and information is in the hands of those that have acquired it, mostly legally, but an increasing trend is emerging highlighting the illegal activities associated with acquiring and trading data that has been taken or acquired without the owner's knowledge or consent. Some unscrupulous individuals consider that they can acquire data through various means and can transfer it without being concerned about issues of information assurance. Such individuals consider that data and information represents a commodity that is owned by those who acquire it and benefit from the use of it without worrying about how it is secured, stored, or traded to third parties.

If data and information is viewed as a commodity, it makes defining who the stakeholders are more difficult. Owning data and safeguarding data is controlled by law, however, individuals, organizations and governments are unlikely to know what data and information exists and who has access to it, if they do not have adequate information assurance procedures in place. Because data can be transferred via the Internet, the true depth of the problem can be realized when one notes that data remains on a number of servers for ever and can be traded and packaged in various ways, and transferred again and again, without those responsible being caught and taken to task for their illegal acts.

In this chapter, first attention is given to security concerns (Section 14.1) and this is followed by consumerization of IT (Section 14.2). The Proteus Envelope (Section 14.3) is followed by integrating security with intelligence (Section 14.4) and this is followed by the benefits of cloud computing (Section 14.5). Reference is made to safeguarding data (Section 14.6) and future working practices (Section 14.7). Issues and concerns to be researched (Section 14.8) is followed by issues related to using cloud computing (14.9). A conclusion is provided (Section 14.10).

## 14.1 Security Concerns

There are a number of traditional security concerns and a number of cyber related security concerns that corporate security staff, risk managers and corporate legal staff are becoming increasingly concerned about. One type of threat has been covered by Mahmood and Hookham (2011: 19) who highlight the fact that over 150 online criminal 'superstores' are dealing in stolen bank details and that websites are trading debit and credit card numbers with their three-digit security numbers included. Mahmood and Hookham (2011: 19) state: 'The names, addresses, dates of birth, email addresses and telephone numbers of British victims who have had their card details stolen are also easily available....Many of the websites operate for only a few months before they are detected by law enforcement agencies and shut down.'

It is not surprising that the UK Prime Minister David Cameron informed those attending the London Conference on Cyberspace, which was held on 1 November 2011, that (http://www.number10.gov.uk/news/cyberspace/ [accessed 4 November 2011]):

*First, we have come together because we passionately believe in the internet as a force for economic, social and political good. The internet has changed the way we change our world. Go to Cairo or Tripoli and you'll meet people whose lives have been transformed because technology gave them a voice. Go to the poorest parts of Kenya and you'll find people accessing financial services for the first time via their mobile phones, finally getting a foot-hold in the economy.*

*And the internet has profoundly changed our economies too. Studies show it can create twice as many jobs as it destroys. It's estimated that for every 10 per cent increase in broadband penetration, global GDP will increase by an average of 1.3 per cent. So to grow our economies and get our people back to work, we've got to push harder than ever for wider access – and that's what we're doing in the UK.*

*Second, we have come together to tackle cyber crime. This costs the UK an estimated £27 billion a year. Globally, it's as much $1 trillion. It costs just 69p – about the price of a song on iTunes – to buy someone's credit card information online. Cyber criminals have their own 'online shopping websites' where they can buy and sell stolen credit card details in just the same way you'd buy a book from Amazon.*

*And threats come not just from criminal gangs. Every day we are seeing attempts on an industrial scale to steal valuable information from individuals and companies. Britain will shortly set out a new approach for better online security, crime prevention and public awareness. But a cross-border problem needs cross-border solutions, which is why the world needs to act together.*

*Third, we are here because international cyber security is a real and pressing concern. Let us be frank. Every day we see attempts on an industrial scale to steal government secrets – information of interest to nation states, not just commercial organisations.*

*Highly sophisticated techniques are being employed. This summer a significant attempt on the Foreign Office system was foiled. These are attacks on our national interest. They are unacceptable. And we will respond to them as robustly as we do any other national security threat.*

*So Britain has prioritised cyber attacks as a tier one threat – and put £650 million towards improving our cyber defences. And internationally, we're inviting others to join us in a network wide enough and powerful enough to face this threat down.*

*So our task today and in the future is to strike a balance. We cannot leave cyber space wide open to the criminals and terrorists that threaten our security and prosperity.*

*But at the same time we cannot go the heavy-handed route. Do that and we'll crush all that's good about the internet – the free flow of information, the climate of creativity that gives life to new ideas and new movements. Governments must not use cyber security as an excuse for censorship, or to deny their people the opportunities that the internet represents.*

In the case of a consortium that does business with other consortiums, it is likely that data and information become the common trading link between partners. Data and information are used by those that are determined to benefit or seek a strategic advantage from their use. Some might argue that the issue of trust is no longer a bonding force and in the process of data and information transfer and usage, trust is replaced by ownership and exploitation. Should this be the case, a key point to note is that the ultimate owner of data and information will not be held accountable for their actions because they already have transferred ownership to another entity. At this juncture it is important to note that as regards technological breakthroughs that witness social interactions among individuals and the exchange or sharing of data and information, where data and information is stored and protected is not an immediate concern and consumers in particular do not accept responsibility for what happens to it. Although laws are in place to protect individuals and ensure that they do not suffer from identity theft, it can be argued that more needs to be done by public sector and private sector organizations, because the objectives and motives of stakeholders overlap. This is something that our political masters and their policy advisors need to be aware of.

Consider this example: a dissatisfied employee decides to manipulate an organization's customer database (dataset of customer details that are password protected) and at the same time transfer a copy of the dataset or a section of data from the same dataset to a third party, without internal approval. In this case, the insider is disrupting the internal database and gaining a financial advantage from selling quality data on to a competitor, without understanding or being concerned about the implications of such action. There is both an economic and psychological element to what a criminal insider does.  For example,  it is possible to adequately assess the motives and objectives of the insider because  they perceive  data to be  a commodity that can be traded and owned by many. Another example relates to an overseas government that establishes a front company (e.g. a bank) to collect and buy, or acquire illegally, data and information relating to the expansion plans of companies in a specific industry sector, which is used to formulate policy and strategy that later allows the overseas government to penetrate the critical information infrastructure of the nation targeted. What would cause this to happen? How can this be prevented? Are the countermeasures in place sufficient to prevent such behaviour? As regards the latter, it can be argued that no one nation will have on its own, sufficient muscle to prevent such attacks; however, by acting in unison it is possible to put combined pressure on overseas governments to stop this from happening.

There is no doubt that cyber security can be increased through planning and international cooperation, and the Joint EU–US Cyber Security Exercise held on 3 November 2011 has done much to focus attention on what can be achieved, as the quotation below makes clear  (http://www.prnewswire.com/news-releases/first-joint-eu-us-cyber-security-exercise-conducted-today-3rd-nov-2011-133138608.html [accessed 4 November 2011]).

*The first joint cyber security exercise between the European Union (EU) and United States (US) is being held today (3rd Nov.) in Brussels, with the support of the EU's Network and Information Security Agency (ENISA) and the US Department of Homeland Security. The day-long table-top exercise, Cyber Atlantic 2011, is using simulated cyber-crisis scenarios to explore how the EU and US would engage each other and cooperate in the event of cyber-attacks on their critical information infrastructures.*

*In the first scenario, a targeted stealthy cyber-attack (Advanced Persistent Threat – APT) attempts to infiltrate and publish online, secret information from EU Member States' cyber security agencies. The second simulation focuses on the disruption of supervisory control and data acquisition (SCADA) systems in power generation infrastructures.*

*More than 20 EU Member States are involved in the exercise, 16 of them actively playing, with the European Commission providing high-level direction. Cyber Atlantic 2011 is part of an EU–US commitment to cyber security which was made at the EU–US summit in Lisbon on 20 November 2010. The aims are to 'tackle new threats to the global networks upon which the security and prosperity of our free societies increasingly depend.'[1] The exercise draws on lessons learned in the first pan-European cyber security 'stress test' exercise, Cyber Europe 2010, which was facilitated last year by ENISA.[2] ENISA's role involves supporting EU Member States in organising cyber security exercises and formulating national contingency plans, with good practice guides and seminars.*

## 14.2 Consumerization of IT

As regards the consumerization of IT and the general topic of information assurance, it is necessary to revisit the issues of availability, integrity, authentication, confidentiality and non-repudiation (Singh et al., 2009: 294–295). Singh et al. (2009: 283) advocate that as well as safeguarding information, information can be 'securely shared, if required, among a set of related groups or organizations that serve a common purpose'.

A number of questions can be posed: What role does the risk manager play with respect to prioritizing the sharing of various types of information? Who will benefit from owning the information? Who is excluded from the information sharing decision making process? Will information increase or decrease the organization's level of resilience? Who are the stakeholders? What are the stakeholders' intentions? What influence do stakeholders have? How do stakeholders use/exercise their influence? Is it in the nation's interest that the information is shared? If a grouping of nations is involved, what are the risks/consequences for each nation?

Other questions emerge relating to the rights of consumers; ethical data handling; and the power of governments to regulate against technological transformation brought about by rapid diffusion and an insatiable consumer appetite (social network apparatus in particular). The picture that emerges is one of confusion, where the owners of technological breakthroughs provide advice to consumers and government representatives and this

---

1    Joint Statement, EU–US Summit, Nov.2010: http://www.consilium.europa.eu/uedocs/cms_data/docs/pressdata/EN/foraff/117897.pdf

2    ENISA Cyber Europe 2010 exercise reports: http://www.enisa.europa.eu/act/res/ce2010, http://www.enisa.europa.eu

goes unchallenged or unnoticed. However, in the case of interactive technologies that operate in real time to counteract cyber threats, the opposite is true.

## 14.3 The Proteus Envelope

It is important to reflect on what Proteus Enterprise™ represents (http://www.infogov. co.uk/proteus_enterprise/index.php [accessed 11 May 2011]):

> *Proteus Enterprise™ is a fully integrated web based 'Information Risk Management, Compliance and Security' solution that is fully scaleable....Using Proteus Enterprise™, companies can perform any number of online compliance audits against any standard and compare between them. They can then assess how deficient compliance controls affect the company both financially and operationally by mapping them on to its critical business processes. Proteus® then identifies risks and mitigates those risks by formulating a work plan, maintains a current and demonstrable compliance status to the regulators and senior management alike. The system works with the company's existing infrastructure and uses RiskView™ to bridge the gap between the technical/regulatory community and senior management by presenting the distilled information in a graphical 'dashboard' placed on their desktop.*

The checklist requirements for Proteus are outlined in Table 14.1.

**Table 14.1  Checklist Requirements for Proteus**

| Category | Selection | Complete or Tick |
|---|---|---|
| Your contact details: | Name: | |
| | Position: | |
| | Telephone no: | |
| | Email address: | |
| Who are you? | Public body: | |
| | Company: | yes |
| What are your information security interests? | Security discovery health checks | yes |
| | Best practice maturity assessments | yes |
| | Alignment of controls and risks | yes |
| | Alignment of network sensors, controls and risks | yes |
| | Integration of network management to controls and risks | yes |
| | Installation of a GRC, sensors/collectors, or iGRC | yes |
| | Other (specify) | |

**Table 14.1**  *Concluded*

| What business problems are you trying to solve? | Protection - of reputation, information, data and IPR | yes |
|---|---|---|
| | Risk avoidance - to impairment of service performance | yes |
| | Prevention and correction - of unwanted events and incidents | yes |
| | Management visibility - of risks to unwanted events and incidents | yes |
| | Other (specify) | |
| What questions do you need answers to? | Ensuring regulation is applied widely | yes |
| | Bridging gap between management and systems | yes |
| | Blocking unwanted system events and incidents | yes |
| | Obtaining external event and incident information and data | yes |
| | Deployment of controls and countermeasures against incidents | yes |
| | Demonstrating governance, risk and compliance regime to your customers | yes |
| | Other (specify) | |
| What business scenario(s) would we like to demonstrate? | Best information security practice versus your current state | yes |
| | Value of integrating an ISMS with network sensors | yes |
| | Moving from spread-sheet to web based compliance | yes |
| | Integrated governance, risk and compliance management | yes |
| | Enhancing managements visibility of their information security operations | yes |
| | Other (specify) | |

*Source*: Infogov. Reproduced with permission.

The term *integrated security mechanism* is alternatively known as the Proteus Envelope. The Proteus Envelope encapsulates the Proteus software tool and its policy and operating environment, which includes the strategic management environment in which security decisions are made and executed. A way in which this can be explained is to understand that the Intelligence Cycle concept is useful but can be extended or replaced with the Critical Thinking Process, the key being to formulate/produce 'an in-depth end product for sound decision making' (Patton, 2010: 139). The difference between the Intelligence Cycle process and the Critical Thinking Process is highlighted in Table 14.2.

**Table 14.2   The Steps in the Intelligence Cycle and the Critical Thinking Process**

| Intelligence Cycle | Critical Thinking Process |
| --- | --- |
| Planning and direction | Purpose |
| Collection | Question at issue |
| Processing | Information |
| Analysis and production | Interpretation and inference |
| Dissemination | Concepts |
| | Assumptions |
| | Implications and consequences |
| | Point of view |

*Source*: Patton (2010: 139). Reproduced with permission. © Kerry Patton, 2010, *Sociocultural Intelligence: A New Discipline in Intelligence Studies*, Continuum, an imprint of Bloomsbury Publishing Inc.

The Critical Thinking Process can be used to identify immediate and future threats, and can provide a basis for integrating management policies, systems and procedures to harness knowledge (both internal to the organization and external to the organization), and to provide a systematic way in which risk and the management and mitigation of risk can be carried out. Patton (2010: 154) is right to suggest that 'The Rings of Defense or Defense in Depth concept is a proven approach to make penetration of an asset much more difficult than without the rings'. The key is to deter, detect and neutralize identified threats through kinetic or non-kinetic manoeuvres (Patton, 2010: 155). Knowledge of the Social Net/Network within which interactions between individuals takes place is important with respect to comprehending the movement of people and data, and how threats materialize. However, complexity is evident because as Patton (2010: 158) rightly points out, 'several networks exist within systems', and relevant analysis often requires that threats are prioritized.

## 14.4 Integrating Security with Intelligence

As this point in the proceedings, it is useful to reflect and take stock of the wise words of Coveney and Highfield (1995: 7–8): '…the majority of real-world problems – and therefore most of those in modern industries and societies – do not fit into neat compartments. To solve them, people must be able to communicate across traditional boundaries, to approach issues in a collaborative, integrated way.' For this reason, it is important to adopt a multi-disciplinary approach to counteract threats posed by cyber attacks and to ensure that the issue of organizational resilience is addressed not just by the organization's risk manager, but by the whole of senior and junior management. In order to do this effectively, it is important for the security and intelligence models that are in existence, or being developed, to be refocused so that they place cyber security at the centre of the transformation process evident within the organization. Indeed, the GISES (Global Intelligence and Security Environmental Sustainability) Model outlined by Trim (2005) warrants that managers develop a security–intelligence interface and also, the SATELLITE

(Strategic Corporate Intelligence and Transformational Marketing) Model (Trim, 2004) can be used to link more firmly environmental issues with business intelligence planning.

Trim and Lee (2010: 4) have recognized the importance of an organization developing a security culture:

> It can also be stated that by integrating security more firmly into the organization's structure, it should be possible to reduce the organization's level of risk and facilitate information sharing. Information sharing should enhance co-operation between partner organizations and add to the defensive capability vis-à-vis establishing effective counter-cyber attack measures.

## 14.5 The Benefits of Cloud Computing

As regards the benefits of cloud computing, Clapperton (2010: 17) has stated:

> In general, though, cloud specialists provide more efficient environments than their customers could achieve in-house, Craig-Wood says, not just through virtualisation improvements, but also through investing in mass automation of data centres, which results in reduced power and hardware requirements. Companies should consider outsourcing to the cloud via two routes, she advises: IaaS (infrastructure as a service), which involves renting servers that reside in the cloud; and SaaS (software as a service), where email hosting and other applications are provided as a cloud service.

This raises a number of interesting and linked topics: data storage and the use of a data centre, and the energy savings that can be made which translate into carbon savings. For example, Bray (2010: 19) states:

> Within the data centre, organisations need to consider two aspects: the IT equipment itself (servers, storage, networking equipment, etc.), and the infrastructure that supports it (cooling, ventilation, humidification, power supply etc.). As a rule of thumb, for every pound you spend buying a server you can reckon to spend another pound to manage it and two pounds to power and cool it, so energy considerations should be an important part of the procurement decision.

The process of virtualization is, according to Hamilton (2010: 41), 'a technology that allows firms to abstract IT services from an underlying infrastructure' and 'in simple terms, offered a trustworthy path to slashing energy costs and reducing data centre space', and needs to be placed in the context of an organization's long–term IT strategy. More generally, Hamilton (2010: 41) has explained this by stating that:

> Boards understand cost, but they also understand that in today's world you need to be more responsive and that means having the ability to release new financial products that meet rapidly changing market demands. To enable these core demands to be met, other key elements in the migration to the cloud will be critical. These include refreshing older applications, some of which can't handle the demands of cloud computing, and equally important, ensuring that, for example, IT operational processes are optimised to reflect the importance of on-demand computing in the private cloud.

*What are some practical actions you can take to start achieving these objectives? Assessing the readiness of your IT infrastructure and processes to deliver cloud-based services is a good place to begin. Many firms are also developing financial models and business cases to determine the feasibility of cloud for their operations. Workshops with application and business stakeholders can establish priorities for cloud-enabling applications, align business requirements to IT service levels, and clarify compliance and security requirements.*

## 14.6 Safeguarding Data

It has been suggested that the cloud will 'revolutionise traditional outsourcing models' (Quillinan, 2010: 32) and it has to be remembered that not all managers are familiar with the benefits and potential risks associated with cloud computing. Indeed, it has been suggested that some managers need specific and detailed guidance as regards what may be suitable for their organization and in the case of storing highly sensitive data and information, a proper risk assessment and analysis needs to be undertaken in order to ensure that if a data breach does occur it will not put the organization at risk. When considering issues such as the cost of storing data and information, physical location of the data is an issue but so too is the possible threat from insiders. Issues such as geographical proximity (Quillinan, 2010: 32) may be deciding factors, along with the issue of compliance (Quillinan, 2010: 33) The degree of interoperability, the way in which user behaviour creates security issues, needs attention (Adams, 2010: 49) and as well as cost being considered important, so too are ethical issues (Winston, 2011). For example, it should not be the intention of senior management to cut costs if it means data is placed at risk/high risk.

## 14.7 Future Working Practices

The issues and challenges associated with changes in working practices also need attention. For example, remote working cannot be considered without paying adequate attention to security and counter-intelligence work. Intelligence work is likely to be given a higher platform within an organization as it becomes increasingly obvious that those intent on gaining an advantage from industrial espionage will carry on using illegal business practices to do so. Remote working is also considered to have economic and environmental benefits (Rosch, 2010: 35).

### MAIN THEMES IDENTIFIED

Will cloud computing provide all organizations in the value chain (supply chain and marketing channels) with an opportunity to be more profitable?

The possible questions to be addressed are:

- Question 1.   Will cloud computing transform existing business models into more profitable business models?
- Question 2.   What new management systems and structures will need to be invested in by the host organization that provides the hardware and the associated software,

bearing in mind customers will have access to the data and information they have stored with the provider via the Internet?

- Question 3: Can cloud computing adequately provide an opportunity for organizations to reduce their energy costs and enhance the image of the corporation's brand by linking reduced carbon emissions with a corporate social responsibility programme that is linked with government policy relating to protecting the environment?

Is it a correct assumption to suggest that by implementing virtualization (e.g. reducing the number of an organization's servers) energy costs will be reduced but the costs relating to additional security to protect data and information stored will increase?

The possible questions to be addressed are:

- Question 1.   Are the potential energy savings exaggerated?
- Question 2.   What security issues will need to be addressed in the next 10 years?
- Question 3.   How useful are existing international standards with respect to ensuring that compliance and governance are adequate?

How can the various stakeholders engage with each other to ensure that the priorities for cloud computing, however defined, once agreed and acted upon, result in an enhanced IT strategy for all the organizations availing themselves of the cloud?

The possible questions to be addressed are:

- Question 1.   How adequate are existing enterprise risk management approaches, concepts and models?
- Question 2.   How can risk be communicated more widely?
- Question 3.   What new forms or partnership involving industry, academia and government are needed in the foreseeable future?

## 14.8 Issues and Concerns to be Researched

A range of issues are evident including: how cloud computing can result in scaleable services; pricing in the context of public and private sector customers (especially in relation to infrastructure provision and cost); supply chain vulnerabilities; the SARS level of service and the fact that a multi-level set of users exist and a different set of tools are needed for different users; flexibility in market approach and in particular the need for customization; the role of the platform provider and who owns what; the need for adequate software interface; the need to structure the data; the quality of service in terms of SLA (Service Level Agreement); the risks and threats in relation to the opportunities and challenges identified – basically the fact that an organization's data may be held hostage; how current and future regulations will effect access to data, the backup of data; and future trends in cyber crime and risk mitigation.

The range of security issues identified is increasing. For example, the nature of cloud computing and the context within which it is placed; architectural and data requirements and operational issues linked to who in the organization does what; internal vulnerability and insider threats; the fact that there is no generally accepted common language for everyone so people view matters differently and interpret situations and events in different ways; malicious alert, criminal activity in the cloud, and issues of controlling identity management, linked with integrated liability and who owns the data (individual or cloud operator) – all need urgent attention and solutions need to be implemented sooner rather than later. Another important point is causal relationships between measurement and the software framework, and underlining causes, software service contracts and how a successful and sustainable business model can be created. Economic issues and comparability of services will be a distinct feature and providing access to roaming services and software licensing are expected to be part of the business equation. More generally, issues relating to software development and how to identify truthful providers that can be integrated into service provision needs urgent attention.

The delivery of a service will differ across industries. There are a large number of service characteristics for measuring the quality of service and cultural and industry factors need to be taken into account. Who sets the standard for a given quality of service needs attention also. Intelligence can be built into the system – operability and flexibility. Operating partners need to think in terms of IP risk; risk in the cloud (the type and form of electronic contracts and the influence of European/international law). The role of middlemen and the risk associated with trading across borders (compliance and accountability) are not to be underestimated. A number of questions surfaced. What happens if data providers or owners go bust? How can domestic companies work in areas of computer knowledge and skill development and not lose IPR to foreign competitors?

As regards the questions cited, it was noted that an emerging service is a collaboration of social networks which need to provide a common proof of service. Being a collaborative provider in a global market place means that there are a number of security issues related to SLA scalability and measuring service provision. As regards security, identity and authentication are crucial and the level of authentication required, the level of service provision that is deemed acceptable when a service provider fails and what can be done about it are aspects that senior management should address from the start in their contingency planning. Furthermore, are management in a position to know why something failed? Are they aware of the immediate and long-term consequences? The issue of reputational damage is important and so too are the knock-on effects vis-à-vis share value.

Trustworthiness is a predominant feature and how trustworthy relationships are developed and then maintained through time needs to be thought through. Human factors, perception, human interaction and intercepts are important considerations. The liability model, economic aspects of trust, SME and corporate level security awareness issues, how trust can be incorporated in technology or a technological tool are issues that constantly surface. What constitutes a trusted service, and the trustworthiness of a company takes into account measurability and value for money.

Cloud computing needs to be addressed from the perspective of how society embraces ICT and a range of socio-cultural and politico-economic situations. Summarizing the above it can be argued that managers at both the strategic level and the operational level will be concerned about: configuration requirements, storage, data security, scalability, more services online, service level agreements, dependable services and penalties, portability of data between service providers, boundaries of law enforcement, imbalances, intelligence services, security, identity, authority, recruiting policies, denial of service attacks, black and grey clouds, failure models, government ICT strategy and what happens when a service provider goes bust.

The future issues that managers need to take on board and plan for include: social and cultural feedback, the mix of networks, different technologies, emergency services, sensor networking, protocols, networking between different services, content user wants, combination of different networks (fibre, remote, satellite, fixed), industry needs, technical needs, negative resilience and availability, e.g. every 10 years a new generation of networks, scaled, interoperability, UK and EU, other parts of the world – US, China, Japan, manifest and have a technological impact.

At this stage in the proceedings, it is useful to reflect on the Sequence-of-Events Model and how it can be used. The Sequence-of-Events Model can be used to identify security related questions. For example:

- What is the purpose of security?
- What is the context of security?
- What is the scope of security?
- What is the scope of counter-intelligence?
- How broadly defined is the organization's security policy?
- How does the risk management process relate to the security objectives of the organization?

Bearing the above in mind, it is possible to revisit the issue of risk and state a number of facts.

- Risk management is not something that is done in isolation, it is organization specific and within an industry context.
- Risk communication is part of the security communication strategy, for the simple reason that each partner organization is subject to known and unknown impacts of varying intensity.
- Risk managers need an internal definition of security; an external definition of security; and an integrating or integrated definition of security.
- The analysis of risk is within the context of integrated security.
- A security plan is composed of a number of components or elements or defined in stages and the hub of all security activities emanate from an information security management system, e.g. the organization/extended organization is security focused.
- Business continuity is an important component and links with security awareness and training and education, and is underpinned by business impact analysis and includes all aspects of disaster recovery.
- Corporate governance needs to be viewed as flexible and a flexible approach is needed to understand and make sense of impacts, and so an emergency planning framework is to be incorporated within a corporate governance framework. Should this be the case, it is possible to suggest that the SATELLITE Model (Trim, 2004) can be viewed as a foresight and response oriented approach to dealing with a crisis/emergency. For example, as regards a response to an incident(s):
  - Apex and control: Senior management is classified as (GOLD and SILVER)
  - Hands-on management and technical: middle management (SILVER and BRONZE)
  - Operational and active: operational specialists (BRONZE)

Reflective stance:

- Have the assets been correctly defined?
- Are the assets listed given a value?
- Are the current threats and potential threats listed/known?
- Are the known threats prioritized?
- Are all the vulnerabilities known?
- Are the criticalities classified appropriately?
- Have the potential impacts been assessed in terms of impact, probability and intensity?

The Generic Cyber Security Management Model (GCSMM) featured in Figure 10.1 was modified and an updated version, known as the Modified Generic Cyber Security Management Model (MGCSMM) was produced (see Figure 14.1). As a result, the Integrated Security Mechanism was derived (see Figure 14.2).

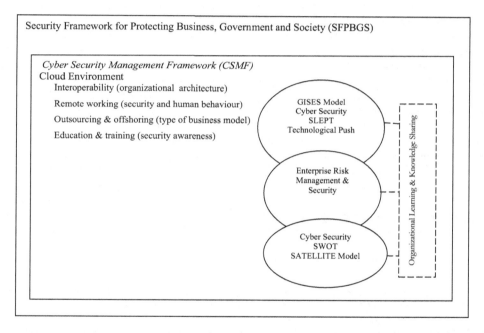

**Figure 14.1 Modified Generic Cyber Security Management Model (MGCSMM)**

(Incorporating the Sequence-of-Events Model, a Modified and Extended Generic Cyber Security Management Model (MEGCSMM) and the Proteus Envelope)

*Sequence-of-Events Model*

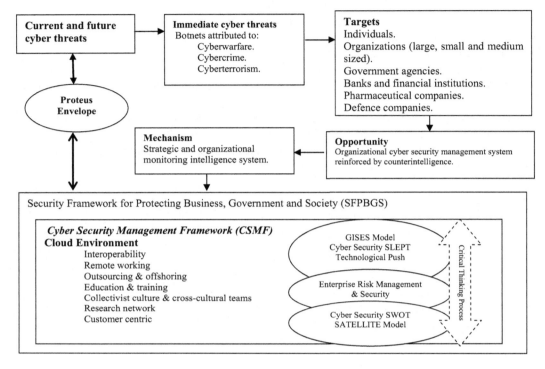

*Modified and Extended Generic Cyber Security Management Model (MEGCSMM)*

## Figure 14.2: Integrated Security Mechanism

*Note*: in Figure 14.2 the MGCSMM has been extended and becomes the MEGCSMM.

## 14.9 Issues Related to Using Cloud Computing

The dynamic business environment is providing opportunities in the form of unmet needs but also threats in the sense that if we look at the business environment now and we move forward in time to look at how we can satisfy unmet needs, without understanding the types of risk the organization faces, it is possible that future business objectives will not be satisfied (Trim, 2011). There are various forms of business model in place that link risk with product-market integration, however, do managers need to apply a quantitative or a qualitative form of risk assessment and is one risk approach better than any other? For example, technology led consumerization sets frontiers that we cannot imagine or if we can, we cannot necessarily interpret.

Are consumers the best judge of what they want and how they will consume what they think is good for them? Matching product capability with cost effectiveness seems ideal but is the context within which relationships are built, for example a dynamic, changing and somewhat unpredictable business environment, helpful or a hindrance to seeing what constitutes reality.

As regards the threats identified, some may be criminal oriented and some may be government orchestrated, and the concept of trusted partnership, when there is so much uncertainty, needs to be given better consideration than is the case at present, because getting the relationship wrong can prove expensive over the long term.

The rapid rise in mobile related technology and working arrangements sets forth a range of questions relating to the production, storage, utilization and transportability of data, and it may not be possible to predict what type of business model, on an industry-by-industry basis is more beneficial than any other. The different approaches to cloud computing means that managers will be provided with choice, but it is doubtful that managers will fully understand the implications of what is at stake. And will they be interested or motivated to ask the right questions?

What needs to be borne in mind is that data is owned, traded, stored and sometimes forgotten, but it is only when it is lost that people make a fuss. So issues of information assurance, governance and compliance all have meaning when one considers that data is translated into information and can be interpreted from the stance of a product specification, a technology and/or intellectual property rights, all of which suggests that stakeholders can be defined from the perspective of power and authority and the strength of the business relationship.

As regards cloud computing, it may not be possible for managers in an organization to fully understand what is going on, and this is dangerous because people at the apex of the organization may make a strategic choice for all the wrong reasons.

Is the real issue, not about technology and what technology can or cannot do, but about security and the fact that making technology central to how a person undertakes their work, produces a technology led focus that assumes that people will adapt to and embrace the positive aspects of the innovation. However, will less informed individuals embrace consumerization and see it as enhancing their lifestyle? Strategists expect consumers to consume, inventors to invent, entrepreneurs to take risks, and entrepreneurs to develop new business models that assume security is built in and that the potential threats and their associated impacts can be visualized and understood, and will anyway be less harmful than first thought.

But complications exist. By entering the cloud, a manager gives up the right to undertake an adequate risk assessment because suddenly they are too confident a blow-back resulting from the manifestation of threats will not be attributed to them because the decision to engage in cloud computing was made by staff at the top of the organization.

Policy advisors and their political masters may assume that putting in place a framework to support the development of cloud computing is as far as they should go because the market will decide. What goes on within the cloud is not visible and many questions will remain unanswered. Because of this, those supporting the development of the cloud are not responsible for the entrepreneurial behaviour of others and the resulting consumerization process, which will in turn give rise to a higher level of consumerization which unfolds much more rapidly than the previous stage of consumerization.

Will regulators be able to comprehend this emerging dynamic and uncertain trust based environment? And will the sharing of information between partner organizations be accelerated or result in confusion as to how to place a new business model within the context of a holistic security approach?

Virtualization will require a different view as to what security is and who will take responsibility for it. Managers may have a reasonable understanding of what the physical and virtual networks within the organization and partner organization look like, but will they understand how cloud computing will change business-to-business relationships in view of the fact that different forms of working and different accountability and responsibility levels, and greater movement of people between organizations and industries, is likely to stimulate the development of a range of business models, most of which are not sustainable?

Are the issues relating to cloud computing too diverse and complex in the sense that individuals, organizations and government departments have different needs and motivations, and because of this, trust cannot be viewed in the way that we now define trust? The context, rationale and capability of the infrastructure itself can be viewed from different perspectives. By eradicating known organizational vulnerability, new vulnerabilities may be created; hence the business risk model that we have in our minds may no longer be relevant. How can management identify the risks associated with cloud computing, when little is known about developing business relationships that may not be sustainable anyway?

Possibly, the unmet need referred to at the beginning can be thought of as, not from a specific company's situation, but found in a new security provision, or looked at from the perspective of the cloud provider, and the need for a new cloud security business model. In other words, security will predominantly be centred on and around the cloud owner/ provider and trust will be redefined so that the cloud provider is perceived as having authority and being a knowledge enabler. In which case all those that consume a cloud service (directly or indirectly) will be advised by and influenced by the cloud provider. Should this be the case, managers based in organizations that consume cloud services will no longer be required to think through complex situations regarding risk, ownership of the data, storage of data, the legitimate use of data and how the cloud can be made more secure, because this will no longer be something they are concerned with.

In their paper entitled 'Common and shared services in the context of cloud computing', Trim et al. (2011) posed five questions, which were posed at an IAAC workshop on 17 November 2011. The five questions were: What are the main issues relating to shared cloud computing services that are relevant to consumerization? What factors do policy makers need to take into account when sanctioning the use of public and private owned clouds? Is there an appropriate business model that can be utilized to benefit from cloud computing? Are the rights and privileges of individuals and organizations at risk from the vulnerabilities associated with cloud computing? If individuals and organizations are prevented from using shared services, what are the consequences likely to be?

Three papers were presented at the workshop which provided insights into cloud computing. The subject matter of the papers were as follows: 'Issues that management need to consider when contemplating using cloud computing' (Trim, 2011); 'Placing shared services in context: A technology-management perspective' (Austin, 2011); and 'The benefits and pitfalls that industry, government and academia need to be aware of when championing the use of cloud computing' (Aston, 2011).

The aim of the workshop was satisfied, namely to gain insights into the current and evolving complexities associated with shared services, and to highlight the issues and opportunities associated with cloud computing, so that managers working in the public and private sectors are better informed about the pitfalls and opportunities associated with shared services. A number of operational, organizational and professional issues were raised and discussion encapsulated the challenges that managers and policy makers are being confronted with. The work of Clapperton (2010) was drawn on and reference was made to real world situations and examples.

The workshop lasted three and a half hours and 22 people attended. The breakdown of those attending was as follows: government (32 per cent), academia (27 per cent), the private sector (23 per cent) and a small group of people (18 per cent) represented various not-for-profit organizations.

The main points stemming from the papers presented were as follows. Trim (2011) indicated that the dynamic business environment is providing opportunities in the form of unmet needs but also threats are evident. For example, managers do not always understand the type of risks the organization is confronted with and the situation is compounded by the fact that there are different business models for the same industry as well as different business models for different industries. Because managers can adopt either a quantitative or a qualitative approach to risk assessment, it is not always possible to establish which risk approach method is applicable. The real issue tends to be not about technology and what technology can or cannot do, but about security itself. Owing to the fact that individuals, organizations and government departments have different needs and motivations, trust cannot be viewed in the way that we now define it. This will no doubt provide management with much food for thought, as they will have to work out which relationships are sustainable in the long run.

Austin (2011), in his paper entitled 'Placing shared services in context: A technology-management perspective', concentrated on how data in the cloud would be looked after and how it would be safeguarded. Managers will need to carry out a security analysis of data needs at various levels and will also need to address the issue of how the information architecture takes account of various types of risk. As a consequence, top management will need to be aware of a number of factors, which are (listed in priority): data governance; identity management; an overarching security policy (people, process, technology, end point environment); type of possible solution: enterprise solution versus consumer solution; the logic associated with an organization having a kill pill that can be used to solve 'the basic problem' and eradicate the problem completely; and the need for monitoring to be constantly applied. Aston (2011), in his paper entitled 'The benefits and pitfalls that industry, government and academia need to be aware of when championing the use of cloud computing', focused attention on a number of issues relating to relationship building involving the service provider; for example, trust in relation to cloud computing; and how managers will work with law enforcement staff.

Following the presentation of the three papers by Trim (2011), Austin (2011) and (Aston, 2011), two groups were established to talk through the subject and provide answers to the five questions set. The information below represents a summary of what the two groups came up with. The small group discussions lasted 35 minutes and were highly interactive. Brief answers will now be provided for each of the five questions posed (Trim et al., 2012).

### Question 1. What are the main issues relating to shared cloud computing services that are relevant to consumerization?

Trust in the provider, due diligence to assess the capability of the provider and whether the provider has sufficient brand reputation to withstand reputational damage in the case of a data loss, are important factors for management to consider. Another question can be posed: What is the risk of not using the cloud service? For example, the cloud provider may be better able to protect data against attack. This is because the provider has better business continuity and recovery backup systems in place than the customer organization.

**Question 2. What factors do policy makers need to take into account when sanctioning the use of public and private owned clouds?**

Managers may have different interpretations of what the cloud represents, what the scope of cyber is and issues of education and awareness in behaviour surface. Risk, access and control are important considerations, and managers need to establish appropriate controls to deal with the various risks identified. Pressure can be exerted on providers to ensure that the shared elements of risk are known and that an outsource provider puts the necessary controls in place.

**Question 3. Is there an appropriate business model that can be utilized to benefit from cloud computing?**

As regards the type of business model, issues such as a collectivist decision making process and internal IT services versus outsourcing are key considerations. There is room for more than one type of business model and the flat fee versus transaction approach does take account of business costs and expected returns.

**Question 4. Are the rights and privileges of individuals and organizations at risk from the vulnerabilities associated with cloud computing?**

The answer is yes and people should be made more aware of the threats that exist. Being able to predict day-to-day service levels is important and consideration is also needed as regards what level of disruption is acceptable if a service fails. Management need to be aware of internal governance issues and identity protection and data backup in particular.

**Question 5. If individuals and organizations are prevented from using shared services, what are the consequences likely to be?**

People may be prevented from using a shared service as opposed to being deterred from using a shared service. Controls and leadership models are in place to prevent individuals and organizations from using shared services; however, this may result in a loss of productivity. In a situation where people are blocked from using a shared service or deterred from using a shared service, ways may be found to use it. Ultimately, managers will be asked to undertake a risk assessment in order to explain how critical the service is to the organization and also, what would happen should the service fail, result in non-delivery of a service, and what the outcome or consequences would be.

## 14.10 Conclusion

Placing security in context is paramount, if, that is, an organization is to continue to operate effectively. Risk managers in particular are charged with understanding the threats posed by current and evolving complexities in the business environment; however, cyberspace requires that attention is also given to the socio-cultural factors and issues that are shaping the environment in an economic and political context. Opportunities associated with cloud computing, cyber security and information assurance abound. Managers need to stand back and think of how to highlight and reinforce the link between information assurance and cyber security, and promote a security culture that permeates from one sector to another. The logic of this is that both public sector organizations and private sector organizations will be involved in various aspects of harmonizing security practices and policies.

## References

Adams, D. 2010. Virtual reality. *Financial Sector Technology*, 16 (4), 48–50.

Aston, S. 2011. The benefits and pitfalls that industry, government and academia need to be aware of when championing the use of cloud computing. *Second Information Assurance Advisory Council Consumerisation Research Workshop: Common and Shared Services in the Context of Cloud Computing*. BCS, Chartered Institute for IT, London (17 November).

Austin, J. 2011. Placing shared services in context: A technology-management perspective. *Second Information Assurance Advisory Council Consumerisation Research Workshop: Common and Shared Services in the Context of Cloud Computing*, BCS, Chartered Institute for IT, London (17 November).

Bray, P. 2010. Getting down to brass tacks. *The True Cost of Your IT: A Guide to Environmentally Friendly Computing*. London: Lyonsdown Media Group, 18–20.

Clapperton, G. 2010. Clouds, not smoke. *The True Cost of Your IT: A Guide to Environmentally Friendly Computing*. London: Lyonsdown Media Group, 16–17.

Coveney, P., and Highfield, R. 1995. *Frontiers of Complexity: The Search for Order in a Chaotic World*. London: Faber and Faber Limited, 7–8.

Hamilton, S. 2010. Private clouds. *Financial Sector Technology*. 16 (4), 41.

Mahmood, M., and Hookham, M. 2011. On sale at £3.70: your stolen credit details. *The Sunday Times*, (6 November), 19.

Patton, K. 2010. *Sociocultural Intelligence: A New Discipline in Intelligence Studies*. London: The Continuum International Publishing Group.

Quillinan, J. 2010. Austerity rules. *Financial Sector Technology*, 16 (4), 32–33.

Rosch, V. 2010. Living the dream. *Financial Sector Technology*, 16 (4), 34–36.

Singh, P., Singh, P., Park, I., Lee, J-K., and Rao, H.R. 2009. Information sharing: A study of information attributes and their relative significance during catastrophic events, in *Cyber Security and Global Information Assurance*, edited by K.J. Knapp. Hershey, PA : Information Science Reference, 283–305.

Trim, P.R.J. 2004. The strategic corporate intelligence and transformational marketing model. *Marketing Intelligence and Planning*, 22 (2), 240–256.

Trim, P.R.J. 2005. The GISES model for counteracting organized crime and international terrorism. *International Journal of Intelligence and CounterIntelligence*, 18 (3), 451–472.

Trim, P.R.J., 2011. Issues that management need to consider when contemplating using cloud computing. *Second Information Assurance Advisory Council Consumerisation Research Workshop: Common and Shared Services in the Context of Cloud Computing*, BCS, Chartered Institute for IT, London (17 November).

Trim, P.R.J., and Lee, Y-I. 2010. A security framework for protecting business, government and society from cyber attacks, pp. 1–6. *5th IEEE International Conference on System of Systems Conference (SoSE): Sustainable Systems for the 21st Century*, Loughborough University (22–24 June).

Trim, P.R.J., and Lee, Y-I. 2011. Cyber social science and information assurance: A generic cyber security management model (GCSMM). Poster paper presentation. *The IAAC Symposium: Information Assurance: Meeting Challenges of Changing Times*, College of Physicians, London (7 September).

Trim, P.R.J., Lee, Y-I., Austin, J., and Aston, S. 2011. Common and shared services in the context of cloud computing. *Second Information Assurance Advisory Council Consumerisation Research Workshop: Common and Shared Services in the Context of Cloud Computing*. Pre-Workshop Briefing Paper. London: BCS, Chartered Institute for IT (17 November).

Trim, P.R.J., Austin, J., Aston, S., and Lee, Y-I. 2012. Common and shared services in the context of cloud computing: Analysis and interpretation. *Information Assurance Advisory Council Research Workshop Report*. London: Information Assurance Advisory Council.

Winston, Lord. (2011). Scientists & Citizens. St George's House Annual Lecture 2010. *St George's House Annual Review, 2009–2010*. Windsor: St George's House, Windsor Castle, 4–11.

## Websites

Source: http://www.infogov.co.uk/proteus_enterprise/index.php [accessed 11 May 2011].

Source: http://www.number10.gov.uk/news/cyberspace/ [accessed 4 November 2011].

Source: http://www.prnewswire.com/news-releases/first-joint-eu-us-cyber-security-exercise-conducted-today-3rd-nov-2011-133138608.html [accessed 4 November 2011].

# **15** *Modified and Extended Generic Cyber Security Management Model (MEGCSMM) and Strategic Management Framework, and Project Liaison Team Management*

## 15.0 Introduction

Trim and Lee (2010: 4) have recognized the importance of an organization developing a security culture, and by integrating security into an organization's structure it should be possible to reduce the organization's level of risk and at the same time facilitate information sharing that is aimed at establishing an effective counter-cyber attack strategy. The process can in fact be supported and reinforced through a project liaison team management approach. This approach centres around an understanding of, and a commitment to, organizational learning. Such a commitment brings to the fore the benefits associated with organizational learning and the fact that managers need to be committed to raising the skill level of employees, through education and training, if, that is, the organization is to sustain and prevent cyber attacks from penetrating key parts of the organization. Cyber related training has to be planned for and thought through because the resources required to provide adequate staff development programmes can be considerable. Indeed, being committed to making the organization as robust as possible is logical and much thought needs to go into designing an effective security awareness programme. Senior management need to adopt a hands-on approach to training and education, and implement a leadership style that motivates employees.

This chapter outlines how the Modified and Extended Generic Cyber Security Management Model (MEGCSMM) and strategic management framework was produced. First, reference is made to a strategic security framework (Section 15.1) and this is followed by a short section on impact analysis (Section 15.2). Corporate governance (Section 15.3) is given attention and linked with the SATELLITE Model produced by Trim (2004). This is followed by reference to the Modified and Extended Generic Cyber Security Management Model (MEGCSMM) and strategic management framework (Section 15.4). Reference is made to what a learning organization represents (Section 15.5) and the subject of project liaison team management (Section 15.6) is addressed. The chapter ends with a conclusion (Section 15.7).

## 15.1 Strategic Security Framework

Coveney and Highfield (1995: 7–8) have indicated that solving real-world problems is complex and requires a multi-disciplinary approach. Hence risk managers need to know how to use the security and intelligence models that are in existence, or being developed, and refocus their efforts so that cyber security is the centre of attention.

The systems-of-systems approach has been heralded as a possible way forward as regards a methodological process and framework for bringing together various stakeholders to produce a strategic security framework of relevance to counter the growing threat from cyber attacks. The issue of trust is key from the perspective of industry–government relations, government–society relations and company–society relations. The fact that a number of governments are now talking about actively cooperating is important both in terms of raising awareness throughout society and cooperating in order to stop cyber attacks escalating and being concentrated on or launched from countries with ineffectual government leadership. As well as warning people in society about the dangers associated with giving out passwords and sharing data with people they do not know (mostly through social websites), it needs to be remembered that the essence of strategic marketing is to include an unmet needs element (Aaker and McLoughlin, 2010: 35–38). It is this unmet needs element that corporate strategists need to focus on. Aaker and McLoughlin (2010: 35) state: 'An unmet need is a customer need that is not being met by the existing product offering.'

## 15.2 Impact Analysis

As well as external threats there is a growing threat from internally orchestrated attacks, and this has been given attention (Trim, 2008; Koo, 2011). Strategists need to monitor the external environment and identify and rank the strategic uncertainties and establish how they are to be managed through time (Aaker and McLoughlin, 2010: 93). Decisions regarding which threats are to be watched more closely than others is done in the context of rating priorities and the costs associated with further investigation. However, Aaker and McLoughlin (2010: 93) have indicated that strategists need to think in terms of (i) what a strategic uncertainty is related to (trends or events impacting a business, the importance of the business and the number of businesses likely to be affected); and (ii) the immediacy of a strategic uncertainty and what it is related to (the probability that something will occur, the time frame involved and the reaction time necessary to develop and implement an appropriate strategy).

# 15.3 Corporate Governance

Corporate governance is a well known and well understood subject; however, Fahy et al. (2005: 2) state that a more holistic approach is needed to the subject because 'Enterprise Governance is based on the principle that good governance alone cannot make an organisation successful'. Bearing in mind the point about unmet needs, Trim (2004) has produced the SATELLITE (Strategic Corporate Intelligence and Transformational Marketing) Model, which allows security to be built into the strategic management process of an organization (see Figure 15.1). The SATELLITE Model specifies the type of work to be undertaken and identifies who will undertake the work. For example, various groups of specialists are in existence and include: a Corporate Intelligence Staff Support Group; a Strategic Marketing Staff Support Group; a Corporate Security Management Group; an Internet Marketing Group; a Relationship Marketing Advisory Group; and a SATELLITE Advisory Group. The SATELLITE Model is used by senior managers to integrate all aspects of corporate intelligence and security work, and incorporates and links with staff based in stakeholder organizations. Most importantly, the work undertaken by organizational strategists is focused not just on marketing strategy formulation and implementation, it is also linked with organizational design and most importantly, ensures that data and information are protected (Trim et al., 2009: 351). It is suggested that the Corporate Security Management Group take responsibility for devising a cyber security programme, which is composed of a cyber security strategy, the cyber security policies and plans, the cyber security practices, the cyber security controls, and the practices and cyber security supporting controls (Mehan, 2008: 189). As regards the Internet Marketing Group, Kendrick (2010: 10–11) has outlined how Internet technologies have given rise to enhanced email enabling communications; marketing and transactional opportunities via websites; the development of intranets that facilitate the recording and archiving of an organization's intellectual property; the development of extranets that facilitate links with strategic alliance partners and provide access to customers; Internet technologies that enable economies of scale of the production of goods and services; Internet technologies for use in specialist and niche markets; and web 2.0 technologies that provide an opportunity for further business opportunities.

In order that senior managers are able to devise realistic defensive strategies based on counter-intelligence, security needs to be viewed as a core activity (Trim, 2005b). Should this be the case, a proactive as opposed to a reactive security culture will be produced that ensures that the organizational security awareness programmes are as effective as possible. It is also necessary for strategists within the organization to be able to work with colleagues and implement an effective learning organization culture. Should this be the case, various security awareness policies and programmes can be developed and made public through well crafted internal marketing orchestrated promotional campaigns. The security awareness programmes can be adapted and made available to partner organizations. This should result in trust based relationships being formed that become strategic intelligence focused partnerships (Trim and Lee, 2008b).

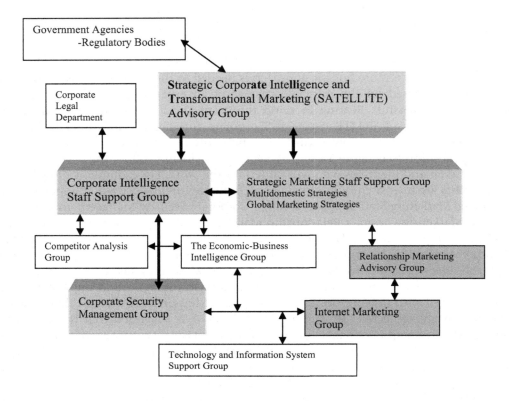

**Figure 15.1 The SATELLITE (Strategic Corporate Intelligence and Transformational Marketing) Model**

*Source*: (Trim, 2004: 246). Reproduced with permission.

## 15.4 Modified and Extended Generic Cyber Security Management Model (MEGCSMM) and Strategic Management Framework

Trim and Lee (2010: 5) state:

> *By encouraging greater linkage between commerce and industry, government and academia, it is hoped that a more pro-active approach to cyber security will be established. This being the case, it can be argued that a hands-on approach to making an organization resilient will be needed, in the sense that resilient management systems and processes will provide greater protection against multi-dimensional attacks.*

Senior managers can devise a Modified and Extended Generic Cyber Security Management Model (MEGCSMM) that ensures that the issues relating to cloud computing and cyber security are given the attention needed in order to put in place a counter-intelligence operation to thwart cyber attacks. The Sequence-of-Events Model (Figure 2.1) and the Global Intelligence and Security Environmental Sustainability (GISES) Model

(Trim, 2005a) are integral parts of the strategic management framework and so too is the strategic marketing intelligence framework (Trim and Lee, 2007a) (Diagram 3.1) and the strategic marketing intelligence and multi-organizational resilience framework (Trim and Lee, 2008a) (Figure 4.4). More attention does need to be given to the role played by various stakeholders associated with cyber security (government, industry, universities for example) and it is for this reason that the authors have adapted the GISES Model (Trim, 2005a) and placed it in context (see Figure 15.2).

With respect to the MEGCSMM, it is important to note that there are three points of immediate focus:

1. the linkage and improvement and refinement through time between a company's cyber security strategy and the company's ability to attract and maintain cyber security specialists;
2. the cyber skill base of the specialists employed and how they influence policy in the context of the integration of cyber security management systems, processes and procedures throughout the organization's operations and functions; and
3. the linkage between the company and the stakeholders in the industry and how a government influences cyber security initiatives to ensure that the organization develops and maintains a sustainable competitive advantage.

Underpinning the MEGCSMM and strategic management framework (Figure 15.3) is an organizational commitment to security as a core activity (see Diagram 15.1).

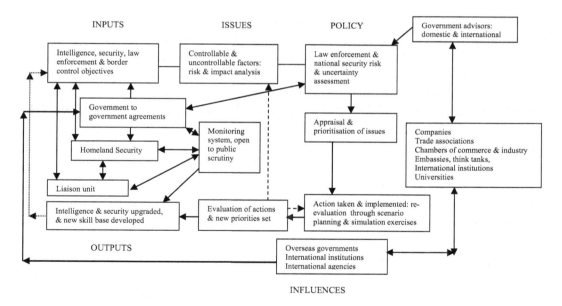

**Figure 15.2 The Global Intelligence and Security Environmental Sustainability (GISES) Model in Context**

*Source*: Adapted by the authors from Trim (2005a: 456).

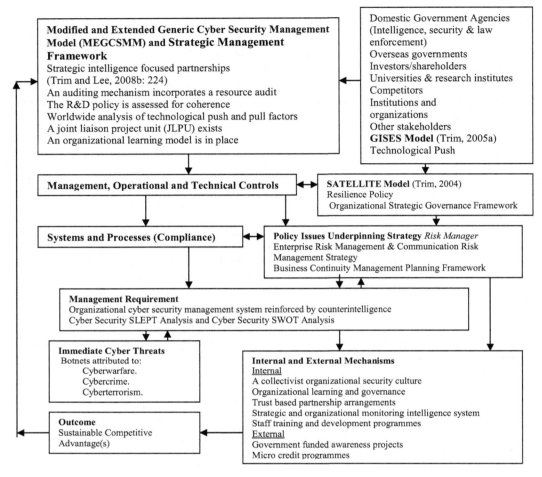

**Figure 15.3 Modified and Extended Generic Cyber Security Management Model (MEGCSMM) and Strategic Management Framework**

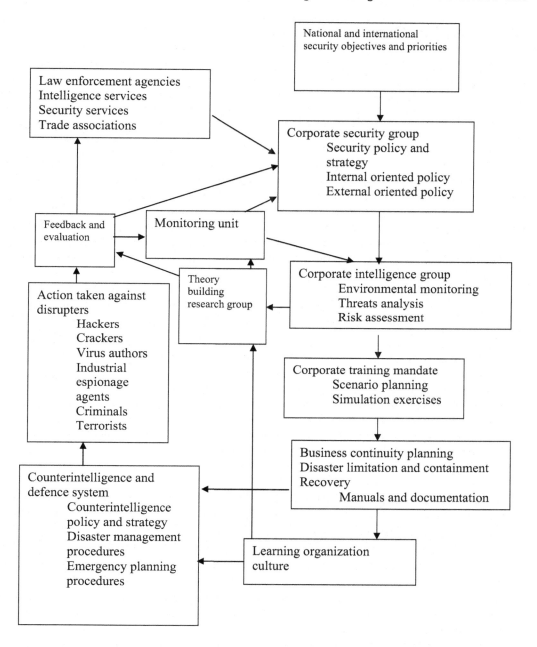

**Diagram 15.1  Security as a Core Activity**
*Source*: (Trim, 2005b: 502). Reproduced with permission.

## 15.5 Learning Organization

Appelbaum and Gallagher (2000) have provided guidance as to why senior managers need to embrace training and they argue that training is very much concerned with organizational transformation. Senge (1999: 14) has provided useful insights into what a learning organization represents: 'an organization that is continually expanding its capacity to create its future.' It is important to remember that Morgan et al. (1998: 357) have indicated that the process of organizational learning is facilitated by: (i) adaptive learning (existing knowledge is embraced in order to improve existing operations) and (ii) generative learning (this represents the next stage of the learning process and deals with cognitive learning and intellectualizing). Organizational learning can help managers to create uniqueness and the organization can develop a sustainable competitive advantage (Trim and Lee, 2004: 286). It is at this point that mention can be made of the international project group approach, which can be used by organizational partners to pool knowledge. According to Trim and Lee (2007b: 337), the main purpose of an international project group is:

> to work on 'secret' projects that are deemed essential to the future survival of the organization. One can think in terms of new products for existing markets, new technology for an evolving market, new technological processes that improve manufacturing capability, and new distribution arrangements that enable the organization to provide a high level of customer service (after-sales service) on entry to the market.

> The senior manager(s) responsible for the functioning of an international project group need to ensure that those given the responsibility to discuss matters in an open and frank manner, and reach the deadlines set, are able to do so. It is because of this that the concept of organizational learning needs to be thought of as a tool for facilitating the management of change, and providing future leaders.

Diagram 15.2 outlines the link between organizational learning and the development of strategy otherwise known as the strategic management process. The strategic project groups identified may not be permanent in nature. Some will be permanent and some will be put together on an ad hoc basis. Training and staff development programmes will take into account the skills required and as a consequence new human resource management polices will be devised and implemented. The key point to note is that rather than reacting against change, change will be embraced and a change management process will be put in motion. Furthermore, as Trim and Upton (2013: 177–178) point out, international project groups can be used to harness both knowledge and expertise throughout an organization, and in addition, can be used to implement plans and strategies.

## 15.6 Project Liaison Team Management

The three strategic project groups identified in Diagram 15.2, relate to three main areas: (i) business continuity, (ii) risk and (iii) IT. The first strategic project group, under the business continuity manager, is responsible for a number of internal, organizational duties and externally orchestrated duties. The internal duties include: working with risk and

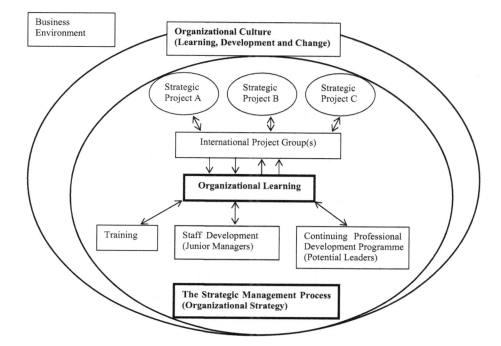

**Diagram 15.2 A Conceptual Model Outlining how Organizational Learning Underpins the Strategic Management Process**

*Source*: (Trim and Lee, 2007b: 341). Reproduced with permission.

IT staff to develop cyber security inter-organizational and intra-organizational policies and procedures; information assurance policy and educational and training programmes, which have as inputs foresight planning and scenario analysis. Contributing to risk assessment is vital and staff are very much concerned with issues relating to damage limitation, recovery and reputational management. Various marketing initiatives (e.g. identifying unmet needs) receive attention. The external duties of this strategic group include monitoring behaviour within social networks and working with marketing personnel *vis-à-vis* integrating a response in the context of integrated, multi-media channels and the deployment of multi-media tools. It is suggested that staff associated with this group are involved with and cooperate with personnel in the military and civilian sectors in order to identify and quantify potential incidents and impacts. The organizational learning value added manifests in improving situational awareness tools and techniques, and initiating a common strategic intelligence forum, thus creating and sharing cyber security knowledge with a wide audience.

The second project group, under the risk manager, is very much concerned with risk assessment, risk analysis and liaising with experts (both at home and abroad) who deal with threat prevention. One way to highlight the need for continual security awareness is for staff in this strategic group to work with peer groups concerned with devising cyber security training and staff development programmes. Staff also need to show a commitment to influencing social networking policy (this can be done by working with university research groups to monitor and appraise trends in social networking).

Monitoring both the internal and the external environment (e.g. to anticipate human behaviour change and its consequences) is critical as regards preventing acts of disruption. Furthermore, staff in this strategic group need the capability to monitor the organization and its partners for vulnerabilities (especially the supply chain) and mobile devices in particular; and need to devise effective risk management strategies that take into account interdependencies between organizations. Information sharing is considered essential (with organizations and governments) and this suggests that organizational learning needs to be concerned with providing a proactive organizational culture.

The third strategic group is headed by the IT manager and is very much concerned with all the technical and technological aspects of cyber business and work and management practices (BYOD for example). An appreciation of and ability to defend against state orchestrated industrial espionage and a clear commitment to protecting the organization against information breaches is required. Staff in this group need to provide guidance to staff in the other strategic groups with respect to the implications of changing regulations and their consequences, and ethical issues associated with public and private clouds for example. It is not possible always to differentiate between internal and external considerations in the sense that IT is very much concerned with operational factors in real time, and staff need to keep up with issues such as platform vulnerability and managing assets safely. Staff also need to be aware of technical capabilities and the role that standards play, and initiatives to stop malware doing damage. It can also be suggested that staff need to update themselves vis-à-vis debates regarding cyber weapons and their deployment and take note of changes in the geo-political arena.

Reflecting on the above, it is possible to conclude that senior management, in order to produce an appropriate cyber security culture, need to engage with external partners including government policy advisors. The formation of an international project group(s) to deal with cyber security policy is necessary if a cyber security strategy is to be viewed as globally oriented. Diagram 15.3 below indicates how a cyber security culture can manifest.

**Diagram 15.3 Cyber Security Culture Model**

## 15.7 Conclusion

The GISES (Global Intelligence and Security Environmental Sustainability) Model outlined by Trim (2005a) will assist managers to develop a security-intelligence interface and  a hybrid security culture. In addition, the SATELLITE (Strategic Corporate Intelligence and Transformational Marketing) Model (Trim, 2004) can be used to link more firmly environmental issues with business intelligence planning, and will reinforce the organization's hybrid security culture. The organizational learning concept can be utilized to provide a holistic approach to training and can also provide a foundation from which a project liaison team management structure can be built. This being the case, a cyber security culture can be developed that reinforces security awareness and ultimately influences the organizational value system and the value system of partner organizations.

## References

Aaker, D.A., and McLoughlin, D. 2010. *Strategic Market Management*. Chichester: John Wiley & Sons Limited.

Appelbaum, R.S., and Gallagher, J. 2000. The competitive advantage of organizational learning. *Journal of Workplace Learning: Employee Counselling Today,* 12 (2), 40–56.

Coveney, P., and Highfield, R. (1995). *Frontiers of Complexity: The Search for Order in a Chaotic World.* London: Faber and Faber Limited.

Fahy, M., Roche, J., and Weiner, A. 2005. *Beyond Governance: Creating Corporate Value Through Performance, Conformance and Responsibility.* Chichester: John Wiley & Sons Limited.

Kendrick, R. 2010. *Cyber Risks for Business Professionals*. Ely: IT Governance Publishing.

Koo, M. 2011. An information war? Balancing national security, trade secrets and the rights of the individual. The Strand, London: Australia House (19 May).

Mehan, J.E. 2008. *Cyber War, Cyber Terror and Cyber Crime: A Guide to the Standards in an Environment of Change and Danger.* Ely: IT Governance Publishing.

Morgan, R.E., Katsikeas, C.S., and Adu, K.A. 1998. Market orientation and organizational learning capabilities. *Journal of Marketing Management*, 14, 353–381.

Senge, P.M. 1999. *The Fifth Discipline: The Art & Practice of the Learning Organization.* London: Random House.

Trim, P.R.J. 2004. The strategic corporate intelligence and transformational marketing model. *Marketing Intelligence and Planning*, 22 (2), 240–256.

Trim, P.R.J. 2005a. The GISES model for counteracting organized crime and international terrorism. *International Journal of Intelligence and CounterIntelligence*, 18 (3), 451–472.

Trim, P.R.J. 2005b. Managing computer security issues: Preventing and limiting future threats and disasters. *Disaster Prevention and Management*, 14 (4), 493–505.

Trim, P.R.J. 2008. Effective communication and persuasion for behaviour change. *Master Class session, The Malicious Exploitation of Information Systems Conference*, University College London (7 November).

Trim, P.R.J., and Lee, Y-I. 2004. Enhancing customer service and organizational learning through qualitative research. *Qualitative Market Research: An International Journal*, 7 (4), 284–292.

Trim, P.R.J., and Lee, Y-I. 2007a. A strategic marketing intelligence framework reinforced by corporate intelligence, in *Managing Strategic Intelligence: Techniques and Technologies*, edited by M. Xu. Hershey, PA: Information Science Reference, 55–68.

Trim, P.R.J., and Lee, Y-I. 2007b. Placing organizational learning in the context of strategic management. *Business Strategy Series*, 8 (5), 335–342.

Trim, P.R.J., and Lee, Y-I. 2008a. A strategic marketing intelligence and multi-organizational resilience framework. *European Journal of Marketing*, 42 (7/8), 731–745.

Trim, P.R.J., and Lee, Y-I. 2008b. A strategic approach to sustainable partnership development. *European Business Review*, 20 (3), 222–239.

Trim, P.R.J., Jones, N.A., and Brear, K. 2009. Building organisational resilience through a designed-in security management approach. *Journal of Business Continuity & Emergency Planning*, 3 (4), 345–355.

Trim, P.R.J., and Lee, Y-I. 2010. A security framework for protecting business, government and society from cyber attacks, pp. 1–6. *5th IEEE International Conference on System of Systems Conference (SoSE): Sustainable Systems for the 21st Century*, Loughborough University (22–24 June).

Trim, P.R.J., and Upton, D. 2013. *Cyber Security Culture: Counteracting Cyber Threats through Organizational Learning and Training*. Farnham: Gower Publishing Limited.

# **16** *Recommendations for Counteracting Cyber Threats*

## 16.0 Introduction

This chapter builds on the information contained in previous chapters and includes recommendations for counteracting cyber threats. It can be noted that both technological factors and human/behavioural factors have been taken into account when addressing the issues and problems in cyber space, and also, when a country such as South Korea comes into the frame, geo-political factors also surface and can be considered central to the development of a national/international cyber security strategy. Separating out companies and government(s) is not possible as much of the critical national infrastructure is owned by the private sector and it is generally agreed that those in the private sector and those in the public sector need to work together in order to provide workable solutions to very serious, recurring cyber threats.

The recommendations put forward here are based on a logical and extended argument. however, only broad based recommendations are offered because only recommendations that are considered to effect stakeholders equally are perceived as a shared responsibility and are likely to be turned into policies to counteract the increasing sophistication of those launching cyber attacks.

This chapter is composed of the following sections: Thinking through the complexities of security and intelligence (Section 16.1); recommendations (Section 16.2); and a conclusion (Section 16.3).

## 16.1 Thinking Through the Complexities of Security and Intelligence

It is useful to reflect and suggest that, as well as developing relevant theory, academics are required to undertake work that can "guide future generations", a point taken from Wonderpedia (2013: 19) and one which can be placed in the context of academia-industry-government cooperation. Whether we call this foresight or something else is up for discussion, but Leonardo da Vinci had the strength of character to be able to design and invent and also, appreciate the consequences of the technologies he was explaining (Wonderpedia, 2013: 24). As we look at the role of the intelligence, security and law enforcement agencies, we can see that science, something that Leonardo da Vinci devoted his whole life to, is pivotal to their ability to find solutions to technological threats.

Richard Aldrich (2012: 56) explains that the intelligence agencies are moving from 'retail surveillance' (warrants or court permissions are needed to observe individuals/small groups) to 'wholesale surveillance' (the use of algorithms to search though large data groups/sets in order to identify patterns), otherwise known as robotic spying, facilitated by supercomputers. It has to be recognized that governments around the world have become familiar with the benefits provided by supercomputers, and Parsons (2012: 48) has indicated that quantum computing, which uses parallel processing, will provide new opportunities in the area of data security.

The work undertaken by Trim and Lee (2008, 2010, 2013) relating to the strategic marketing approach, marketing intelligence, resilience and cyber security, can be considered important from both a technological and a human/behavioural perspective. The authors make the case for senior management to put in place an effective cyber security management strategy that incorporates marketing intelligence focused partnership arrangements. The objective of a cyber security defence mechanism is to reduce an organization's vulnerability, by strengthening its business-to-business, business-to-consumer and business-to-government links. A cyber security management strategy can and should be devised in order to make an organization as resilient as possible. One such area of focus is incorporating risk assessment and risk analysis within the strategic marketing planning process. Indeed, Trim and Lee (2010, 2011) have provided insights into how marketing strategists can engage with their peers from different functions and develop a strategic marketing intelligence cyber security framework that embraces mutuality. Following a massive cyber attack on South Korea and the US in 2009 that resulted in disabled online networks and hard drives in PCs being hijacked and remotely controlled, and document files and programs being erased, an investigation was carried out by authorities in Japan as it was found that eight servers in Japan had been used as stepping stones for the attack (Andreasson, 2012: 61–63). This places the material in context and makes it known that all types of organization, in every industry sector, in any country are open to attack. Hence the problem as we know it needs to be viewed as internationally focused and not nationally focused.

## 16.2 Recommendations

It is clear from this that a number of problems are evidene: (1) managers have an outdated view of risk; (2) risk management is inadequate; (3) risk assessment is inadequate; (4) risk analysis is inappropriate; (5) there is a limited pool of cyber security experts in existence; (6) there is a lack of well informed specialist research groups in existence; (7) there is a limited number of cyber security training programmes available; (8) there is a limited appreciation of defective software and its consequences; (9) there is a limited appreciation of how an information management system can help transform a business model; (10) there is confusion and misconception amongst the media regarding the complexity of cyber; (11) senior management are unaware of the need for adaptive leadership; (12) cyber security awareness programmes are in short supply; (13) the information in specialized reports needs to be more holistic; (14) the seriousness of cyber threats needs to be better communicated to sections of society; and (15) government, industry and academia have different objectives. Bearing these points in mind, the following recommendations are proposed.

## RECOMMENDATION 1.1

The cyber security educational and training programmes for managers (especially IT and finance managers in SMEs) need to be extended in number and scope.

## RECOMMENDATION 1.2

A more holistic cyber security educational and training programme provision is needed in order that the needs of the risk manager (and equivalent) are integrated with other risk areas in other business functions.

## RECOMMENDATION 1.3

A cyber security awareness programme should be introduced to increase substantially the number of IT managers and finance managers in SMEs attending cyber security educational and training programmes over the next 1–24 months.

## RECOMMENDATION 1.4

By encouraging senior managers in organizations to promote a company security culture, a deeper interest in security should be forthcoming from in-house personnel and staff based in partner organizations.

## RECOMMENDATION 1.5

By increasing significantly the number of cyber security experts available it should be possible to link more effectively cyber security educational and training programmes with the use of relevant software security tools.

## RECOMMENDATION 1.6

A range of cyber security educational provision (certificates, diplomas, degree and above) and short specialized cyber security training courses and programmes for general staff and managers, of varying cyber security ability, needs to be available from various educational and training providers.

## RECOMMENDATION 1.7

Additional information sources need to be made available to staff as there is a limited number of organizations that are making available cyber security information that can safeguard the organization against persistent cyber attacks.

## RECOMMENDATION 1.8

Managers in SMEs in particular need to be made aware of the need for adaptive leadership and how this can assist staff to establish organizational priorities and improve risk judgements.

## RECOMMENDATION 1.9

A better appreciation of risk assessment and a more appropriate form of risk analysis are needed and this can be linked more firmly with foresight planning.

## RECOMMENDATION 1.10

Managers, especially in SMEs, who are not fully aware of the growing seriousness of the threats posed by cyber attackers need to be informed about the national security implications associated with certain types of attack and the loss of intellectual property and its consequences.

## RECOMMENDATION 1.11

An integrated management guideline needs to be produced that can be used by managers in organizations to understand how to deal effectively with what can be deemed inappropriate behaviour of staff that results in data breaches.

## RECOMMENDATION 1.12

Managers in organizations need to develop an organizational learning framework for the development of new cyber security knowledge and knowledge transfer between academia and partner organizations.

## RECOMMENDATION 1.13

Managers in organizations need to develop an organizational learning framework for the development of new cyber security knowledge and knowledge transfer between academia and government agencies.

## RECOMMENDATION 1.14

Managers in organizations need to develop a foresight planning mechanism to better understand/anticipate the immediate (short-term), medium-term and long-term effects associated with a sophisticated cyber attack(s).

## RECOMMENDATION 1.15

A limited number of case studies need to be produced outlining best cyber security practice, cyber security training, security management training and its connection with educational provision (degree and above).

## RECOMMENDATION 1.16

A limited number of case studies can be produced outlining the problems associated with defective software.

## RECOMMENDATION 1.17

A cyber security management system needs to be developed that adequately deals with risk and risk communication, governance and compliance.

## RECOMMENDATION 1.18

A society security mandate needs to be agreed that eradicates identity theft.

## RECOMMENDATION 1.19

All organizations in the public and private sectors need to undertake an up-to-date cyber security SLEPT and SWOT analysis and link with assumptions and risk mitigation strategy in the organization's strategic plan.

## RECOMMENDATION 1.20

University researchers and cyber security writers involved in quantitative and qualitative research need to join appropriate networks and involve themselves in government initiatives and produce a cyber security exploitation and publication strategy document.

## RECOMMENDATION 1.21

Managers, cyber security practitioners and interested parties need to get involved in foresight planning and undertake a sustained cyber vulnerability and threat analysis and contribute findings to the appropriate trade organization/government agency or department.

## RECOMMENDATION 1.22

Managers in various organizations need to produce an industry specific organizational strategic governance framework.

## RECOMMENDATION 1.23

Managers in various organizations need to produce an industry specific business continuity management contingency planning framework.

## RECOMMENDATION 1.24

Managers in various organizations need to produce an industry specific communication risk management strategy.

## RECOMMENDATION 1.25

Managers in various organizations need to produce an industry specific Generic Cyber Security Management Model and Strategic Management Framework.

## RECOMMENDATION 1.26

Managers in various organizations need to engage in resilience policy and strategy mapping.

## RECOMMENDATION 1.27

Managers in various organizations need to produce an industry specific risk assessment policy.

## RECOMMENDATION 1.28

Managers in various organizations need to produce an industry specific integrated governance mechanism.

## RECOMMENDATION 1.29

Managers in various organizations need to produce an industry specific integrated security mechanism.

## RECOMMENDATION 1.30

Managers in various organizations need to engage in threat identification.

## RECOMMENDATION 1.31

Managers in various organizations need to produce an industry specific integrated resilience management model.

## RECOMMENDATION 1.32

Managers in various organizations need to produce an industry specific integrated management model and system.

## RECOMMENDATION 1.33

Managers in various organizations need to produce an industry specific unmet customer needs identification profile.

## RECOMMENDATION 1.34

Managers in various organizations need to produce an industry specific competitor and marketing analysis.

## RECOMMENDATION 1.35

Managers in various organizations need to produce an organization specific project liaison team management.

## RECOMMENDATION 1.36

Managers in various organizations need to produce an industry specific governance and compliance decision-making process.

## RECOMMENDATION 1.37

Managers in various organizations need to produce an organization specific communication of risk management strategy.

## RECOMMENDATION 1.38

Academics involved in cyber security need to work with people in academia, industry and government to produce a relevant Masters Degree in Security Management (i.e, Corporate Intelligence and Cyber Security/Resilience).

## RECOMMENDATION 1.39

Managers in organizations need to provide timely feedback regarding existing or new cyber security standards and/or government initiatives (education, training and research) to prevent existing and evolving types of cyber crime.

## RECOMMENDATION 1.40

Managers in organizations need to provide feedback to and cooperate with professional associations and institutions regarding the tasks and duties of staff in relation to cyber security policy, systems and procedures, in order to ensure that ethical issues are addressed adequately.

## RECOMMENDATION 1.41

Managers in organizations need to work with in-house human resource management specialists to ensure that staff are adequately vetted, qualified and aware of appropriate and inappropriate behaviour as regards outsourced operations and offshore operations, and BYOD, and are held to account by appropriate clauses in contracts binding the parties concerned.

## RECOMMENDATION 1.42

Managers in organizations (IT, finance, marketing etc,) are required to work closely with the risk manager to ensure that the enterprise risk model/risk per function is prioritized and documented in the risk register and an appropriate risk communication strategy is in being and also, that there is adequate cyber insurance cover of assets and facilities.

## RECOMMENDATION 1.43

Managers in organizations (IT, finance, marketing etc,) are required to work closely with the risk manager to ensure that there is a pro-active and international outlook as regards cyber security and that the law associated with protecting and valuing assets, data and information is not confined to national law/boundaries.

## 16.3 Conclusion

The premise underpinning the central argument in this chapter is that marketing strategists can play a more visible role within an organization than is the case at present by adopting the strategic marketing school of thought, and by linking corporate intelligence with corporate security. The reason why a collectivist organizational culture can be considered necessary is that the various business functions require staff to deal with data that is of a highly sensitive nature. Data needs to be collected and analysed, and the findings need to be interpreted and the outcome used. The strategic marketing approach requires that marketing strategists think in terms of using a formal strategic decision-making process that places marketing oriented decisions in a policy oriented context.

The strategic marketing approach can be utilized by senior managers in an organization that operates in different parts of the world to link more effectively their marketing, intelligence and security operations than is the case at present. However, in order to achieve the objectives set, senior management will in the years ahead need to place more emphasis on training and staff development, the central theme of which is facilitating organizational transformation and managing cultural change. There are three main reasons for this. First, cyber security training and staff development programmes will need to take into account the higher skill levels associated with interconnectivity that is reshaping the work environment. Second, professional development in the workplace is increasingly being linked with the motivation of staff in order to attain higher personal goals. Third, the increasing vulnerability of staff in the workplace due to the sophisticated nature of social engineering attacks means that management need to devise and implement security awareness programmes (through internal marketing programmes) that are aimed at eradicating data breaches

## References

Aldrich, R. 2012. The ultimate spy. *Focus*, Issue 248 (November), 55–59.

Andreasson, K. 2012. *Cybersecurity: Public Sector Threats and Responses*. London: CRC Press.

Parsons, P. 2012. The quantum revolution is here. *Focus*, Issue 249 (December), 46–51.

Trim, P.R.J., and Lee, Y-I. 2008. A strategic marketing intelligence and multi-organisational resilience framework. *European Journal of Marketing*, 42 (7/8), 731–745.

Trim, P.R.J., and Lee, Y-I. 2010. A security framework for protecting business, government and society from cyber attacks, pp. 1–6. *5th IEEE International Conference on System of Systems Conference (SoSE): Sustainable Systems for the 21st Century*. Loughborough University (2–24 June).

Trim, P.R.J., and Lee, Y-I. 2011. Cyber social science and information assurance: A generic cyber security management model (GCSMM). Poster paper presentation: *The IAAC Symposium:*

*Information Assurance: Meeting Challenges of Changing Time.*, College of Physicians, London (7 September).

Trim, P.R.J., and Lee, Y-I. 2013. How the strategic marketing approach can underpin cyber security in partnership arrangements involving European and Asian organizations. *2013 CAMIS, KSMS and GAMMA Joint Symposium.* Birkbeck, University of London (4 January).

Trim, P.R.J., and Upton, D. 2013. *Cyber Security Culture: Counteracting Cyber Threats through Organizational Learning and Training.* Farnham: Gower Publishing Limited.

Wonderpedia. 2013. The Da Vinci Universe. *Wonderpedia*, Issue 8 (January), 18–28.

# Index